CFO

ARCHITECT OF THE
CORPORATION'S FUTURE

CFO

Architect of the Corporation's Future

Price Waterhouse Financial & Cost Management Team

JOHN WILEY & SONS
New York • Chichester • Weinheim • Brisbane • Singapore • Toronto

Published in 1997 by John Wiley & Sons

John Wiley & Sons Inc.,	John Wiley & Sons Ltd,
605 Third Avenue,	Baffins Lane,
New York,	Chichester,
NY 10158-0012,	West Sussex PO19 1UD,
USA	England

Tel (+1) 800 225 5945   Tel (+44) 1243 779777
Fax (+1) 212 850 6135   Fax (+44) 1243 775878

e-mail (for orders and customer service enquiries):
bstahoski@wiley.com *or* cs-books@wiley.co.uk

Visit our Home Page on http://www.wiley.com

Other Wiley Editorial Offices

Weinheim • Brisbane • Singapore • Toronto

Library of Congress Cataloging-in-Publication Data

CFO : architect of the corporation's future / Price Waterhouse
    Financial and Cost Management Team
        p.   cm.
    Includes bibliographical references and index.
    ISBN 0-471-97599-0
    1. Corporations—Finance—Management. 2. Chief financial officers.
    I. Price Waterhouse (Firm). Financial and Cost Management Team.
    HG4026.C428 1997   97-26644
    658.15—dc21   CIP

British Library Cataloguing in Publication Data

A catalogue record for this book is available from the British Library

ISBN 0-471-97599-0

Typeset in 11/13pt Rotis by Footnote Graphics, Warminster, Wiltshire
Printed and bound in Great Britain by Butler & Tanner, Frome, Somerset

PREFACE

In a recent issue, *Fortune* magazine ran a cover story about 'Super CFOs'. The article's thesis: that a new breed of chief financial officer is revolutionizing the traditional position occupied by the finance function in the corporation. Presiding over processes that cut across the business, these CFOs set strategy, lead crucial change initiatives and act as real partners in decision-making with their CEOs.

Fortune's article was just one of the signs of a sea change occurring in the perception of the CFO's role. Then celebrating its 10th birthday, *CFO* magazine had already increased its readership to 360,000 – making it the largest controlled circulation magazine in the US. The number of MBAs going into finance and related disciplines was, and still is, rising, outpacing all others.

Yet little research had been done on the growing part played by the CFO on the corporate stage. So we began a worldwide study. Working in conjunction with the Conference Board, and learning from our engagements with major multinationals, our aim is to explore how the best CFOs make a fundamental difference in their corporations – in particular how they:

- design routes toward maximizing shareholder value on a sustainable basis

- make the concept of globalization work, building world-class business support

- champion a more positive approach to structural and process streamlining.

This book reports the results so far. In doing so, it attempts to meet the need – confirmed by our research – for a comprehensive set of guidelines for finance professionals wanting to be ready for the next millennium's challenges. Many of the approaches it describes have been on the *boardroom* agenda for some years, but are still only rarely seen in action *at the operational front line.* Where we've lacked the necessary space – or powers of prediction! – to suggest complete solutions for the future, we've aimed at least to pose questions likely to provoke fresh, profitable lines of thinking. Intending to cater for *dip-in* readers as well as any inspired to move cover to cover, the book highlights practical lessons in imaginary and real-life anecdotes, diagrams and checklists.

We'd like to thank all the people who shaped the chapters – starting with the hundreds of CFOs who offered views in our survey, interviews and case studies. We hope they'll continue a dialogue with us in our ongoing investigation of finance best practices. Within Price Waterhouse, thanks are due to Jon Green for helping to structure everyone's ideas and make sure that *CFO: Architect of the Corporation's Future* has a coherent beginning, ending, and themes linking the two. Subject experts led teams working on the guts of the book, as follows.

Value based management	Michael Donnellan, Likhit Wagle
Performance management	Dan Keegan, Jon Green
Activity based management	Bob Eiler, Stephen Justice, David Pettifer
Risk management	Mark Stephen, Fred Cohen, David Knight
Streamlining	Graeme Cottam, Stewart McCulloch
Shared services	Clive Johnson, Ray Trakimas, Richard Sandwell
Systems	Nigel Candelot, Tyler Prince
Finance change	Stewart McCulloch, John King, Jeremy Hopwood

Valuable input was supplied by countless individuals, inside and outside the firm. Those who gave special help include: Nick Burt, Nick Chipman, Andy Embury, David Fincher, Stephen Gates, Tom Jones, Erik Klinger, Tim Lott, Steve Lukens, Joe Ness, Juan Carlos Palomo, Susan Ragan, Bob Russell, Simon Street, Andrew Strivens, Bob Sullivan, David Swann, Ian Tong, Guy Walker, Tim Whiston, John Wynn, Tara Yamashita.

Not least of the creative challenges was to give one voice to the thoughts of so many contributors: we're grateful to Linda Gatley, an independent consultant, for sensitive editing and support throughout.

Cedric Read and Scott Kaufman
August 1997

Cedric Read, a senior partner in Price Waterhouse and global leader of the Financial & Cost Management (FCM) consultancy team, can be contacted on +44 113 244 2044. Scott Kaufman, a senior partner and US leader of the FCM team, is on +1 213 236 3000.

Contents

Contents

Chapter 1
Leading Corporate Change

Imagine you're the CFO of a multinational with operations in the Americas, Europe, Asia and the Pacific Rim. The corporation employs 200,000 people but not all are in the right places. For while you do everything possible to hold on to market share in the US and Western Europe, the real opportunities lie in dramatic growth projected for developing nations. A high proportion of fixed cost investment and supporting infrastructure is sunk in mature markets. But the future capital expenditure program is filled with projects for China, Mexico and Indonesia. Streamlining the old organization, shifting decision-making power and capital to the new: all this must happen – and fast.

Shareholder value tops the corporate agenda. Half the worldwide product portfolio generates cash but is subject to mounting cost competition. The other half consumes cash but enjoys higher margins and brighter prospects.

You can see the big picture. You have all the figures. How can you, through the finance function, intervene in the management process to ensure that investments and resources aim at value creation? You're proud of finance's capabilities. Most divisional finance officers around the world are your personal appointees. And you believe many finance processes are

> *world-class. Yet you sense that the skills and influence of your people will have to grow if the corporation is to gain its global ambition.*

Jettisoning the baggage of the past, today's multinationals concentrate their efforts on globalization, maximizing shareholder value and exploiting core competencies across the corporation. How can *you* make a difference? Many CFOs act to develop world-class finance functions. But often this is too little, too late. How do you *really* build value in the business? How can you work proactively to reconcile external investors' expectations with what internal managers do day-to-day? What does it mean in practice for finance professionals to realize their full potential as business partners?

This book challenges you to complete the difficult task of transforming finance's role and ways of working: from command and control in a vertical hierarchy, to enterprise-wide decision support through horizontal processes. Introducing our *CFO 2000* research program, Chapter 1 explores the implications of this shift for tomorrow's finance activities and skills. And it describes the *finance value line* – showing how you can shape corporate strategy *and* make vital connections to operational reality, to achieve superior returns. At the end of the chapter, a checklist of the book's best practices points the way for the CFO leading change as *architect of the corporation's future.*

CHALLENGES FOR THE CFO

When most people in the world of financial management talk of being world-class, they have in mind benchmarks for best practices and metrics that deal principally with transaction processing, controls, budgeting and the more routine reporting activities. Some also refer to the cost of the finance function and its effectiveness as an internal service supplier. But few think about what world-class really means in terms of decision support. And even fewer about the CFO's potential role as *corporate architect*: a designer, who shapes the business to meet the demands of global markets and oversees execution of the new design – to build shareholder value.

Hundreds of CFOs contributed their views to this book. As you'd expect, their attitudes and standing differ from country to country. In the US, most CFOs see themselves as primary players in devising and implementing strategy. With costs already cut to the bone, the pressure is on to find opportunities for growth. But for many CFOs in Western Europe, reducing costs remains a priority. In Germany, they often see their role fundamentally as one of controller. Developing nations, such as Taiwan and the Philippines, offer a further contrast: spontaneous revenue growth has CFOs scrambling merely to staff a professional finance function to cater for the basics.

Despite variations, the prevailing shift in focus of the CFO and finance function is *away* from transaction processing and control, *toward* decision support and greater involvement in developing global strategy. Our *CFO 2000* survey, covering CFOs of 300 leading multinationals worldwide, confirms this trend.[1]

While 34% of respondents say decision support has been their top priority in the past three years, 74% rank it as their highest priority for the next three years. A similarly high proportion indicate that finance remains under pressure to trim its cost base: finance functions are becoming smaller but the quality of service is improving as the headcount drops (Figure 1.1). Our research shows that the cost of less efficient finance functions tends to be in the region of 3% of turnover. World-class finance functions are nearer 1%.

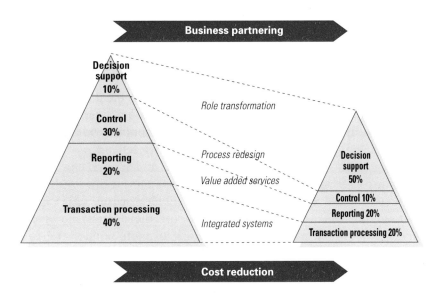

Figure 1.1 **Refocusing the resources of the finance function**

Two messages come across clearly from all parts of the world.

- ***What keeps CFOs awake at night is fear of failing to control the business*** Avoiding nasty surprises in financial reporting, conforming to laws and regulations, sustaining strong credit ratings – all suddenly become important if things go wrong. And, all the time, there are the uncertainties and pressures of change – for the corporation and its people. Asked to name his biggest concern, one CFO says: 'Will the company change, both operationally and functionally, quickly enough to compete and build shareholder wealth?'. Another pinpoints: 'Dealing with rampant egos!'.

- ***What excites CFOs during the day is the prospect of adding substantial shareholder value*** Restructuring, mergers and acquisitions, seeking out new revenue-generating opportunities – all are routes to value creation. Mega-deals can sharply raise the CFO's profile and perceived contribution to the business. This book echoes the ambitions of finance executives who say they concentrate on 'implementing global strategies', 'emerging market growth', 'delivering and integrating major acquisitions', 'crusading for shareholder value'.

Balancing these two sets of priorities is difficult, and depends on the skills and mindset of the CFO's first-line reports. Senior finance executives tend to come from one of two backgrounds. Either they train in financial or industrial accounting and rise through the *internal* ranks of company management – becoming steeped in the corporate culture and gaining deep knowledge of the business. Or they're raised in the *external* world of corporate finance – picking up experience in handling investors and leading tough negotiations. The most successful CFOs marry the two types of skills, bringing together the external world of investors with the internal world of company management *on an international basis.*

They seem to do so intuitively, through people or structural change. For example, one CFO says he rotates his senior finance executives through various external and internal facing roles. And he expands their experience through placements in different parts of the world. Another CFO has restructured his finance activities to combine treasury with transaction accounting in one function, and investor relations with management accounting in another.

What lessons do these examples offer? In our research we came across much evidence of finance functions adopting proactive initiatives to become *more engaged in the business*. These initiatives tend to operate at process level – getting finance out of its functional *silo* and into multi-disciplinary teams to perform process re-engineering or implement systems. But the value of such projects is limited by the constraints of the existing business design. For example, re-engineering the supply chain for a mature product in a declining market might bring short-term cost savings but can have no lasting impact on the inherent value of the company.

CFOs playing for the really high stakes throw resources into generating headlines like these...

- *Yet another merger to consolidate our standing as biggest in the industry. This deal will immediately enhance shareholder earnings.*

- *Already most efficient in our sector, we plan a further $1.5 billion cut in operating costs over three years to prepare for future competition.*

- *We will operate only in markets where our brands can hold number one position. We've begun rationalizing our product portfolio to achieve this goal.*

- *Following takeover of this business, we intend to retain parts that will add to our shareholder value and dispose of the rest.*

In such cases, the CFOs seem better prepared: they're ahead of the game. The decisions that their CEOs and fellow executives are making relate directly to strategic positioning and value to shareholders. These CFOs anticipate rather than react. They're quick to play their part in targeting ways to improve shareholder value – and prepared to make bold changes to the business structure.

RAISING THE BAR ON WORLD-CLASS FINANCE

Of course, everyone would like to achieve world-class in finance basics. The dream of most CFOs! But they're never enough. To counter competitive forces, a world-class CFO crafts a financial strategy that matches investor aspirations and supports delivery of the business strategy.

Consider what Dudley Eustace has done to improve the quality of the finance function at Philips, the electronics conglomerate, where he was formerly CFO and is now vice chairman and executive vice president. And how, with parts of the business under severe competitive pressure, Eustace's team plays a vital role in the program to transform the business.

CASE STUDY: Helping to Make Things Better at Philips

In common with other US and European multinationals, electronics giant Philips ran into problems in the 1980s and early 1990s, with increasing competition from Asia and recessionary conditions in major markets. Like many, the company found it had become insular and inward-looking. Philips relied heavily on internal appointments to senior positions, but in 1992, it broke from tradition to bring in Dudley Eustace as CFO. Just then, with negative cash flows and declining shareholder value, the group's problems were peaking.

Eustace's first priority was to focus operating management on the importance of generating cash. He also set about restructuring the group's debt financing, placing it on a longer-term, more secure footing, and cultivating stronger external relationships with banks. Internal priorities were to improve the speed and accuracy of reporting and develop a high caliber team of finance professionals. All these objectives have now been achieved.

One big win was re-engineering the reporting and accounts closing processes to world-class standards. Today, results from as many as 1200 reporting units, covering 125 businesses, are available within a week of month end.

But Philips continues to suffer with slim margins in consumer electronics. Even the more profitable semi-conductor business, which helped balance the profitability picture in the past, has been under some pressure. Consistently meeting financial forecasts provided to investment analysts proves difficult, jeopardizing management's credibility. Consequently, the share price is discounted.

Recent changes are beginning to have an impact, increasing the investment community's confidence: Eustace is working closely with newly appointed chairman Cor Boonstra to put in place an improvement program. Its goals are to:

- *tackle the 'bleeders in the company', through the turnaround, sale or closure of underperforming businesses*

- *sustain investment in businesses with future growth potential, and sharpen the focus on marketing to the end consumer to further exploit the Philips brand*

- *reduce overheads, and build both senior management's commitment to new financial targets and accountability for results.*

The most urgent issues on the finance function's agenda for tomorrow are achieving greater accuracy in forecasting and further improving management's credibility with investors. Boonstra, Eustace and, more recently, division vice presidents, hold frequent briefings with investors and analysts to communicate the company's position and plans – helping to prevent surprises in future.

In pursuing the longer-term goal of improved share price performance, Eustace and his finance team help management adopt a shareholder value based approach – identifying which business units create or destroy value. Philips already uses cash flow as a key metric for performance measurement and budgeting. The objective is to shift the group's emphasis to a portfolio of businesses, all producing cash returns that exceed the cost of capital invested.

Eustace needs to move finance even closer to the business: 'What we must do is bridge the divide between the twin pillars of corporate finance and management accounting'. Re-shaping the finance organization to make it more respon-sive to internal customers, Eustace uses regional shared service centers in Asia, Europe, North and South America to provide corporate finance, treasury and cash management services. He adds: 'We are trying to strike a balance between providing corporate direction and empowering the business units'.

Tomorrow's finance agenda at Philips and those being developed by other multinationals have many similarities. Three themes keep repeat-ing: world-class CFOs seem preoccupied with *globalization, creating value* and *streamlining the business design*. The scenario that began this chapter illustrates how these converging themes challenge the CFO of any large multinational. And they resound through every chapter. Why are they so important?

Operating in a Shrinking World

Capital and trade have shifted around the world for centuries. But power-ful forces now permanently alter the picture: faster communication and decision-making, emerging global investors and financial markets, and converging consumer expectations across previously distinct regions.

Everyone *talks* of the global company. As Glen Peters points out in his book *Beyond the Next Wave*, a truly global company not only takes advantage of global markets and their economies of scale but is *culturally representative of markets in which it operates.*[2] Many multinationals fail to achieve this: they simply impose the dominant parent culture on their plants or selling operations in other countries. Yet the transition from multinational to global is critical if companies are to command respect and loyalty from people in their new world markets.

For the CFO, this raises thorny issues (Figure 1.2). If your company operates in the world's three main economic theaters, you probably deal with finance markets in London, Tokyo and New York. You need to provide a 24-hour service. How should you structure the treasury management function – globally, regionally or nationally? Your aspiration may well be global: cash management banks like Citibank already provide 24-hour electronic access to their treasury support facilities, 365 days a year. Global restructuring questions also apply to other financial policies and processes. And sometimes, the right answers are inconsistent. In moving to financial shared services, one CFO was happy to regionally consolidate exchequer processes, while encouraging the management accounting activities to follow the new global management structure for product categories.

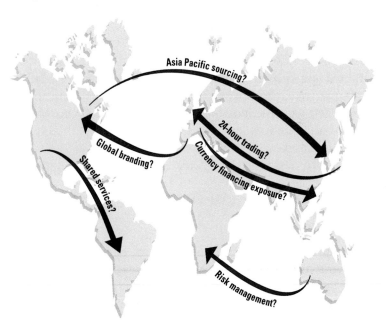

Figure 1.2 **CFOs of global companies are re-evaluating product marketing, sourcing and financing decisions**

Our *CFO 2000* survey uncovers a major structural dilemma: whether to organize the finance function worldwide by business unit or some other way. Two-thirds of CFOs say they've reorganized finance in the last three years in response to business-wide restructuring. As more and more companies move from geographic management to a global product–market approach, finance, too, must reorganize to service newly defined business units that cut across traditional geographic and functional boundaries.

A divisional CFO of a major US based multinational comments on his changing role: 'Three years ago, I was CFO of all the company's UK operations. The monthly reporting package back to the US, statutory reporting, and local acquisitions were what was important. I felt I was a real company director of UK plc. Today I'm CFO for one product group worldwide. My influence extends beyond Europe to the US and Asia. Serving global customers, worldwide product sourcing, and pooling cash flows internationally have become my priorities'.

> As corporations move from geographic management to a global product–market approach, the finance function, too, must reorganize

Global competition forces CFOs to reduce the cost of financial activity. Two contrasting groups of global companies emerge: those becoming more centralized to support global integration of production and sales, and those with relatively independent foreign subsidiaries in which the finance function is increasingly decentralized.[3] The former group tends to make relatively bigger cuts in finance staff. Their CFOs say their highest priorities are mergers, acquisitions and divestments – a more strategic role emphasizing corporate finance.

Perhaps your toughest challenge as CFO of a global company relates to your external, not internal, role. The powerful institutional investors that today own large slices of companies are themselves shedding their national traditions and becoming more global. So the typical CFO reports financial results and projections to a mix of shareholders. Some are global in outlook, others more parochial, and all may have differing objectives: you need to tailor investor relations accordingly.

How should you communicate to these investors the risks of doing business around the world? For example, a multinational operating from a fixed asset base in a stable currency, and trading in more volatile foreign currencies, will be exposed to exchange rate fluctuations. Much of this exposure could be hedged, at a cost. Yet sophisticated institutional shareholders may be prepared to take such risks – the upside and downside – within a geographically diversified investment and trading portfolio.

Maximizing Shareholder Value

Accounting conventions – different from country to country – tend to be subjective. What's more, there's now considerable evidence showing that earnings derived from reported profits hold scant relation to share price movement. In contrast, cash and share value correlate tightly.

In the US and Europe, more and more institutional investors base their valuation of companies on projected cash flow performance, not reported earnings. This trend is taking root in Japan too, where companies beginning to suffer competition from lower cost economies regard generating cash as more important than merely taking market share through strategic investment.

In response, many CFOs wanting insight into how the market values their business now use the free cash flow valuation techniques discussed in the next chapter. But doing this at just *corporate* level often proves more an academic than a practical exercise. *Within the business*, which operating units or products create shareholder value? Which parts of the business destroy value by consuming excessive capital to generate less-than-acceptable market returns? What really delivers results is using this more detailed knowledge to target and communicate changes across the enterprise, to improve shareholder value.

In our research, maximizing shareholder value stands out as CFOs' number one priority – with managing investor relations not far behind. Yet few have a sound understanding of how major strategic change can affect value. The minority of companies that link individual change initiatives to value drivers are at the leading edge. So too are companies that have successfully institutionalized value based management. Many try to link shareholder value targets, through corporate strategies, to scorecards for performance measurement. What still lies ahead is the challenge of making value principles visible in the heart of the business – in culture, systems, incentive schemes and decision-making at every level.

In our research, maximizing shareholder value stands out as the number one priority of CFOs worldwide

More familiar sources of success, thanks partly to media reports, are companies' efforts to improve share price performance through well planned mergers and acquisitions – often followed by disposal of those parts of the target company seen to be non-value adding. Key decisions for CFOs:

- *how much to pay and for which parts of the business* – again, their answers now rely less on historical accounting values and more on predicted cash flow performance

- *how to release synergistic benefits through integration* – creating new value depends on grasping the relative values of the organizations' core competencies and underlying business processes.

Streamlining the Business

Schooled by their business process re-engineering experiences – good and bad – today's CFOs seek ways to give a hard kick to shareholder value and investor perceptions. Often, opportunities lie in restructuring the business, to cut costs and, more importantly, boost revenue. The hunt is far-flung: CFOs look domestically *and* internationally, within business units *and* across them. Some whittle down the value chain to more tightly define business processes. Many renew concentration on fewer, more valuable core competencies, sometimes using shared services or even outsourcing. For successful players, the rewards are enormous. And the most adroit let the finance function itself lead the way, for example as an early candidate for shared services.

Making such solutions work is far from easy. Corporations with long-established, substantial international operations face problems breaking down bureaucratic infrastructures, ingrained corporate cultures and carved-in-stone internal boundaries. While capital investment can be quickly shifted to where it's needed most, the attendant middle management baggage, seemingly immovable, may not be needed at all.

The finance function is well placed to influence the outcome. Transforming the business means transforming measurements and the way performance is reported. When the consequences of change are built into budgets and operating plans, that change is more likely to happen. Unwittingly, finance could *add* to the ever-growing complexity in business: the hazard is overlaying one set of measures or systems on another, to absorb new structures. More often, finance intervenes successfully to *cut* complexity – anything from simplifying the chart of accounts to reducing the number of suppliers or management layers – bringing great benefits.

The CFO must weigh trade-offs. Outsourcing manufacturing, for example, can reduce capital expenditure but will increase operating expenditure. It cuts management's workload but may introduce new kinds of business risk. Whether such moves create value overall depends on the corporation's ability to differentiate between those processes that genuinely add value in-house and those that don't. In these mold-breaking decisions, the CFO becomes the arbiter.

YOUR PIVOTAL ROLE IN THE BUSINESS

In any corporation, the CFO plays a pivotal role – aligning shareholders' demands for value creation with, in turn, the CEO's leadership of the business, operating units' strategies and the finance function's capabilities. Our *CFO 2000* survey shows that CFOs spend a growing proportion of their time with the CEO and business unit executives. They participate in all enterprise-wide improvement initiatives and lead many. Why?

The most obvious answer is that CFOs hold the financial key to all critical decisions. But that's only part of the story. To design effective internal responses to marketplace change, executive managers need a *process* view: structural, people and technological changes all tend to follow implementation of newly designed business processes. So, more and more corporations are adopting a business process approach. This puts CFOs in an even stronger position. They sit in the *cross-hairs* of corporate change, where pressures exerted by the old-style, hierarchical elements of the organization intersect with the forces of new-style, process based elements (Figure 1.3).

> In any corporation, the CFO plays a pivotal role – aligning shareholders' demands with business strategies and capabilities

Successful corporate change depends on the associated infrastructure of business plans, finance, systems, measures and controls. 'Nothing gets done around here without my sanction and a lot of extra work for my people,' comments one CFO.

World-class companies recognize that their finance functions, in the cross-hairs of change, can help make big things happen – as in the case of Ericsson.

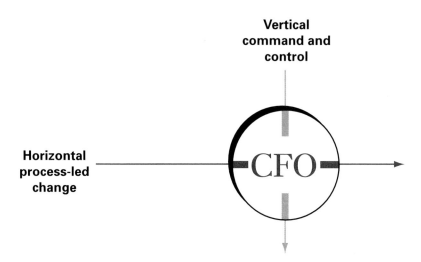

**Vertical
command and
control**

**Horizontal
process-led
change**

CFO

Figure 1.3 **The CFO is in the *cross-hairs* of change**

CASE STUDY: Building an Economic Engine

In mid-1996, Ericsson's Business Area Mobile Phones and Terminals decided to strengthen its organization and improve internal processes: it needed to manage expansion of the mobile phone business and increase its focus on the full lifecycle returns of product investments. Shaping Ericsson's play in this explosive-growth market – demand was rising by over 30% a year – president Johan Siberg asked new CFO Lars Lindqvist to step in to continue improving the business control function.

Lindqvist saw finance as uniquely positioned to pool knowledge and information to create value for the business – integrating its components into one 'economic engine'. Moving swiftly, he recast the function as three activity groups: financial control, business planning and decision support. Then he launched the most ambitious element of the reorganization program: an innovative business management process.

Under the banner Linking Strategy with Action, *a specially formed team concurrently designed and implemented the new process, creating strategic and tactical plans for coming years. Devolving decision-making from a common strategy, the process incorporates the value drivers of business performance, takes a scenario based approach to identifying current and future competitive capabilities – and then measures actions to make sure they're aligned with the strategy.*

Already, the team's business management process is prompting far-reaching changes. It has helped develop a shared business language and awareness of the value outcome of decisions – liberating previously untapped staff potential. Critically, in the world's fastest growing industry, it lets the company delegate with confidence while maintaining strategic direction.

Here, and in many other examples, today's finance function fulfills a bigger role in managing the business. As management shifts to a business process approach, finance professionals, less concerned with vertical command and control, focus on supporting horizontal process-led change. Indeed, the best CFOs view the finance function itself as a sequence of processes – through which they can exert influence and implement change.

Any change to one finance process affects others. And all finance processes affect business processes, to some degree, for example through performance reporting, transaction accounting or decision support. Yet our work with CFOs restructuring and re-engineering their finance functions makes clear that *there is no generally accepted definition of finance processes that covers the CFO's full remit.*

To fill the gap, we developed a simple framework for understanding finance processes, the connections between them and their links with the business value chain.

Why Define Finance Processes?

If the finance function is to add value as it becomes more embedded in the fundamentals of the business, finance processes must change, both in their own right and in the way they relate to the business they serve. The *finance value line* is a high level definition of processes that finance professionals normally undertake in an industrial company (Figure 1.4). Driving from *financial strategy* – the process of planning shareholder value improvements – through to predominantly operational processes, it proves a powerful tool for exploring finance's role.

Financial strategy influences each subsequent process in the finance

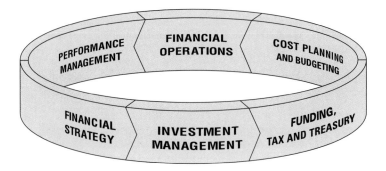

Figure 1.4 **The finance value line**

value line, especially *investment management* (capital appraisal and allocation, investor relations and external transactions) and *funding, tax and treasury* (including risk management). Next in line – mirroring the sequence of the business planning cycle – are *cost planning and budgeting* and *financial operations* (accounting and transaction processing). Finally, shaped by the budgeting process and delivered through transaction processing systems, performance measures serve the business through the process of *performance management.* With finance people combining all measures – external, internal, financial and non-financial – *performance management informs strategy*: the finance value line wraps around to complete the finance process cycle.

The *CFO 2000* survey asked CFOs how their finance functions divide their time across the finance value line – and how they think this will change in the next three years (Figure 1.5). Already expending significant effort upstream, in the more strategic activities, finance people will in future spend even more time on financial strategy and investment management – as well as performance management. They'll spend less time on the routine of downstream financial operations.

Why do CFOs and their finance teams find this framework useful? The short answer is because it encourages you to think big. It prompts you to see your prime role as shaping financial strategy to improve shareholder value – reinforced through investment management and business planning cycles. It emphasizes the importance of regular intervention by the finance function, for example to ensure that shareholder value targets are used in medium-term planning, annual budgeting and continuous performance measurement. In an acquisition, the finance value line

Financial strategy (shareholder value)	Investment management (M&A, capital expenditures)	Treasury/tax management (including pensions)	Cost planning/ budgeting	Financial operations (GL/purchase payables etc)	Performance management
In the past three years…					
13%	13%	14%	20%	24%	16%
In the next three years…					
18%	15%	14%	17%	18%	18%

Figure 1.5 **CFO 2000 survey: What proportion of time/human resource does the finance function spend on these processes?**

framework helps you align the finance processes of the two parties and guide business integration.

When it comes to major change, this process view shapes the questions that determine how you will move from strategy to operational reality (Figure 1.6). The strategic answers set out the battle plan and help marshal the resources, while the operational answers guide you in managing the plan and its results. The following case study illustrates the benefits.

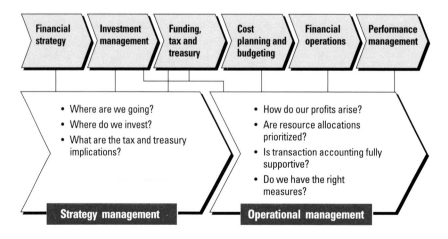

Figure 1.6 **Moving from strategy to operational reality: The big questions**

CASE STUDY: Multinational Doubles Its Share Price in Two Years

A consumer products company with operations in the US and more than 90 subsidiaries worldwide formed a new business strategy aimed at improving profitability and cash generation. Its reorganization to focus on three core businesses meant management accepting more accountability for results. But the finance function had lost touch with the business. And it was falling down on the basics: often, accounts were late and carried unwelcome surprises.

The new CFO took a double-barreled approach to change. He had to gain the confidence of senior managers and, in doing so, encourage them to concentrate on where performance improvements were most needed: ambitious targets for positive cash flows and improved return on net assets provided a rallying call. In parallel, he had to fix the finance function. The CFO decided to structure the change program according to the finance value line.

Starting with financial strategy, he used shareholder value analysis techniques to benchmark the company against peer group competitors, revealing major opportunities for value creation. In brainstorming workshops, top executives set themselves targets. Besides 25% growth in net margin, the bulk of capital expenditure was to shift from one part of the company to another, reducing it overall from 15% to 9% of sales. Working capital would be cut by a third.

Strategy implementation involved overhauling the capital investment appraisal process and incorporating new, value driven targets in medium-term plans and annual budgets. Accountability was sharpened by overturning the performance measurement system, company-wide – replacing it with a smaller number of more strategically relevant measures, linked to target shareholder value improvements. Taken down to personal level, this meant even relatively junior front-line managers now had clear goals, harmonized with overall strategy.

After a global review of treasury risk, new hedging policies were introduced, reinforced with systems that provide an up-to-the-minute picture of worldwide exposures. A stronger mix of debt-to-equity funding cut the cost of capital.

By this stage, the CFO was seen by colleagues to be ahead of the financial markets, thanks to improved investor relations and his full participation in the corporate agenda. The company's share price began to climb fast. At the same time, the internal credibility of the finance function was being restored.

Again using the finance value line framework, the CFO targeted process improvements for financial operations, *based on external benchmarks. More than 75% of the cost of transaction accounting processes was found to be non-value added. The budgeting cycle and accounts closing process were shrunk, giving management quicker access to more reliable information.*

Many changes initiated at strategic level began to flow smoothly into operational changes. Since direct savings were brought by pilots of activity based costing techniques in non-value adding corporate overhead areas, the outdated cost accounting *systems are being replaced with full blown activity based management. Needing new financial systems, the company chose a package giving enterprise-wide coverage. For the first time, the right financial and non-financial information for performance monitoring could be brought together in one place.*

The planned *upshot of this portfolio of initiatives was a 25% rise in the share price over two years. In fact, the stock nearly doubled in that period. Though this was due, in part, to a general rise in the sector, the finance function has certainly made its mark. Far from being cash negative, the company has built a* war chest *for focused acquisitions.*

This company's experience shows what can be achieved relatively quickly. Though only a snapshot of its work, the case study offers some powerful learning points.

- The case for change must be based on numbers – and big ones.
- Managers need to get out of their *silos* and work together on the economics of the business as a whole.
- To grab the attention of the rest of the business, finance managers must lead by example.

So How Can Finance Drive Change in the Business?

Finance processes are inextricably entwined with business operations. So a step change in the performance of the finance function invariably leads to a step change for everyone.

Financial managers perceived to be the true drivers of change are those who understand the cash generating potential of the business value chain, and stimulate concrete action (Figure 1.7). Our research confirms this over and over. What's needed is a new breed of financial officer, with a new set of skills, and a grasp of how finance processes that add real value can be integrated with others in the business at large.

Consider costing: if historical manufacturing costing systems, based on direct labor and overhead, are thrown out and replaced with forward-looking activity based management techniques for resource allocation, the finance function is bound to make a difference. One CFO asked: 'When I sell the rights to this product, and dispose of the manufacturing operations to a third party, what proportion of corporate and management overheads can I cut out of next year's budget?'. Activity based costing gave the answer.

The best CFOs take a rigorous approach to embedding finance processes in the business value chain. A new policy and process for capital investment management, for example, can have a major impact on manufacturing. Similarly, operational financial processes – even something as simple as payables – can be integrated with purchasing activity, under in-bound logistics in the business value chain, to achieve markedly lower costs and better supplier performance. A cross-functional process re-engineering team that combines financial and purchasing resources can achieve a step change in purchasing strategy.

In one case, the number of suppliers was cut from 17,000 to 1500: this

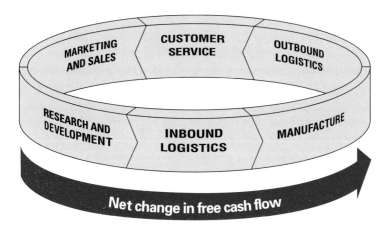

Figure 1.7 **Generating continuous cash flow through the business value chain**

reduced the downstream workload in the payables cycle, delivering big clerical savings. More importantly, concentrating the company's buying power by using fewer suppliers led to a $40 million saving in purchases.

Making connections between finance processes and business processes – and so finance systems and business systems – creates a more horizontally structured organization. But that's not all. What matters most is closer interaction between people from different functions, at all levels, based on a common shareholder value agenda. Talking about this is not new: *doing* it is.

The challenge for the chief financial officer is to drive fundamental process–led change, to benefit the business

Typically, CFOs see change as a series of external transactions, with or without internal structural alterations – all having hard financial consequences. They give less attention to the important soft issues of envisioning, communicating, changing culture and addressing individuals' needs.

This book draws a thread between your major challenges: meeting the objectives of external investors... reconciling these with internal management's agenda for change... facilitating improvements by introducing financial management best practices. Each chapter, with practical case studies, shows how you can drive fundamental, process-led change, to benefit the business.

Use traditional analytical skills to improve performance... No-one argues with an analytical role for the CFO on shareholder value. But to enter the corporate debate on value creating strategies, and make those strategies happen throughout the business, you need a *value based management* system (Chapter 2). You'll also need to intervene at every level, particularly front-line operations, to influence managers' behavior through new *performance measures* (Chapter 3). One mechanism you could use to prompt change is *activity based management* (Chapter 4). Going way beyond just costing, ABM lets you allocate resources for the future, based on a clear understanding of the activities that make up business processes.

Use specialist knowledge to support decision-making... Building on your role as protector of the company's assets, you could become the natural focus for *business risk management* (Chapter 5). Join the CFOs who – by embedding treasury, tax and insurance expertise in the decision-making process – turn risk into an asset exploited for gain, rather than something to be controlled at all costs.

Use your unique organizational position to influence structural change... Recognizing the links between finance processes and all other business processes, you should integrate changes in the finance function with changes in the business: *streamlining the organization for value creation* (Chapter 6), *sharing services* (Chapter 7) and introducing new decision support *systems* (Chapter 8). Create a model change process for the rest of the organization by transforming the finance function – its services, skills, structure and technology – in line with a new *vision* (Chapter 9).

The book ends with a look at the personal characteristics and competencies that will differentiate the best CFOs in the 21st century – challenging you to develop your capabilities as *corporate architect* (Chapter 10).

Like all chapters, this concludes with a checklist of best practices to point your way.

CFO's CHECKLIST

PURSUE VALUE Do you understand how the market values your company? Have you set stretch targets, using external benchmarks, for shareholder value improvement? Do you know which parts of the business create value and which destroy value?

DRIVE HOME STRATEGY WITH PERFORMANCE MEASURES Do you have so many measures they rob the company of focus? Are your performance measures tailored to current strategies? Do they link to the drivers of shareholder value? Could you implement a value scorecard?

DEVELOP A NEW GENERATION OF ACTIVITY BASED MANAGERS Do you use activity based costing to make big ticket decisions? Are your activity measures integrated with process measures? Are budgets based on activities? Have you gone beyond the pilot stage to full blown activity based management systems?

INTEGRATE FINANCIAL AND BUSINESS RISK MANAGEMENT Do you understand the full scope of your business risks? Have you quantified your *value at risk*? What is your company's appetite for risk? Does your corporate culture encourage risk-taking?

RE-SHAPE THE BUSINESS FROM A VALUE PERSPECTIVE Are you battling growing complexity? Could you shorten the business value chain? Have you rationalized customer and supplier lists? Could you streamline sales operations and back office services by creating virtual organizations? Are you making the finance function the Trojan horse for change?

BREAK DOWN BORDERS USING SHARED SERVICES Are your finance processes simplified and standardized according to best practice? Would you benefit from a move to shared services, across geographical boundaries? Or across business units? Have you thought through the business case?

STEP UP DECISION SUPPORT WITH SYSTEMS CHANGE Have you moved to integrated enterprise-wide systems? Do your decision support systems facilitate value based management, performance management and activity based management? Do you have a data warehouse?

DELIVER A VISION FOR FINANCE Does your vision for the finance function support the overall business vision? Have you confronted the reality of where you are today? What do finance's customers think of the service you provide? Do performance measures for your finance executives encourage the right behaviors?

BECOME THE ARCHITECT OF YOUR CORPORATION'S FUTURE Do you act as the *alter ego* of the CEO? Are you the driving force behind value creation? Do you have skills that will allow you to succeed in the 21st century? Does your service contract mean you can build personal wealth in line with that of the corporation?

CHAPTER 2
In Pursuit of Value

The date: 1 February 2004. Jan McNally sits down with a smile. She's just addressed the annual stockholders' meeting of Mediatronics, the global manufacturer of state-of-the-art semi-conductors, communication devices and Internet software she joined as CFO back in 1997. Her ears ringing with applause, McNally reminds herself of the skepticism at her first meeting when she'd outlined plans to 'create the future business history' of Mediatronics. There wasn't a single skeptic in today's audience.

Mediatronics' credo had always been delivering value – for its customers, employees and investors – making it a keen proponent of shareholder value management when this became the rage in the early 1990s. The CEO knew he had to keep investors happy if the corporation was to raise the huge amounts of capital it needed to continue funding its exponential revenue growth. It had not taken McNally long to convince him that delivering value to shareholders on a sustained basis meant much more than using discounted cash flow techniques to evaluate big ticket decisions. She argued that all decisions – investment, financing and operational – must be consistent with achieving Mediatronics' value objectives. And that managers at every level must view the corporation in the same light as its investors did. Winning the board's approval in 1998, she set about operationalizing value based management.

    McNally supervised the analysis that showed where Mediatronics was – and was not – creating value. A radically new investment management system soon followed. Planning and budgeting would no longer involve tortuous annual negotiation of incremental improvements, but would be conducted in the context of a five-year plan driven by a target return to shareholders. The entire decision-making process was overhauled to align targets being set inside the guts of the business with the overall shareholder value target. Then, employees could be incentivized based on measures they understood and were able to control. The end game was value reporting, which went live in 1999.

    Today, the benefits of the approach championed by McNally are clear: in each of the seven years since her appointment, Mediatronics has delivered a total shareholder return in excess of 30%, making it one of the NYSE's best performers and America's most respected corporations.

As *maximizing shareholder value* emerges as a key corporate objective the world over, so *value based management (VBM)* is becoming an imperative for the CFO. Highlighting the growing influence of institutional investors, this chapter explores the implications of their increasing use of cash flow based techniques to evaluate investment options.

The chapter focuses on the CFO's pivotal role in making VBM an operational reality. What methods should you use to analyze where your corporation is creating or destroying value? How can you introduce the fundamental changes needed to ensure that your corporation's decision-making processes – at all levels – are consistent with shareholder value principles? How can you transform your current financial systems into *integrated value planning and reporting systems*? Equipping the CFO with tools to penetrate the damp course of middle management, VBM is a powerful way of energizing the whole corporation in pursuit of value.

INVESTORS INVADE THE BOARDROOM

Originating in the US, the trend for investors to flex their muscles in company boardrooms is sweeping through capital markets worldwide. How come?

Share ownership has undergone a fundamental shift. In the US and Europe, individual investors once owned more than 50% of stock directly, but are now less significant than institutional investors such as pension funds, mutual funds and insurance companies. The same change is taking place in the Asia Pacific region. Controlling much bigger stakes in companies, institutional investors have correspondingly greater power over them. Their mounting strength – and the pressure felt by multinationals – is being magnified by a number of allied factors: rapid globalization of capital markets, a low inflation environment across the world, relatively anemic growth prospects in continental Europe, and strong competitive performance by companies operating in low labor cost countries.

> The trend for investors to flex their muscles in company boardrooms is sweeping through capital markets worldwide

Institutional investors are themselves under pressure to deliver high returns to their own investors, over sustained periods. Their uncompromising remit is to ensure a consistently high *total shareholder return*: they want the company's executive management to concentrate on maximizing the combined dividends and share price appreciation that shareholders can expect during their period of share ownership.

For example, some investors, including US fund manager Oppenheimer Capital, invest primarily in corporations that make an explicit commitment, in their annual accounts, to enhancing shareholder value. Moreover, they may insist that the corporation returns money to shareholders if management is unable to find investment opportunities capable of generating their targeted rate of return.

Where management teams look like failing to meet investors' requirements for above average returns, institutions are becoming more interventionist. Chrysler, Chase Manhattan Bank and Saatchi & Saatchi are among blue chip corporations to experience the leverage that big investors now have in the boardroom.

Even seemingly invulnerable senior level jobs can come under intense pressure. Sir David Sainsbury, CEO of well known UK retailer J Sainsbury, has had clear notice that the company is being given only a small window of time to improve its performance before institutional investors push for changes in top management. And this is in a company where the Sainsbury family still owns a substantial shareholding. Similarly at Philips, while recently appointed chairman Cor Boonstra has initially received a positive reception from his investors, there can be little doubt that they're looking for tangible signs of improvement during 1997.

The overriding message to executives everywhere is clear: create value or your shareholders will get someone else in to do it for you.

Implicit in that message is another, and it's equally compelling: you can't hide from investors any more. Influential publications such as *Fortune* magazine and *The Sunday Times* publish league tables ranking companies that have created shareholder value – and pointing the finger at those destroying it. Recent lists of high performers contain names like Coca-Cola, Monsanto, Intel and Microsoft.

At Endesa, a $20 billion Spanish corporation and one of Europe's five largest utilities, director financiero Jose Luis Palomo describes his team's experience of the transparency demanded by the international investment community – following flotation, 10% of the company's stock is in the hands of US investors. 'When we first went for listing on the NYSE, we found a group of investors who were prepared to back us. They were bright, articulate and penetrating in their analysis, and they surprised us when they began tracking us more closely than we were used to. Then they also began to intervene in our routine management process. We decided the only way they were going to stay with us was if we opened up fully to them, letting them know the good points and bad. We told them: "This is your company, not ours, and we don't expect you to buy a stock that's unfairly priced one way or the other". Ten years on, they're still with us. Our experience overall, while sometimes uncomfortable, has been positive.'

> The overriding message to executives everywhere is clear: create value or your shareholders will get someone else in to do it for you

Looked at from the other side of the corporate equation, this new breed of shareholder has little choice but to intervene. Unlike most private investors, they cannot simply dump stock if they think a company is being badly managed – the size of their stake means any attempt to sell could in itself damage the value of their shares. Instead, the investment philosophy they're adopting is to engage proactively with executive management, pushing through needed changes in strategy, to deliver returns in line with aggressive expectations.

Witness the track record of the largest US public pension fund, the California Public Employees Retirement System (CalPERS), which in the last few years has trebled its assets to more than $100 billion. A study of

42 companies targeted by CalPERS for investigation in 1992 showed that in the preceding five years their stock had underperformed the Standard & Poor's 500 index by 66%. In the five years following CalPERS' intervention, the same stock outperformed the index by 41%.[1]

Mergers and acquisitions provide particularly fertile ground for the growth of the interventionist investor. In the UK, the Mercury Asset Management Fund – among the country's largest institutional investors – supported Granada's hostile bid for Forte: Mercury had more confidence in the Granada team's ability to deliver value from the Forte businesses. This was despite Forte's mounting a spirited defense, including significant action to reduce costs and make the business as a whole more focused. Elsewhere, ITT – owner of Sheraton Hotels and Caesar's World Casinos – is having to fight hard to retain its independence in the face of a $6.5 billion hostile bid launched by Hilton Hotels. ITT had seen its share price substantially underperform the Standard & Poor 500 since the beginning of 1997. Only now, as part of its defense strategy, has it identified and sold off non-core assets, among them its ownership of the *New York Knicks* – moves that shareholders had been recommending for some time. Hilton's bid, well received by institutional investors, is led by new CEO Stephen Bollenbach, formerly CFO of Disney, who has a formidable record of enhancing shareholder value.

Of course, investors' influence can equally be used to step in and *prevent* unwanted takeovers. A striking demonstration was provided by Fleming Investment Management when it led a successful campaign to stop BBA making a hostile bid for Lucas, the UK based automotive brakes manufacturer. Lucas subsequently merged with Varity in the US.

Without doubt, institutional investors consider that their responsibilities extend well beyond the doors of corporate governance. Today's more powerful, more demanding investor is not shy to force management to change its ways.

As a result, maximizing shareholder value is becoming the number one priority for most publicly listed corporations – not just in the Anglo-Saxon world but also in the Asia Pacific region and continental Europe, particularly Germany, where top companies such as Veba, Hoechst and Daimler Benz have embraced the concept. Recognizing that short-term value gains achieved at the expense of, say, customers or employees are unlikely to lead to sustained value creation in the longer term, they regard *all* stakeholder objectives as consistent with their overriding shareholder value objective.

IT'S CASH THAT COUNTS!

Institutional investors' growing influence has been accompanied by another big change – in the way they appraise investment options. Traditional methods of evaluation, based on accounting concepts such as earnings per share (EPS), return on equity, and return on investment, are being replaced by cash flow based, economic methods.

Behind this trend lies what has become overwhelming evidence from empirical studies showing that there is a significant relationship between a company's share price and its cash flow performance – much stronger than the relationship between share price and EPS performance. In Figure 2.1, based on a recent study in Europe, the correlation of share price movements with EPS is negligible at 0.01, while the correlation with cash return on invested capital is 0.77.

The shortcomings of EPS as a basis for judging corporate performance should come as no surprise to CFOs. International accounting conventions tend to be subjective: EPS calculations for the same company in the same year can vary significantly from country to country. Generally, EPS based valuation techniques do not take account of inflation, or the different levels of business risk associated with different companies.

Spectacular illustrations are provided by, for example, Maxwell Communications and Coloroll – companies that collapsed despite high reported profits and revenues looking good. Only days before it went bust, another UK company, Polly Peck, reported profits of £161 million – a 70% growth in earnings on the previous year. When Daimler Benz registered on the NYSE in 1993, having been highly profitable according to German accounting rules, it appeared to turn into a heavy loss-maker under US GAAP.

Finding it hard to make comparative judgements based exclusively on EPS performance, institutional investors are building shareholder value models that forecast future cash flows for each of their investments. In our recent survey of 30 leading US investment management firms, one senior analyst sums up the views of the majority when he comments: 'Cash flow is typically a better and cleaner number by which to value a company, from both accounting and economic standpoints. On the accounting side, there are fewer manipulations that can take place, and on the economic side, cash flow is ultimately the value of what the shareholder gets when buying a share of stock'.[2]

Their move toward cash flow based valuation makes institutional

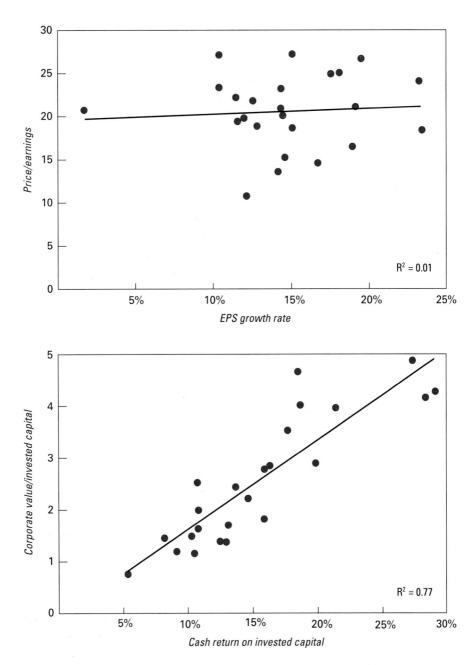

Figure 2.1 **Cash flow measures show a greater correlation with share value**
Source: Credit Suisse First Boston

investors even hungrier for information. Acting on a global stage, they want to be able to compare companies' performance across sectors and countries, on an equitable basis. They understand better than ever before the competitive fundamentals of the industries in which they have interests. And they commit huge amounts of resource to keeping abreast of who's doing what and why – intelligence that lets them make highly informed judgements on the appropriateness and sustainability of a corporation's strategy and management.

AIMING AT TOTAL SHAREHOLDER RETURN

How are progressive corporations responding to these pressures?

Monsanto showed the way when it replaced its return on equity targets with cash based, economic value targets. CFO Robert Hoffman says: 'We needed to find a financial metric that would create new levels of share owner value by being more directly correlated with stock price. It had to be a measure that's economically based and tied to cash flows, rather than accounting based'. Monsanto aims to generate a 50% increase in its stock price by 2000: from $30 per share, reflecting the current market capitalization of $18 billion, to $45 per share – a market capitalization of $27 billion. This means cash flow return on investment should increase from 9% to 13% in real terms, linked to a longer-term 10% asset growth. Monsanto believes that acquisitions will play a major part in its growth. Value creating strategies also include cutting costs and re-purchasing stock when debt levels merit a strong single-A rating.

The CFO of another US corporation comments: 'We are much more closely aligned to shareholders than 18 months ago, when we were driven more by return on assets than cash. Only if you know what drives share-holder value can you be successful, and all the studies seem to indicate that cash flow is the biggest driver, not bottom line. Now, we measure our business units on cash flow, rather than just earnings. The top 40 managers have their business and personal targets aligned to this new measure'.

Like these CFOs, many others are leading their businesses away from conventional targets, including return on capital employed (ROCE) and return on net assets (RONA). Eager to satisfy institutional investors' demands, they now aim at total shareholder return (TSR) or other value based targets, such as cash flow return on investment (CFROI), free cash flow (FCF) and economic value added (EVA™).[3] Often, the shift is reinforced by introducing value based compensation packages for senior managers.

Debate continues about which of these new metrics correlates most closely to shareholder value. Whichever you choose, your shareholder value measure must be forward looking and established for a reasonable period – at least three to five years. Don't lose sight of the fact that ultimately what's important is your company's cash flow performance, and how it compares with that of other companies competing for the same investment funds.

But setting targets alone – even when soundly based on value principles – won't automatically deliver the *desired* result. Without a business and financial management system to back up shareholder value measures, many companies have difficulty explaining them and obtaining buy-in. Critically, they struggle to establish the new measures at divisional and strategic business unit level. A divisional manager at one major European multinational told us: 'The CFO is really hooked on this shareholder value thing. Out here in operations, where it counts, it means nothing. It simply hasn't been translated into terms that we relate to. We haven't got a clue how to put it into practice'.

'We're much more closely aligned to shareholders than 18 months ago, when we were driven more by return on assets than cash'

The challenge, then, is to forge a link, from value based strategy, through to operations and the actual value being created by executing management's plans. In short, you need to install a *value based management* system.

WHERE ARE YOU IN THE VALUE BASED MANAGEMENT LIFECYCLE?

Many companies claim they already manage for value. In our *CFO 2000* survey, nearly 70% of companies say they use shareholder value analysis at corporate level for strategic planning. At operational line management level, a smaller proportion – one third – say they have deployed shareholder value analysis in budgeting and setting performance measurement targets.

Our experience in the field suggests a similar picture. Certainly, most companies in the US – and increasing numbers in Europe and Asia Pacific – do use shareholder value analysis to drive strategic decision-making. But only a minority have begun to think seriously about how to make the more fundamental shifts involved in deployment at lower levels. Often, attempts to operationalize value principles seem, in reality, to have involved little more than a change of metrics.

So what does it take to put value based management (VBM) into action? VBM is about analysis and management of operating free cash flows, risk and time adjusted. It's also about changing the mindset of people within the business, from short-term profit horizons to long-term value creation. Orienting management toward improving the position of shareholders, VBM has a profound influence on business strategy, plans and budgeting – helping to ensure the future success of the company. By constantly reinforcing the shareholder value theme and motivating individuals' behavior, VBM helps all employees achieve corporate goals.

> Value is created or destroyed at the point where decisions are made – and not just big strategic decisions, but operational ones too

Few investment opportunities have a higher payback. That's why enlightened CFOs of companies including Monsanto, PepsiCo, Boots and Lloyds Bank have turned to the VBM approach. For them, it really is cash that counts.

As one CFO points out: 'To get excellence, the greatest source of untapped resources is from middle management down'. More than once in this book we stress that value is created or destroyed at the point where decisions are made. The extent to which people throughout your company use shareholder value thinking in *decision-making* is a good test of where you stand in the VBM lifecycle (Figure 2.2).

VBM adds transparency to decision-making processes across the enterprise: it lets you see the likely impact of specific decisions on the value of the business – not just big strategic decisions, but operational decisions too. What will be the impact on shareholder value of, for example, reducing lead time? Or reconfiguring the supply chain? Or rationalizing the product range? Or focusing on a smaller number of key customers?

Expressing shareholder value in terms that everyone can understand, VBM helps re-energize middle managers – bridging corporate and front-line managers, strategy and implementation.

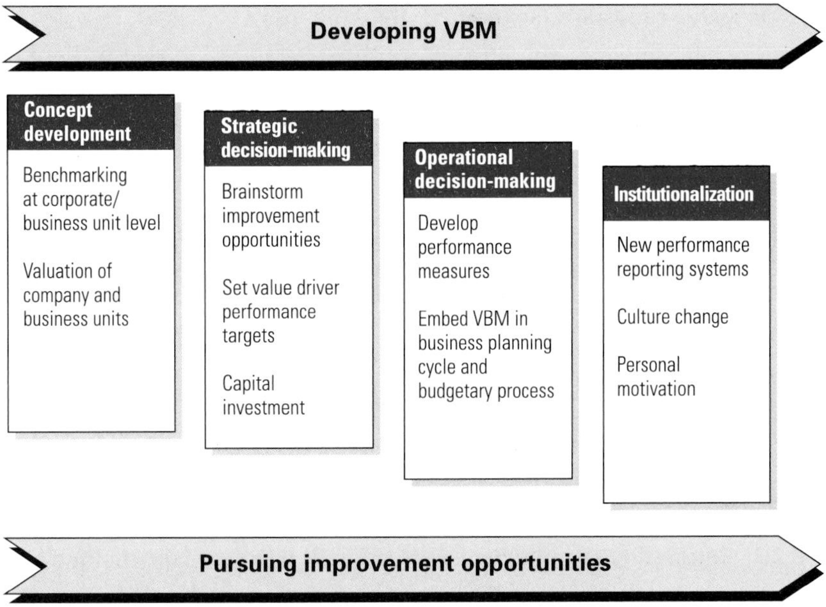

Figure 2.2 **The value based management (VBM) lifecycle**

MAKE VBM AN OPERATIONAL REALITY

The VBM system needs to combine historic *and* predictive views with financial *and* non-financial drivers of the business. It needs to incentivize people at all levels to pursue the overriding objective of improving shareholder value.

To make your VBM system operational, take four essential steps:

- understand your value drivers

- find where value is created or destroyed

- take value based decisions

- embed the VBM system.

Step 1: Understand Your Value Drivers

First you must understand the sources of value in your business. Comprehensive and practical, the analytical framework in Figure 2.3 is based

Shareholder value = corporate value - debt

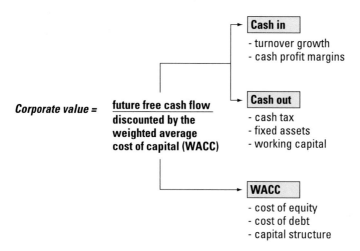

Figure 2.3 **Calculating shareholder value using the free cash flow method**

on work in the 1980s by US economist Alfred Rappaport.[4] Shareholder value, in this simple definition, is equal to total corporate value less debt, where corporate value is no different from the economic value of any asset – that is, the future *free cash flow* that investors expect the company to generate over a defined timeframe, discounted by the cost of capital appropriate for the business.

This means you need to consider seven *value drivers* – macro level factors, varying between industries, that determine shareholder value. Five are operationally based. *Turnover growth* and *cash profit margins* drive the amount of cash coming into the business. The *cash tax* rate (actual tax paid) drives the amount going out. So does investment in the business, in terms of *fixed asset* and *working capital* expenditure. In addition to these, there's the *weighted average cost of capital (WACC)*: the rate of return demanded by investors – in relation to both debt and equity – based on the risk associated with the business and its capital structure (ratio of debt to equity).

The company creates shareholder value only if it generates returns in excess of its cost of capital. So the seventh value driver is the timeframe over which the market expects your business to achieve this, known as the *competitive advantage period*.

Rappaport's approach proves extremely powerful in practice. Our experience in over 100 cases involving listed companies in the US and Europe – using publicly available information in brokers' and analysts' reports to derive assumptions for each company's value drivers – amply substantiates its credibility. Valuations are typically within 3–5% of a company's market capitalization.

Yet even the most sophisticated companies pay too little attention to key drivers of shareholder value. Our survey of leading US investment fund managers highlights the competitive advantage period as among the most important of the value drivers: it's also the driver on which respondents say they receive *least* useful information from companies. Perhaps the most difficult driver to estimate, competitive advantage periods can vary from just a few years, in industries like software development (where technology changes rapidly), to much longer periods, in industries like oil and gas (where barriers to entry are higher and competitive conditions inherently more predictable). Generally, the markets estimate competitive periods of around ten years.

> Using the value drivers, the CFO can communicate with managers about shareholder value in terms they're already familiar with

Calculating WACC can also be troublesome. For example, few companies make adequate adjustments to reflect the varying levels of risk – particularly political and economic risks – that can result in markedly different costs of capital for different operations across businesses and geographies (Chapter 5). And often, companies *destroy* value by failing to invest in projects where expected returns exceed their cost of capital.

Intending to be seen as prudent, one company set a hurdle rate for project evaluation by adding a buffer of 5% to its cost of capital. Not only did this result in missed opportunities, but, because the company appeared to be accepting projects with higher levels of risk than its existing business, the market increased the risk it attached to the business overall. Investors didn't regard management as prudent – in fact, the opposite.

CFOs who break down shareholder value using the value drivers can begin to view the business from the inside exactly as it's viewed by external investors. Gaining a tangible feel for market expectations of the company's performance on the seven drivers – and using this to model assumptions for each – the CFO can better guide financial strategy and implementation. Most important of all, the CFO can communicate with managers about shareholder value in terms they're already familiar with. Able with relative ease to judge the impact of their decisions on the value drivers, managers throughout the business can more readily contribute to value creation.

The company in the case study used shareholder value analysis to make needed improvements in performance – and prevent the market getting a rude shock.

CASE STUDY: Overhauling the Capital Investment Program

To develop shareholder value models, a manufacturing company asked managers at its two strategic business units and head office to forecast performance against their respective value drivers, over a ten-year period. The combined results established the value of the company as a whole – and were reconciled to its current market capitalization by comparing managers' forecasts with those published by brokers and analysts.

Then the company did some external benchmarking. The value drivers of each business unit were compared with those of companies that it would have competed with for investment funds had it been a separate listed company. This revealed that, compared to industry high performers, one of the units required 40% more fixed capital investment to generate each dollar of sales income.

The company had been investing heavily in new plant and machinery to increase capacity in this business unit. But margins in the unit were under pressure. Management's predicted returns from the fixed capital investment program were significantly below both the unit's cost of capital and investors' expectations. Destroying rather than creating value, the investment program needed urgent attention to prevent the 15% depreciation in company share price forecast by the combined value models.

The program's negative impact on value was further stress-tested by a sensitivity analysis. It emerged that if the business unit could reduce its capital investment by just 1% of turnover through efficiency improvements, and main-tain the same level of sales income, its value would rise by 17%. After margins, fixed capital expenditure was the most sensitive value driver for this business!

Eighteen months on, the company has implemented a new, integrated investment management system in which all capital projects undergo rigorous appraisal and monitoring. Projects in non-core areas have been scrapped. Overall, the company's capital expenditure as a per cent of sales income has dropped to the average for its peer group. And its shareholder value has increased by over 33% – well ahead of the industry.

Value drivers at micro level, too, vary from sector to sector. Figure 2.4, based on the telecommunications sector, illustrates how micro value drivers can be linked to the shareholder value model. This helps management to demonstrate the value impact of potential performance improvement initiatives, such as re-engineering processes, changing pricing or launching a new marketing strategy.

Using an industry specific micro model alongside ValueBuilder™ modeling software, CFOs can attach *coefficients of value* to individual strategic or operational decisions – quantifying them in shareholder value

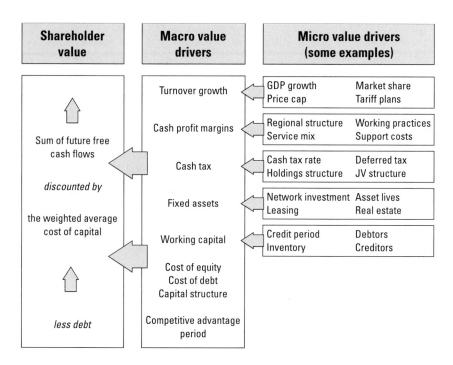

Figure 2.4 **Micro value drivers for a telecommunications operator**

terms.[5] They can also evaluate the consequences of changes in external competitive conditions – for example, the impact of losing customers.

A telecommunications company wanted to assess exactly how its value would be affected by deregulation: future revenues would be driven by competition and downward pressure on prices. Creating coefficients of value, management could see that every 1% loss of *market share* by 2001 would cause shareholder value to diminish by $227 million. Each 1% drop in annual *price tariffs* would cost $444 million in value. But on the upside, if the company reduced annual *operating costs* by 1%, or $83 million, it stood to rebuild value by $1 billion. The company now uses coefficients of value to prioritize all proposed change projects. Implementation is monitored through a combination of operational and value creating reporting metrics.

Step 2: Find Where Value Is Created or Destroyed

Convert the results of your shareholder value analysis into a *value map* – plotting, for each strategic business unit, the value generated against the level of investment needed to generate it (Figure 2.5). Giving a vivid picture of which business units create value and which consume value, this technique can open up a whole new perspective for executive managers. Confronted by a value map, they're prompted to challenge

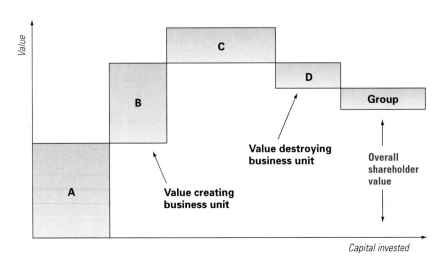

Figure 2.5 **A value map pinpoints the sources of value creation**

basic assumptions that govern the way they constitute, structure and manage the enterprise – as the following case study shows.

CASE STUDY: Using a Value Map to Make Investment Trade-offs

A global player on the high-tech scene analyzed the shareholder value performance of each of its three main businesses – semi-conductors, PCs and telecommunications – as well as group headquarters. Mapping the results raised important issues.

Semi-conductors needed significant capital investment *Sales turnover in this business was expected to grow substantially. But the group was already highly leveraged: debt had been used to fund growth, to the point where capacity was exhausted. And with its share price languishing, raising more equity looked an unlikely option. How could the group fund semi-conductors' expansion? Should it look for a joint venture partner?*

PC margins were under serious downward pressure *It seemed it would be difficult – if not impossible – for the PC business to secure returns above its cost of capital on any additional capital investment. Should capital be rationed? If so, what changes would be needed in the existing worldwide manufacturing infrastructure to keep returns above the cost of capital?*

Expanding telecommunications would mean boosting R&D *The fight was on to keep the new, rapidly growing telecommunications business ahead of competitors. Since capital was constrained, could it be diverted from the PC business into R&D at telecommunications? Or would using it to expand semi-conductors deliver more value?*

Headquarters was having a drag effect on shareholder value *Finding headquarters and corporate support services to be non-value adding, management launched Project ValMax. With duplicated overheads identified in the center and business divisions, potential solutions included outsourcing and other kinds of restructuring.*

Interpret your shareholder value analysis and associated value map in a *competitive* context. Some companies use a tool known as the *corporate power index (CPI)*.[6] Scores are calculated by dividing the company's market value by sales income generated over, say, a year. For example, Microsoft's 1996 market capitalization of $64.7 billion and revenues of $5.9 billion gave it a CPI score of 10.9. A year later, with the company's 47% revenue growth (to $8.7 billion) viewed alongside its 82% increase in market capitalization (to $118.1 billion), its CPI has improved to 13.6. In the same period, Monsanto's CPI improvement from 2.0 to 2.5 reflects revenue growth from $8.9 to $9.3 billion and a rise in market capitalization from $17.8 to $23.3 billion.

Routinely tracked over time, against competitors, the CPI is particularly useful for monitoring the flow of market value between your own company and others. Quantifying where shareholder value is being won and lost, it lets you gage the company's position in its value cycle:

- *are you on an upward value creation curve*, with a vibrant product and service offering that customers are willing to pay a premium for?

- *or have you entered an intensely competitive phase*, with margins squeezed and the value created for investors diminishing?

- *even worse, is value seeping out of your business into competitors' businesses*, so they become stronger at your expense?

After value mapping at business unit level, you may need to dis-aggregate value further, examining lower level *value centers* – these could be product or customer groups, or even groups of processes such as a supply chain.

For example, to develop a better picture of its overall value, a mutual insurance company analyzed the value of its main service groups: core services such as life insurance and health care, along with a diversified portfolio of non-core activities. The company's aim was to create value for policyholders (in effect its owners) by balancing competitive strength and risk-taking across its activities. Combining the free cash flow valuation method with a bottom-up risk analysis, the company made preliminary estimates of attributed capital for each service group – factoring in the relevant assumed risks.

In Figure 2.6, using illustrative data, one axis shows the share of total capital allocated to each service group. The other shows the returns, alongside the marginal cost of capital (the risks). Policyholder value is created when a service group produces risk-adjusted returns in excess of attributed and actual capital costs. Where this exercise helped most was in surfacing, for all to see, the specific value characteristics of each

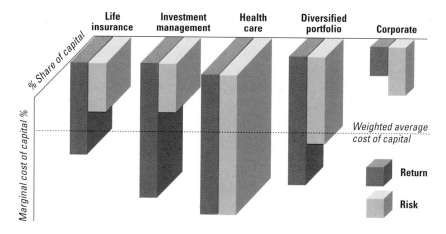

Figure 2.6 **Finding opportunities to enhance policyholder value in a mutual insurance company**

service group: its key value drivers, the sources and concentrations of risk (quantitative *and* qualitative), the relative benefits of the diversification program and, above all, long-term issues of investment and divestment.

For real insight, combine your disaggregated value map with corporate power index calculations similarly disaggregated down to value center level. Now you can make timely adjustments to capital intensity across the business portfolio, based on the relative free cash flow potential of proposed investments. The power index tells you where your company is in its value cycle: the value map guides you in managing the capital investment program and selecting the most appropriate change initiatives. With limited amounts of capital to allocate, the skill of maximizing shareholder value is in the timing – deciding where *and* when to throttle or re-direct investment.

Step 3: Take Value Based Decisions

Corporations take three types of decision: investment, financing and operational.

To evaluate *investment* and *financing* decisions, most use reasonably sophisticated discounted cash flow (DCF) techniques. But often, they're applied on an incremental basis. They may cover only some of the value drivers – and so fail to pick up the full impact of a decision on the business as a whole. For example, conventional investment appraisal of a proposal to build a new factory would not normally reflect its implications for the company's competitive advantage period.

When it comes to *operational* decisions, companies seldom look at these in shareholder value terms at all. Yet establishing a value creating strategy – though clearly important – is not on its own enough to secure success in today's investment climate. The CFO must keep in mind that value is created or destroyed at every point where decisions are made. To be certain that value creation can be sustained and improved operationally by front-line managers, you need a framework that gives *managers at all levels* a coherent understanding of how to take value based decisions.

Disaggregating the corporation's value into value centers (Figure 2.7) may not prove straightforward. You need financial data that's not always readily available: you may have to construct it specially for the purpose. But once you've developed a lower level value model, you can use it to test the impact on shareholder value of operational decision-making scenarios – as illustrated in the next case study.

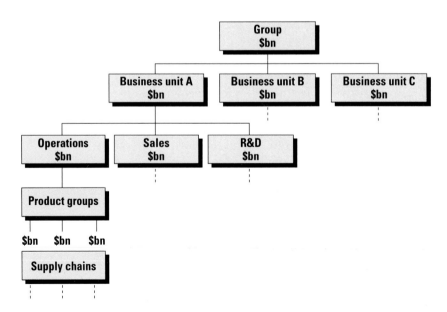

Figure 2.7 **Value by business component**

CASE STUDY: VBM as an Operational Decision-making Tool

A major global manufacturer of branded consumer goods, based in the Asia Pacific region, had recently reorganized one of its divisions along product lines. Separate supply chains were being established for each product group. The division's head of manufacturing was keen to develop models for value analysis that would let his team take product-specific decisions within a common system.

One particular product, manufactured at a single plant in Taiwan, contributed some 15% of the division's worldwide sales. With lower cost producers beginning to appear, especially in China, competition was quickly hotting up. Determined to cope, the manufacturing team knew it should focus on improving efficiencies and lead times. But without a framework for rationalizing its efforts, it continued to wrestle with various, sometimes conflicting, performance improvement projects.

Once VBM was installed, choosing the best projects to pursue became easier. Three were shortlisted:

- *making greater use of external sub-contractors*

- *restructuring parts of the supply chain*

- *laying down new capacity in South America.*

The team created a value model for the product supply chain. Each project's impacts – costs and benefits – were carefully assessed and mapped on to the value drivers. Running these impacts through the model, the team quantified the options in terms of value enhancement.

Two specific solutions now being implemented by the division are forecast to boost the product's value by some 17.5%, having a significant knock-on effect on the company's overall value.

VBM lets you value operational scenarios, select the right option and *then* establish a set of performance measures to monitor day-to-day decisions on the shop floor. Chapter 3 discusses best practice for developing measures from value creating strategies – and for reinforcing value improvement through reward and incentive mechanisms.

What's different about this approach is that it makes shareholder value targets meaningful to front-line managers. Individuals responsible for slices of the working capital pie – inbound logistics, manufacturing, outbound logistics, sales and finance – all know precisely what they must do to deliver the targets, and how their efforts will be measured and reported. Via metrics like receivables, debtor days and lead times, linked to value, the company can see how well it's doing in operationalizing value strategies. And it can begin to develop an integrated performance measurement system covering *all* decisions – investment, financing and operational.

By aligning routine measures with value drivers, managers at this electronics company were able to position a major improvement initiative within the business's overall value framework.

CASE STUDY: Cash Accounting on the Production Line

The performance of a company that designs and manufactures mass spectrometry equipment was fast deteriorating. Backorders were growing: it was taking over six months to produce and ship a product. Shipments were regularly late. Costs and working capital were escalating.

A manufacturing benchmarking study yielded a solution. The company needed to introduce just-in-time production techniques to assemble the final product. It also needed a new system to schedule the 2000 or so piece parts in each product through the various electronic, metal fabrication and optics workshops. It had to abandon its philosophy of maximizing utilization of all resources all the time – and instead concentrate on sequencing and releasing piece part batches through production centers, at rates that maximized throughput only in bottlenecks.

Improvement targets were set: cut the production and delivery cycle from 26 to eight weeks, quickly work off backorders, raise delivery reliability to 96%, virtually eliminate overtime and sub-contract manufacture, and dramatically reduce inventory levels. These targets were translated into routine measures. Then, managers prioritized the measures by linking them to value drivers at business process level: margins and working capital were found to be most critical. The company could assess, using cash as a common denominator, the benefits of minimizing lead times, improving customer service and reducing inventories.

The approach made plain that although plant utilization figures had previously looked great, most departments' overhead absorption ran ahead of budget. The business had actually been bleeding cash, in the form of overtime payments, unnecessary use of sub-contractors, lost and canceled orders, and excessive working and fixed capital consumption. Today's factory is leaner in more ways than one: under the new system, managers found they could get more volume out with less floor space.

The best shareholder value modeling tools support decision-making by mimicking the intricacies and interrelationships of the real world.

A pharmaceutical company succeeded in developing a supply chain model that connects dynamically to its shareholder value model. Using these as a kind of value calculator, managers can test out detailed plans and scenarios, built bottom-up – exploring the likely knock-on effects of decisions, for example about resource consumption. The models give them a more robust basis for devising medium-term plans: they're better able to understand the investment and resources needed to deliver the company's market share and sales forecasts.

CFOs leading their companies to the final stage in the VBM lifecycle should integrate their value models with other decision support tools – by linking them to business planning and performance measure reporting systems, for example, and drawing source data from underlying trans-action processing systems, possibly via a data warehouse (Chapter 8).

Step 4: Embed the VBM System

You'll experience plenty of barriers to implementing VBM. So it's as well to prepare for them now. From marketeers, you may hear: *'It's a narrow financial view of the world. What about our markets and products?'*. From others: *'Shareholder value management treats employees as money-making machines rather than as assets to be nurtured'*. Almost certainly expect this: *'You're obsessed with shareholders. We have to consider government, unions, community, suppliers and customers too'*. And there's always the procrastinators: *'We'd love to install VBM but we don't have the people or systems. Come back in 2010!'*.

The business case for VBM is a highly persuasive one, but you're going to need the strongest possible buy-in from your board colleagues, right from the outset. To become operational, value principles have to be embedded in the company's culture. And that means roll-out must be an evolutionary – not revolutionary – process.

Fully-managed stakeholder communication – with investors, management, employees, customers and business partners – is critical for success. You'll need to strike the right balance between concept and reality too: VBM can all too easily smack of academic theory if it's not presented in the down-to-earth context of business decision-making.

But the real secret to winning the necessary commitment and ownership, at all levels, lies in making it possible for people to participate – in a way that connects the *value* agenda to *their* agenda.

THE 21ST CENTURY FINANCIAL MANAGEMENT MODEL

An embedded VBM system takes the corporation – and the CFO as its architect – into a new, very different world. As the shareholder value concept comes down from the corporate ivory tower and out into the front line of operational management, the CFO and finance function must drive radical change:

- from incremental DCF project appraisal, to *value based business appraisal*
- from profit targets only, to *targets for each of the value drivers*
- from managing traditional functional structures, to *managing value centers*
- from historical accounting, to *predictive value reporting.*

In essence, this is the shift from number crunching to partnering the business. In an era when dissatisfied institutional investors can vote against them, the CEO and board need a CFO who focuses on *making value creation visible.* To do it, you have to be prepared to tell hard truths. You'll need to put yourself in the cross-hairs of external and internal decision-making. And you'll need not just financial and deal-making skills, but a good grasp of operations.

CFO's CHECKLIST

ASSESS WHERE YOU ARE IN THE VBM LIFECYCLE Be honest: have you really gone beyond the concept development stage? Do you use shareholder value thinking in strategic *and* operational decision-making? Be prepared to institutionalize VBM enterprise-wide – in business planning cycles, reporting, systems, incentives, and the culture generally.

BUILD VALUE PLANNING AND REPORTING SYSTEMS Using appropriate strategic and operational modeling tools, establish your company's *baseline valuation*. If it's below your current market capitalization, maybe your results are going to come in lower than the markets expect – giving investors a nasty surprise. If it's above current market capitalization, the markets could be discounting the stock because the business plan, or management, lacks credibility.

DETERMINE WHAT CREATES VALUE AND WHAT DESTROYS VALUE Disaggregate your corporate valuation to business unit level. Create a *value map* to identify how the various elements of the business portfolio are performing relative to the amount of capital they're consuming.

BENCHMARK EACH VALUE DRIVER FOR EACH BUSINESS UNIT Trace the historical and projected migration of investor capital between your own company and competitors. Use benchmarking data to judge the relative strengths and weaknesses of your approach. If – like most companies – you find inadequacies, renew your strategic response and business design.

ENERGIZE YOUR CORPORATION TO CREATE VALUE Analyze the financial drivers of the company and link these to a set of metrics – a *value scorecard* – that communicates the shareholder value message at all levels in the organization. Use it to modify underlying processes such as goal setting, management meetings, strategic planning, budgeting and executive compensation, so that these continually reinforce the message.

EMBED THE VBM SYSTEM   Introduce the value theme into the corporation's decision-making culture. Have you thought of integrating your value models at corporate, business unit and value center levels? Are the models linked to your operational systems for running the business? Consider connecting your value reporting systems to existing performance measures.

MOVE TOWARD THE 21ST CENTURY FINANCIAL MANAGEMENT MODEL   Examine how your business design impacts on the organization's value creating capabilities. Contrast this with your competitors. Become the architect of value in your corporation: apply value principles to internal and external decision-making. Develop the necessary strategic, analytic, corporate finance and operational skills.

CHAPTER 3
DRIVING HOME STRATEGY WITH PERFORMANCE MEASURES

The CEO of Pharma Industries, John Wright, storms into the CFO's office. 'Brian, we don't seem to be getting anywhere with the new strategy. I thought I set out clearly what was needed at the VPs' Bermuda conference. Get out of non-core businesses, focus on extending core products, invest in high growth territories. The unit heads laid out improvement targets for time to market and capital productivity, everything going the right way. And you capped it nicely with our goals for doubling earnings and a healthy hike in share price within three years. But that was a year ago and nothing's happened since! It's business as usual. So what do we do?'

The CFO thinks he might have the answer. Budgeting and management reporting are almost corporate legends – comprehensive, precise, up to the minute. But piles and piles of data. Too much. And too often measuring the wrong things, reinforcing old behaviors rather than new and lending excuses for non-delivery of results. He replies: 'We need a radical overhaul of our measures and the way we make managers accountable for delivering our strategy. This time we need to go deep – not the high level approach we had in Bermuda. But John, we can't force this on the executive team. They have to live it for themselves and coach their own people to adopt the new measures'.

Why are today's largest companies overhauling their measurement systems? How can outdated measures drive companies in the wrong direction? This chapter makes the case for the finance function to lead the process of selecting the *right* – often revitalized – measures to meet new shareholder value targets. *And to make strategy happen.* It introduces a scorecard linking key shareholder value drivers to measures at each level in the organization, especially the front line – the guts of the business.

But can you have too many measures – or too few? How do you resolve conflicting measurement objectives in different parts of the organization? The process reveals gaps, as well as conflicts, in operating strategies. Case studies demonstrate how companies successfully devise and roll out new sets of measures – and secure buy-in. And to complete the development cycle, the chapter gives guidance on how to move from *measuring* to really *managing* step changes in performance improvement.

YOU CAN'T MANAGE WHAT YOU CAN'T MEASURE

According to a recent survey reported in *CFO* magazine, 80% of large American companies want to change their performance measurement systems. 'No wonder,' the magazine comments. 'Yesterday's accounting results say nothing about the factors that actually help grow market share and profits – things like customer service innovation, R&D effectiveness, the per cent of first-time quality and employee development. Nor do traditional measurement systems help to assure senior managers that workers in the field are actually carrying out corporate strategy.'[1]

Beginning with US companies, this tidal wave of change is now reaching Europe and all developed countries. Our *CFO 2000* global research shows that CFOs rank forward-looking, value adding measures a higher priority in the future than in the past. Worldwide, management's challenge is to understand better the company's value drivers (Chapter 2), establish strategies to raise stock prices, and link these into simple measures that everyone can understand. That done, the company must reward people accordingly.

The best executives link value targets, through corporate objectives and strategies, to development of a balanced scorecard

All this interest in measures is in response to companies' desire for enhanced shareholder value. Frustrated by a failure to convert perceived improvements in operational performance into improved share prices, companies are adopting a value agenda to drive actions through perform- ance measures. They stand to gain on several counts.

- If new measures let executives increase the company's stock price, they will share in this wealth creation – they own stock and hold options for more.

- If management can convey company stock to employees, they too can be rewarded for generating value.

- The era of cost reduction is nearly over for many companies. They've wrung out all the savings to be had. Now, they must attend to revenue lines of the income statement, not cost lines.

- Some opportunities to reduce working capital still exist if everyone in the company concentrates on receivables, inventory and payables.

- The worldwide nature of business is making taxation much more complex – a subject well addressed by the value based approach.

- To create future wealth, companies have to start investing again. In doing so, they need the co-operation of capital markets. And the capital markets are looking for above average rates of return.

Consider a logical approach to managing for value – linking share- holder value targets, through corporate objectives and strategies, to development of a balanced scorecard (Figure 3.1). This is a fairly simple idea. Which is why it appeals to so many executives – the people who set the overall tone of the company and carry the investors' mandate to increase the company's value.

The best executives translate the sometimes confusing mantra of shareholder value into easy-to-understand corporate objectives. They recognize how these goals, once fulfilled, will boost the company's stock price. 'No less than 18% free cash flow growth, 40% market share, 7% EPS growth,' they demand. But they know this is just the jumping-off place. Nothing will happen unless they set the right strategies in motion and energize the company. So they pick specific strategies from the infinite number offered and pursue relentlessly priorities such as globalization, process cost reduction and new product offerings.

Then, some executives wait. And wait. They've missed the important next step: operationalizing strategy by measuring what's happening in

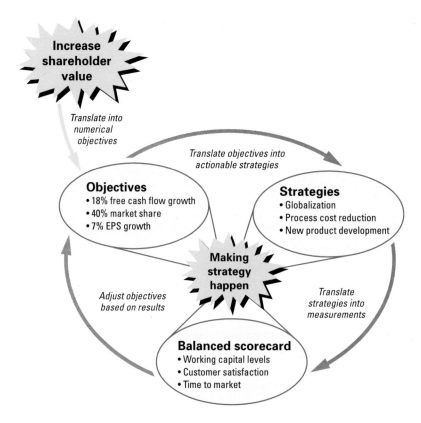

Figure 3.1 **Developing measures from strategies**

the far-flung empire. What gets measured gets managed. Many executives are startled to find what good measures can do, once in place. Measures communicate value creation in ways the CEO's videotaped messages never could – *and* the results tell executives if their goals can be reached in the stated timeframe. The objective–strategy–measurement cycle renews itself regularly, spiraling through time toward shareholder value improvement – with everyone working in unison.

The investment community monitors and benchmarks today's executives – whether they like it or not. Why? Because it's their job to bring about change. To stimulate their own managers to act as if they're all shareholders in the company. To look at themselves as investors do and manage themselves accordingly. This is the performance management agenda for the next millennium. It involves innovative ways of devising strategy, embedding implementation into business planning, and reinforcing it with new ways of measuring activities and reporting results. Future performance management systems will link closely the interests of shareholders, corporate executives and front-line managers – within a common framework of accountability.

Some of the world's best run companies are heralding their success in redrawing the measurement map. When General Motors stated in its 1991 annual report that it was establishing a new performance measurement system to 'facilitate the basic changes taking place' in the business, the company declared: 'This system covers all aspects of the business, including people development, product development, manufacturing, marketing, and shareholder satisfaction. The system includes a focused set of measures that deal with the primary factors influencing quality, customer satisfaction, and financial performance... With full system implementation, we expect a more consistent application of common performance benchmarks across the entire organization'.

Managers at all levels have to develop their own measures – but *within a framework and according to guidelines laid down for the corporation as a whole*. If this is not seen as a corporate-wide exercise, the measures in different parts of the organization will be inconsistent. Often, they'll be over or under-developed. Certainly, they'll be unbalanced – typically, emphasizing mainly financial results.

Management can launch a major overhaul anytime it wants the business to operate better. Other good times to begin are when new strategies are being introduced, when a new executive team is taking over, or when a major interruption to normal business, such as an acquisition or merger, occurs. Consider one company that initiated a new corporate-wide key performance indicator program to coincide with implementing its new business strategy.

CASE STUDY: Enterprise-wide Performance Indicators

A world market leader in producing health products used its new performance measurement system to alter behavior. Under pressure to improve performance, the company's CEO successfully completed a strategic planning exercise and then brought together senior management, including vice presidents from all over the world. Briefing them on what was required, first he made sure they shared his understanding of the financial objectives they needed to achieve, then he reconfirmed the strategies they were all following. Assured that he had their wholehearted support and enthusiasm for a new set of measures, an initiative was launched: the key performance indicator (KPI) program.

Since work on KPIs had already started in some areas, but not others, he brought everyone back to the starting line, proposing guiding principles for the effort. After team-building workshops on how to implement these principles, he secured the needed buy-in to proceed. An enterprise-wide target was agreed for KPI development: only three months allotted for the first cut of KPIs, to be known as Phase 1.

A date was set when the team of some 40 senior managers would meet again to present the results. This process was supervised by a steering committee comprising business unit and functional heads from across the company. But the job of developing measures was carried out by managers – senior and junior – from within the business, facilitated by a central support team. The steering committee's role was to ensure that managers achieved delivery milestones, had adequate resources, and followed the guidelines for developing measures: quality, consistency, balance and integration.

Meeting at the end of Phase 1, senior managers presented their KPIs – developed with a consistent approach to breaking down the value chain and their detailed operating strategies. With results of their work set out on 60 large boards around a conference hall, managers had the chance to cross-examine presenters and satisfy themselves that consistency had been achieved. Eventually, the company sifted measures to obtain a manageable set. For teamwork and pulling together to meet the corporation's performance targets, this initial exercise was generally judged a resounding success.

Two years later, people – from the corporate management team to the front line – are sustaining enthusiastically the subsequent phases of KPI refinement and reporting. High level measures have been translated into individual performance objectives, the final step in the process.

This case offers important lessons. The company has since beaten its performance targets and share price appreciation has been impressive. The CFO puts it simply: 'The performance measurement system is one of management's strongest tools to link a company's vision, its strategy and the actual performance of the business'.

BENEFITS OF EFFECTIVE PERFORMANCE MEASUREMENT SYSTEMS

The essential question, then, is how to drive home management's value creation message throughout the organization – particularly to those unlikely to consult their shareholder value spreadsheets each time they make a decision! An effective performance measurement system should deliver several benefits.

In managing and creating value... By showcasing the most important goals and determining whether objectives are being achieved, an effective measurement system gives senior managers the best way to translate the shareholder value message into action.

In communicating strategy... Performance measurement is far more effective than a company newsletter in giving the organization a *top-down* view of how management wants strategies to be carried out. *Bottom-up*, the measures indicate whether decisions are being made that achieve strategic aims. One large company trained more than 500 people in how to use measures properly – as probes into the organization, telling everyone what's important and how the company's doing. *Facts* on performance against strategy replaced apocryphal stories. And the company could fully understand how well its strategies were taking hold.

In shifting from short-term financial appraisal to longer-term tracking... Effective measurement systems are based on a balanced approach that includes non-financial metrics to track strategic progress, as well as measures that show short-term results. A great example is 3M Corporation. This company states publicly that it wants 30% of revenues from products no more than five years old. It measures this goal and motivates the organization to implement its strategy. But don't think for an instant that next quarter's earnings are not a concern as 3M develops new products for its future.

In looking at the company – entirely differently... The process of refining measures gives the top team a unique opportunity to improve its understanding of what middle managers believe is important and how to motivate them. One airline looks at itself in this way – it established a system of shared goals where each higher level manager sub-divides objectives, negotiating goals with subordinate divisional managers. Sub-goals are, in turn, divided until each unit in the division knows clearly what its responsibilities are. In the process, many fresh issues emerge and are resolved. And the exercise strengthens buy-in and communication generally.

In promoting realistic, demanding goals... Setting stretch corporate goals is necessary. But when those goals are *impossible*, the practice becomes counter-productive. Such goals tend to be set in a vacuum, with little or no thought as to how they're going to be carried out. They de-motivate, rather than motivate, because everyone knows they're unachievable. A well designed performance measurement system gives management the means to meet the objective of shareholder value enhancement, based on realistic appraisal of individual and collective capabilities.

Some companies win, others lose, in a measurement redesign. All companies start out with good intent, acknowledging that what gets measured, gets managed, *gets done.* But few fully understand its real implication. The aim of value based performance management is to get everyone doing things that ultimately create value – and nothing else. So what's wrong with measurement systems in use today?

Better Measurement Results in Better Management

Managers spend far too much time designing new measures, especially when they move to a new position, often giving scant thought to how theirs connect with others in the organization. The result: companies pile measures one on top of another. Before they know it, they have too many – and too many that matter little to anyone but the managers who thought them up.

We were invited to one very large company to talk about measurement. The chairman had met with the CEO of another company, who boasted he'd cut his measurement set to 47. Appalled to think that any company could have so many measures, the chairman related the conversation to his CFO, only to hear: 'That was a real accomplishment. We must have hundreds'. On the spot, the CFO was told to look into the problem.

Too many measures guarantee you have virtually none. Excess measures rob the company of focus. When confronted with a new measure – or a vast array of old ones – people ignore it on the principle that 'this, too, shall pass'! Experience shows that an ideal set consists of around 40 to 60 measures – just five or six for each important process. Only about 15% of these get to executive row. Having such a small set of measures is a revolutionary idea in the corporate world. But the benefits can be enormous.

The opposite problem occurs at the top of corporations. Senior executives tend to be concerned with only a few, broad measures. Results are used for external reporting and internal cheer-leading. These measures can be very sweeping – worldwide earnings, for example. They're too vague and usually mean nothing to employees.

Try asking lathe operators how often they think about shareholder value. OK, how about marginal propensity to consume? *Now* ask how many on-spec things they can make in an hour. Yes, you're still talking about shareholder value, but this time in the right language. What's surprising is the number of companies that adopt the shareholder value mandate but persist in holding training classes to explain value equations to operational people. It's a waste of time. Concentrate, instead, on translating shareholder value into metrics that make sense to the individual's work.

Many organizations can easily discover the flaws in their current measurement systems. The first thing they detect is a snowballing of measures, with no systematic examination of what they mean for the company's fundamental results. Then analysis reveals other problems (Figure 3.2). Some measures are found to be outdated. Often, an imbalance exists because of a tradition of using internally focused, financial measures.

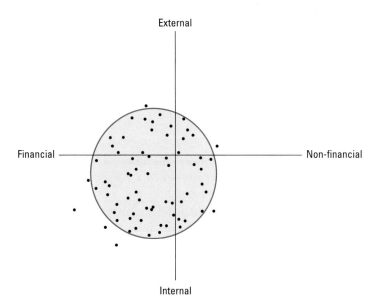

Figure 3.2 **Analyze your measures to see where they need to be updated and balanced**

These are among the most common failings...

Internal bias Measures may be based on traditional operating metrics that remain unchanged even though the company's strategies alter. Labor efficiency, for example, is a manufacturing measure that may represent only a minute fraction of product cost. This measure has one message: *produce*, even if warehouses are full or the customer doesn't want it yet. The labor efficiency measure may well conflict with the company's just-in-time philosophy.

Historical orientation Traditional financial measures go only so far. They must be balanced with an emphasis on the company's under-lying business processes. Results-oriented measures reflect decisions of past management. They should be augmented with predictive process measures that indicate something of the future – for example, time to market.

Over-emphasis on* ad hoc *local activity measures These gage results of only small parts of the corporation. They may be of interest to just one individual and unconnected with strategy. How about cost per invoice processed? The recent wave of re-engineering did much to proliferate such micro-measures.

A plethora of obsolete measures These often result from changes in the environment or organization. One company continues to collect the cost of non-standard shipments for rush orders or production delays – as a measure, rather like trying to figure out what to do if the plane crashes, instead of how to keep it flying. On-time delivery – a success-oriented measure – should be used.

A focus on data, not information Too many managers are buried under a mountain of data that's difficult to use and understand. And it gets worse with each new information system. Complexity chokes many companies. Distinguish between data and measures: a collection of data becomes a measure *when it is accompanied by a goal* and *when management expects the goal to be achieved.*

All too often, the consequence of an obsolete measurement system is unnecessary conflict. The requirements of the new strategy jar with outdated measures that may be driving the company in the wrong direction. Unless the measurement system is re-calibrated to monitor strategy implementation, nothing much will change. The experience of Johnson & Johnson's CILAG subsidiary, in the next case study, shows how new strategies with old measures can give the wrong result.

CASE STUDY: Designing a Consistent Measure Set

At CILAG AG, a pharmaceutical subsidiary of Johnson & Johnson based in Switzerland, vice president of European operations Mike Baronian wanted to improve efficiency and flexibility of the supply chain. Investigation of factors constraining the company's progress showed that different parts of the organization worked against each other, driven by conflicting operating measures.

Baronian explains: 'Down in the factory, the number one objective of production managers was to maximize productivity. And they were doing a great job at this. Because we have a large range of products, their challenge was to minimize disruption during each shift caused by constant juggling of what we were going to make and when. As a solution, the managers were inflating the lot sizes produced, in order to keep run times between line changeovers as long as possible and reduce downtime. But the downside was that we were carrying costly, high levels of inventory.

'On the other hand, the logistics manager, who is responsible for warehousing and distribution, was seeking to minimize time to market so we could get the product out as fast as possible and be flexible. To achieve this, he wanted a continuous flow of smaller lot sizes so he could supply the right mix of products and quickly change order configuration in reaction to changing customer needs. In other words, logistics wanted low inventory – the very opposite of what production managers were aiming for.

'Over in the sales department, our managers were seeking to protect customer service levels across our wide product portfolio, by making sure we always had ample safety stocks of everything. The result: high inventory. So we had people pulling in different directions with some unpleasant consequences.

'We've now changed all that. The supply chain is being driven with a consistent set of measures, with our objective of maximizing cash flow at the core. Manufacturing lead times have reduced from 35 to nine days, efficiency and flexibility are up significantly, and we're running with lower overall levels of inventory'.

The message is clear. If people are to avoid becoming trapped in silo *mentalities, corporate, business unit and operating strategies – and the performance measures that support them – must be consistent across the totality of the business.*

Exercises like the one CILAG went through force the thinking behind strategies and resulting measures. They provide a chance to re-evaluate and test high level assumptions. They focus on front-line experience of middle managers. For example, a company's mission to maximize share-holder value may translate into an objective of increasing cash flows by 30%. Achieving the cash goal could require, among other things, that the company manage its working capital to cut it by 15%. This would require tighter inventory control. What, then, are the key measures of inventory control? Days of sales in inventory? Machine set-up time? Manufacturing lead time? Full-time quality? Or, more likely, a combination of all these?

Then comes the non-financial question. What will inventory reduction do to the company's customer service strategy? Shareholder value improvement is not as linear as computer models suggest. Inventory reduction, while it may throw off cash, may also affect other variables, and these variables may interact. That's why it's important to have a balanced set of measures: so managers can simultaneously assess all consequences of a decision.

IDENTIFYING THE VALUE CHAIN

So what's the way forward for companies prepared to overhaul their measurement systems? Designing an effective measurement system starts with understanding how the company's operational processes deliver benefits to each customer, whether external or internal. Think creatively about your company's value chain (Figure 3.3). As a rule of thumb, an average of eight or nine processes, and result objectives, can provide the basic skeleton on which to build a company's measures. The resulting chain, a blueprint of company activity, describes the functions whose processes the company must optimize in order to succeed. This blueprint guides the process of determining which measures will let the company know when performance is on target.

Once the design team has identified the company's value chain and the most important functions, it can work with senior management to document strategies to deliver shareholder value. These strategies may be

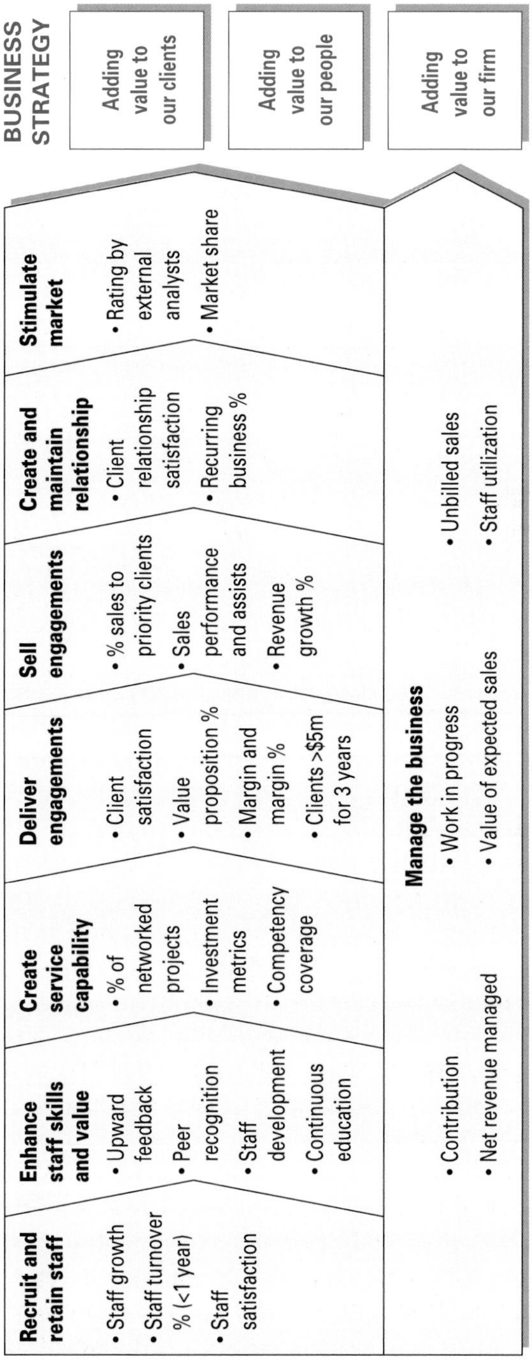

Recruit and retain staff	Enhance staff skills and value	Create service capability	Deliver engagements	Sell engagements	Create and maintain relationship	Stimulate market
• Staff growth • Staff turnover % (<1 year) • Staff satisfaction	• Upward feedback • Peer recognition • Staff development • Continuous education	• % of networked projects • Investment metrics • Competency coverage	• Client satisfaction • Value proposition % • Margin and margin % • Clients >$5m for 3 years	• % sales to priority clients • Sales performance and assists • Revenue growth %	• Client relationship satisfaction • Recurring business %	• Rating by external analysts • Market share

Manage the business

• Contribution • Net revenue managed	• Work in progress • Value of expected sales	• Unbilled sales • Staff utilization

BUSINESS STRATEGY

- Adding value to our clients
- Adding value to our people
- Adding value to our firm

Figure 3.3 **Typical value chain and performance measures for a professional services organization**

directed at a single point or process in the value chain. More often, they will cut across the whole chain, emphasizing the main goals of corporate operations overall.

This exercise forces into the open operating strategies that may conflict with either corporate objectives or each other. *This is where the rubber really hits the road.* Most companies have well developed strategies, thought out carefully by top management. In a few, strategies are poor – outdated, ill thought through, or even missing altogether. In any case, the exercise is useful. The well strategized company needs the lever of measurement to hasten results. Others will see how their strategy gaps make measurement hopeless.

Measures help a company manage both results and the processes by which results can be predicted and sustained over the longer term. Having identified the value chain, the next step is to develop a cascade of measures throughout the organization. Working on the principle that *decisions are the points where value is created or destroyed*, best practice companies frame their measures for the appropriate organizational level. Measures can then be targeted appropriately to indicate the results of strategic, tactical or operational decisions.

Consider the various blocks of decision-making and how they can be used to channel performance measures (Figure 3.4). At strategic level, big issues are market share, strategic alliances, acquisitions and divestments. Decisions such as 'Which market should we be in?' set the scene for the organization as a whole. At business unit level, decisions relate to capital investment – for example: 'Should we invest in a new product distribution network?'. At operational level, planning and budgeting decisions are made, such as: 'Should we put on a night shift to deal with the order backlog?'. These decisions must reflect reality. This is the crux of implementing a measurement system that's meaningful to executives *and* the front line.

Performance measures are best left where action occurs – ensure that your measure set cascades all the way to the individual

Clearly, different measures are needed at various levels of the organization. And they needn't mesh neatly. Take, as an example, first-time quality. It's measured at the end of every stamping press, every paint line, every molding device. This one measure might generate thousands of charts at operational level – but there's no reason to send them to top management, even if it can be done electronically. Most managers don't

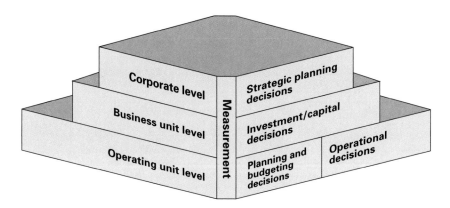

Figure 3.4 **Measures are tailored to specific needs at different levels**

know how to set up lathes or molding machines to improve quality. Instead, they need to know the results of the latest customer satisfaction survey, which reports perceived quality in the marketplace.

Performance measures are best left where action occurs. Despite the clear connection between quality and shareholder value, it's the shift supervisor, not the chairman, who can influence these results. Similarly, high level measures, such as economic profit achieved, have little meaning to workers – but a display at the plant entrance showing the latest stock price will help remind them why the company is in business.

The most progressive companies ensure that the measure set cascades all the way to the individual: job descriptions, team and personal objectives, accountabilities and key result areas should all be aligned with value chain strategies (Figure 3.5). When these objectives and measures are the basis for individuals' performance target setting and appraisal, the business has a powerful means of communicating strategy and putting it into action at personal level.

MEASUREMENT IDEALS: SYMMETRY AND INTEGRATION

Each company's set of measures should reflect its own *processes and strategies*, but as already discussed, some principles of design and categories of measurement action hold true for all companies. While no universal set of best measures exists, there *are* a few best practices for designing them.

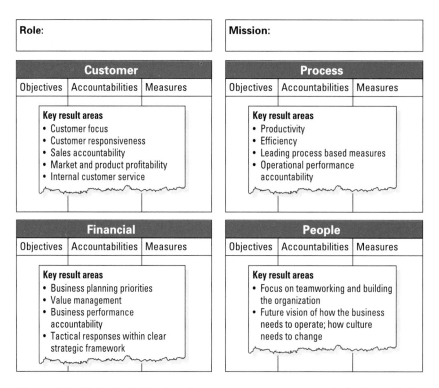

Figure 3.5 **Make individual performance measures part of a balanced job description**

Measures should be *carefully documented* – a task often left undone when a company develops its new measure set. The principles to follow: document strategy; carefully define measures, including how they should be calculated, so they can't be misinterpreted; and show the linkage between strategy and measures. One company published a *white paper* to explain the relation between strategy and measures, then followed up with a pocket booklet demonstrating how each measure interacts with others.

To encourage a symmetrical arrangement and provide structure where none really exists, the best CFOs design the corporate scorecard as a series of measure pairs.

- *Measures should be both leading and lagging* Leading to alert you to immediate results of an operation; lagging to point to results of past decisions.

- ***Measures should mirror both internal and external concerns***
  Internal to reflect achievement of your own objectives for process efficiency, people management and so on; external to reflect achievement of the objectives of key external parties, including suppliers, customers and competitors.

- ***Measures should be both cost based and non-cost based*** Cost measures derive from the resource impact of an activity on the company's performance, while non-cost measures give a glimpse of what drives the costs. The stress should be on processes, rather than cost centers or departments (as in activity based costing, discussed in Chapter 4). Costs neither exist in a vacuum nor are caused by a single department. They cause one another.

- ***Measures should be both quantitative and qualitative*** A great failing of many measurement systems is that they concentrate only on hard measures, ignoring subjective interpretation – ignoring management. An accumulation of measurement data, by itself, is of little value. What's important is what's being done to get a measure back on track. What's the underlying problem? Are actions being taken? What are the probable consequences of these actions?

Only managers close to the process can supply this information. That's why every measurement should be accompanied by a commentary – a proactive discussion sent forward before the telephone call to ask the manager what's happened. Such commentary brings life to the measurement. It pushes decision-making down the organization and takes complexity out of governance. Performance management is not the exclusive duty of executives.

Meeting all these design principles is a prerequisite for success in the measurement exercise. That's why a manageable number of *ideal* measures is so difficult to come up with.

Brainstorming an Ideal Set of Measures

Before executives can begin designing an ideal set of measures, they have to take stock of their existing set. Sifting through existing measures is one of the most difficult parts of the job. An important early step in the process is to survey managers. Ask what they consider to be the problems with the old measures. And what they believe to be the most important things to include in the new set. This provides an X-ray of the company. You find out from the field what's wrong with the current approach and get real suggestions on how to make the new one more effective.

To move from old measures to new, get key functional managers to set out what they'd like to see as an ideal measure, then debate whether to shoot for perfection. Some companies use the *Delphi* approach to select the right measures through ranking and prioritization – this gives managers the opportunity to really understand what's important and what can be left aside. The Delphi process is subjective and, in many respects, less scientific than some would like. But it's an effective way to get the best insights from the best managers. And, as one company's experience shows, it works!

CASE STUDY: Selecting Measures by Priority Ranking

Developing a new set of measures, this multinational company's CEO and CFO drew a selection team of 15 managers from various functional departments – product development, purchasing, distribution, sales and marketing, finance, HR, IT, and manufacturing and international operations. Once the list of potential measures was pared down to about 120, a staff group wrote one or two-line definitions of each and sent these to the selection team, along with a questionnaire. All team members were asked to rank each measure on a scale of 1 to 5, based on specified criteria. For reference, they had the company's value chain – which they'd helped develop earlier – and the company's strategies, arranged by value chain category.

When the team returned completed questionnaires, the staff group used a PC to score and order each measure from most to least favored. The ranked measures were further stratified by the functional background of those voting – so, for example, engineers could see what HR people thought of particular measures, and vice versa. The data passed to selection team members to decide on the measure set.

The first thing that struck the team was how few product design measures appeared in the top 40 – even though revenue enhancement was a well com-municated company strategy. Financial measures dominated the list – though the company already was choked with such data! Obviously, the set was unbalanced.

For two days, the selection team thrashed out measures. At first, members remained true to their functional callings. Days of inventory had little appeal for sales people. The staff training index seemed irrelevant to financial people, while HR thought it critical. But eventually, team members began to see through corporate eyes. Starting to recognize the full ramifications of a particular measure on shareholder value, they debated measures from the perspective of strategy. And, over time, the team settled on a reasonably well balanced set.

Just as important, several members agreed to champion *particular measures, ensuring that their final definition and reporting format would be technically correct. The selection team also became the* inside salesforce *for the new measures, assuring anyone who asked that measures had been selected in a rigorous and fair manner.*

Afterward, the CEO commented: 'I don't know what we did, but we couldn't put our measurement process to bed even if we wanted to. There is too much momentum'.

Who should oversee the performance measure design process? A steering committee composed of senior executives who set the strategies and tone for the company. Who reports to these executives? A design team composed of the company's leading lights – people who'll know what measures might and might not work. This team supports the design process, acting as a sounding board when needed. Together, these two high powered groups ensure that the measures are right. Equally important, they reinforce the message that measures are important. They serve a communication and signaling role, as well as a motivational one. Often, the CFO sets the steering committee's agenda.

Testing Measures Inside and Out

Finally, every measure in the new set should be test marketed. Is it properly defined? Can it be calculated simply and reported effectively? In each case, the design team should get buy-in from the person most familiar with the process whose effectiveness the measure is designed to assess. That person offers a reality check and can tell the team whether the measure is practical and whether data backing it up can be collected easily.

The experience of a major corporation shows why testing is critical. The CEO had decided to move out of a commodity business and re-engineer the product – differentiated, it would presumably command a higher price. For many months, the engineers virtually ignored this strategy. But faced with new measures that would indicate how well the strategy was being achieved, they knew the time for stonewalling was over. A major debate broke out about the strategy. The engineers confessed that, to match what competitors were doing, they would have to add electronic components to the product offerings – and they lacked the design skills to do so. Temporarily shelving his strategy, the CEO set in motion an acquisition plan to obtain technology and skills from outside the company.

An effective performance measurement system brings reality to strategy – and makes strategy impossible to ignore

As this example demonstrates, measurement brings reality to strategy. And makes strategy impossible to ignore.

During measure testing, check shareholder value once again – test that the measures reflect the longer term, as well as the here and now. As discussed in Chapter 2, one of the strongest drivers of shareholder value is the stock market's evaluation of the length of time the company can sustain itself. When the stock market saw that PCs could affect the mainframe business of a computer hardware company, its stock lost much of its attraction. Similarly, the market reacts badly when a pharmaceutical company loses its patent protection. These are longer-term matters, not what happened yesterday. That's why measures of new product development, customer satisfaction and employee training deserve a special place in the overall set.

FINANCE'S KEY ROLE IN METRICS DESIGN AND IMPLEMENTATION

Designing a new performance measurement system can go smoothly, or create dissension and turbulence. In one company, senior management spent two years developing a process-oriented approach – with a new measurement system designed by a team drawn from different functions. But development sessions degenerated into heated arguments about what was a good measure, what should be measured, and what separate components should go into each measure. When the system was finally implemented, employees felt no connection with it. Objecting that their viewpoints had been ignored, they complained of 'death by a thousand graphs' after seeing presentations of the new results. The company's process for identifying measurements may have been right, but it obviously failed to achieve buy-in.

When designing a new measurement system, act like a chess player: remember the end game. Eventually, everyone in the company will be affected by the system. Any apparent shortcuts are likely to lead to a disastrous ending. The company must do it *right first time*. Much more than just a technical activity, redesign is a major change process that requires both technical skill and a broad understanding of the implications of change.

While an effective measurement system touches all aspects of a company's value chain and must be *owned by operating managers*, successful companies rely on the finance function to spearhead implementation of their new systems. Why?

- The more global the company and the more disparate its operations, the greater the need for a mechanism to assess results of management decisions. A ubiquitous function, finance has representatives in every far-flung part of the company. Working to implement the new measurement system, finance staff can also help operating managers interpret what it's saying.

- The greater the mandate to emphasize shareholder value, the greater the need for a framework built on statistical information as well as financial data. Finance staff can quickly assess the relationships between measures, including non-financial ones, and their impact on the ultimate creation of shareholder value.

- Perhaps most important, the finance function has demonstrated its competence in fulfilling the traditional role of scorekeeper. Despite occasional sibling rivalry between finance staff and other organizational groups, operating managers know they cannot go it alone in today's avenging shareholder value climate. They look to the CFO and the finance function for leadership.

Rolling Out the New Measure Set

After a major overhaul of the measurement system – including careful testing – management, through the CFO and finance staff, should put the new measures under lock and key. Refinements should now be made only when measures need to be realigned with new strategies.

In the most successful introductions of new measurement systems, management gives employees a year's grace – an *amnesty period* – during which they're expected to communicate unpleasant occurrences without retribution. In subsequent years, everyone becomes more accountable for their actions and for meeting targets more closely. The purpose of measurement is not to root out and punish *wrong-doers*, but to enhance shareholder value. If something's going wrong in the company, it's better to hear about it, find the root cause and release financial or other resources to fix it.

With the design and testing process complete, implementation begins. The results can be astounding. For example, three years after General Motors announced it was establishing a new performance measurement system, *Fortune* magazine published a gratifying article (Figure 3.6).

Considering the potential impact of a new measurement system, the roll-out must be planned as carefully as the measures themselves. The steering committee should meet regularly to assess preliminary results, discuss any difficulties, and make the connections between measures and executive compensation.

Also, the company will need to understand the stock market's reaction to the greater transparency of action. Communicating the company's intention to adopt shareholder value, buttressed with pertinent measures, management often sees its stock price move upward. They may take some

	1988 Midsize Cars	1997-98 Midsize Cars
Investment costs	$5.9 billion	$1.6 billion
Development time	72 months	37 months
Assembly hours/vehicle	39.0	18.9
Number of parts	3200	2300
Number of plants	5	3
Number of combinations	1,900,000	1000
Unit volume	600,000 per year	700,000 per year

Figure 3.6 **The multi-billion dollar turnaround at General Motors**
Source: Wertheim Schroder, *Fortune*. © 1994 Time Inc. All rights reserved.

joy in this, but for the price to *stay* up, the company will have to *deliver* shareholder value.

Ensure Success with Incentives

Companies always want to know how they should link measurement systems to incentives. This matter is far more complicated than it seems. First, the compensation structure has to be consistent with strategy, relating incentives to the right goals. Policy will be shaped by short versus long-run considerations and by relationships, be they inter-divisional or between parent and subsidiary company.

The short-term versus long-term dimension is the age-old problem of judging where to reward managers for turnaround situations and where to reward them for longer-term growth objectives. The mix of divisions and subsidiaries in the corporate portfolio forces management to tailor schemes according to competitive factors driving each business unit. For example, it would be inappropriate to expect a mature, cyclical chemical business to generate the exceptionally high returns and growth rates of a fast-moving software business. This is where the strategic goals of the business must be matched to a favorable basis for rewarding managers' efforts.

Most early adopters of value based measurement systems have tied an ever-larger percentage of executive compensation to total shareholder return. Different corporations use a mix of current cash, current stock, deferred cash, deferred stock or restricted stock. Some firms establish bonus pools, distributed when certain goals are met. This is quite common in companies like LucasVarity which have adopted EVA™.[2] In these cases, the bonus pool consists of a *bank* of deferred economic profit from which pay-outs are made annually.

At lower levels, the problem is more complex. Systems like those founded on EVA are difficult to cascade through middle management to the layers below. Monsanto attempts to share wealth creation with all its workers by including company shares in its reward system. Others tie the accomplishment of measurement goals into an individual's annual appraisal. The problem is that no one group, much less one person, fully controls many of the company's most important metrics. Take on-time delivery. To get an item to a customer on time requires that the engineers bring it to market when required, purchasing buys the right components at the right time, operations people make it on time, the order entry department correctly records the customer's specifications, and the outbound logistics staff send it promptly. Conceivably, everyone who takes part in this process could be rewarded individually for meeting the on-time delivery goal, but a team based approach – or, better, one tied to overall corporate goals – is more viable.

PERFORMANCE MEASUREMENT OR MANAGEMENT?

The point of talk about measuring performance is simple: *if executives can't measure it, they can't manage it.* Once a company revises its measurement system, it has taken an important first step toward dealing with the real issue of performance *management.* But there's much more to be done. Knowing the company's financial drivers and what's been achieved in the past, management can establish new goals for each measure. Goals are concrete expressions of what is important. They communicate the message of teamwork and accountability. They say, in effect: 'We plan to enhance shareholder wealth and one way to do it is by reducing our time to market to 27 months. Let's work toward that goal'.

Absurd as it sounds, here's an important caution: *the measures must be used.* Managers must revise meeting agendas, making measurement information the main topic of conversation. What are the measures saying? Is the company achieving its quality standards? Are customers satisfied? Do too many engineering changes interfere with prototyping new products? Is the company gaining market share? Has it met its training goals? And, most importantly, is the company generating cash for its investors? Weighty matters, these.

The best run companies focus on measures *in many ways.* They:

- incorporate key performance information in a tailored report that's shared with key managers organization-wide, so everyone sees what's going well and what isn't

- insist on commentary from the measure's keeper to understand the steps being taken to hit targets

- recognize that failure to achieve some goal may be more the fault of company systems and processes than an individual's shortcoming, and invest to rectify the problem

- demand that key managers keep meetings in focus, concentrating on what the measures say and how targets are to be achieved

- adjust their goals and strategies periodically to meet new business conditions

- include measurement target-setting as part of their annual budgeting process, expanding budgeting beyond the traditional halls of accounting

- communicate externally what the company plans to do.

Chapter 1 showed how the CFO can use the finance value line to define finance processes and where they add value to the business. Processes such as capital expenditure appraisal, acquisitions and mergers, as well as budgeting, planning and management reporting, all provide opportunities for the CFO to intervene using the new measures. *Institutionalization* of measures in the business cycle is critical to make change happen. Subsequent reinforcement of measures, through changes to computer systems and culture, completes the picture.

Making use of measurement information – hard work that cannot be done in isolation – really is the *glue* that binds the organization together. It means management must concentrate on things that make the company successful. Often, measurement results indicate a structural deficiency in the company's processes. Products take too long to develop because no process is in place to ensure progress. Or customer deliveries are late because the production planning system is inadequate. Or market share is squandered because the cost system overprices fast-moving items. Here is where performance management really bites.

Correcting a structural deficiency means spending money, perhaps a great deal of it. None of the usual remedies will work – changing the manager, reorganizing the division, tightening the budget, might make everyone feel they've done something, but the measures will continue to tell the unvarnished truth. Structural change, brought about by investment, is the only answer.

In many ways, as shown earlier in this chapter in Figure 3.1, performance management is a circle. Measures are put into place to allow the company to achieve its shareholder value objectives. But these measures, derived from strategy, may indicate that the strategies are flawed – and businesses have to reinvent themselves. Measured performance, good or bad, should tell you whether you're making progress in the right direction. Establishing a new measurement system is one of the most important things the CFO can do.

CFO's CHECKLIST

INTRODUCE THE BALANCED SCORECARD Link business strategies to shareholder value and value drivers. Develop the value scorecard – get it on the corporate agenda.

FOCUS ON DECISIONS Translate high level strategy into detailed operating strategies for each component of the value chain. Frame measures with the strategic, tactical and operating decisions you need to take at the heart of the business. Look for conflicting measures – identify what's missing, the overlaps, and what's new.

BRING IN OPERATIONAL REALITY Make lower level measures part of a consistent set. Use the acid test: do measures really mean something to front-line managers and operatives on a day-to-day basis? Tie team and individual accountabilities and evaluation into the corporate measure set. Use the roll-out to resolve overlaps and duplication in roles and responsibilities – and to communicate business strategy at personal level.

LINK OPERATIONAL MEASURES TO VALUE DRIVERS Map your key operational measures to your value drivers, such as revenue, operating margin or capital expenditure. Experiment with sensitivity analyses. Show your front-line managers the impact on shareholder value of their decisions – for example, to *insource* or *outsource*.

DECIDE ON THE RIGHT NUMBER OF MEASURES Too many and you won't see the wood for the trees. Too few and you won't connect the dots. Make sure they go cross-functional. Maintain a healthy balance between measures: leading and lagging, external and internal, financial and non-financial. Cover the entire enterprise, not just the usual areas.

SEEK OWNERSHIP THROUGH INVOLVEMENT The CEO should lead this initiative from the top. The CFO is ideally suited to oversee the implementation and to ensure that measures are in harmony. Coach both business and functional managers, at all levels, to develop their own collective and individual measures that conform to corporate guidelines.

MAINTAIN MOMENTUM DURING ROLL-OUT Experiment and test. Grant an amnesty period – allow poor performance to reveal itself without punishment! Keep overhauled measures under lock and key, but keep them up to date.

MOVE FROM MEASURING TO MANAGING PERFORMANCE Go for some quick wins. Intervene in the business cycle and introduce new measures in the annual budget round. Link them to incentives. Communicate with investors. Institutionalize measures in *value reporting* systems.

CHAPTER 4
DEVELOPING A NEW GENERATION
OF ACTIVITY BASED MANAGERS

The last two board meetings have been pretty uncomfortable for CFO Lizbeth Jung. Her colleagues are impatient with 'big surprises' and look to her for answers. What sparked the latest flap was a one-off activity based costing exercise which showed that bringing a breakthrough product to market would cost twice what everyone expected. Before that, there'd been nightmare cash flow forecasts for the latest acquisition – with incompatible systems preventing a reliable analysis. But Jung is even more concerned about her cost management information. Based on an archaic cost model, it will be no help in managing global suppliers, products and customers as the company expands its international operations.

In her own mind, the solution lies in activity based management. ABM would add a whole new dimension to ABC studies, taking in resource management and budgeting. Its analytical framework, more attuned to modern competitive conditions, would not only answer many of the current problems, it would put the board in a position to steer the business with more speed and flexibility than ever before.

But if she champions the ABM cause too publicly, it may be dismissed as 'finance theory' or an attempt at empire building. By contrast – and worse, perhaps, given the stamina needed in moving to ABM – she may raise expectations too high, too quickly.

The wise Jung plots a revolution in evolutionary phases. ABC having saved one product misfire, she can get the company to back more extensive use of it. As ABC's full value becomes apparent – for example, in pinpointing product winners as well as jettisoning losers, and revealing what it really costs to service customers – she'll advocate its more general integration into management processes. And finally, when everyone's educated in ABC-related techniques and sees what they can do for the business, she'll push for a wholesale switch to ABM underpinning the company's approach to building shareholder value.

Forward-looking CFOs have known for some time that to help their companies manage mounting competitive pressures, they must find an alternative to traditional methods of cost accounting. Activity based management (ABM) is a powerful candidate for the job. The fact that many who started down the ABM path in the 1980s stopped halfway with activity based costing (ABC) only highlights the difficulty of making a full transition. But those who've persisted, and come out the other side, now reap the rewards. Many others declare themselves ready to pick up again and run with ABM – and this time to stay the course.

This chapter takes a fresh look at ABM – in particular what it brings to the new business agenda of maximizing shareholder value. In place of an abrupt switchover from existing systems – a cause of much past fear – the chapter suggests a three-stage approach, from piloting, through integrating data collection and decision making, to genuine *embedding* of ABM processes into the business and culture. And throughout, it details how CFOs use ABM to convince managers that the finance function, far from being a 'dead hand' on the business tiller, can help chart innovative, profitable new directions for the company.

MEET THE CLASS OF 2000

Companies are always excited by the idea of adopting ABM. For the first five minutes! That's when a corporate sweat breaks out at the prospect of attempting so radical a shift. They look ahead and see initial confusion and defensiveness, endless meetings, and a round of difficult decisions and value judgements. So in the past, understandably, many backed away.

But ABM is starting to look like an idea whose time has come. A new generation of managers, facing a new set of challenges, see the anticipated gain from ABM outweighing the anticipated pain.

ABM Will Separate Winners from Also-rans

In a survey of *Fortune* 500 companies – in the financial services, consumer goods and durable goods sectors – no fewer than two-thirds told us they want to move to more integrated ABM solutions, the sooner the better. They put ABM among factors that will in future separate winners from also-rans when it comes to beating global competition, meeting growing customer demands and improving shareholder value.

In mapping the current state of play on ABM in these companies, our survey also highlights the scale of advantage to be had by anyone prepared to get ahead of the game. A large majority (83%) have so far only experimented with *ABC*, or used it for small assignments – typically *ad hoc* assessments of profitability of individual products and services, and analyses of cost and pricing. Only 17% have integrated, or are starting to integrate, ABC data in existing cost systems. On average their ABC systems are three years old, but only 24% of companies update the information one or more times annually.

In other words, most of them find themselves in the same situation as Lizbeth Jung, the fictional CFO at the beginning of this chapter. Like her, they use ABC on an *ad hoc* basis to model profitability and cut costs. But they want to move to full ABM decision support systems (Figure 4.1) to improve their ability to:

- *analyze profitability* – by product, service, customer, market, distribution method, geographic area, or indeed virtually any profitability dimension or combination

- *manage resources* – reallocate resources, model and budget costs, design products and services, manage processes, and resolve make-or-buy, outsourcing and other supply chain issues

- *measure performance* – benchmark internal and competitive performance to set targets and monitor progress in improving processes for R&D, procurement, manufacturing, distribution, sales or customer service.

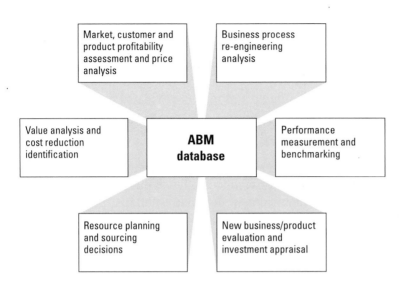

Figure 4.1 **Activity based management (ABM) supplies decision support**

The Best Companies Are Doing It

So who has already signed up for this revolution? And how are they using it? In our *CFO 2000* research some of the most strategically minded global companies confirm their belief in the power of ABM. The best not only integrate ABM into the business cycle itself, to monitor whether operational decision-making is following through on strategy, they use it to fuse the cost perspective to strategic planning. With ABM as the backbone, they develop realistic stretch goals, determine optimal core competencies, effect continuous improvement programs, and stress strategic *action* over strategic planning.

- Chrysler used ABM to support design of the Minivan voted 'Car of the Year' for 1996.

- An internationally renowned truck equipment supplier, mid-way through a 14-plant ABM roll-out to maintain its market leadership, will use it as a common basis for decision-making, profitability measurement and inventory valuation.

- Transco, spawned by ABC analyses that underpinned British Gas's strategy for massive restructuring and delayering, is rolling out ABM as the logical operational cost management and decision support tool to replace foundering 20-year-old systems.

- A major US health insurance company uses its enterprise-wide ABM implementation to analyze profitability of its services.

- In the soon-to-be-deregulated US dairy industry, one dairy stuffs supplier relies on its new ABM system in developing strategies to put it ahead of competitors.

- Iberdrola is integrating ABM as the primary decision support tool to help evolve a common culture and exploit the synergies of its combination of Spain's two largest privately owned electricity companies.

19th Century Costing: It's Over

Most senior executives in first-world countries know that a major shift has occurred in the economics of their business, from direct to indirect cost (Figure 4.2). In the old, predominantly manufacturing based economies, direct labor was the major cost. But as economies move from manufacturing to services, indirect costs skyrocket. Even in manufacturing. Even in labor-intensive financial services. Today, direct labor and related costs account for 20% or less of product cost. For some high-tech companies, they're as low as 3%.

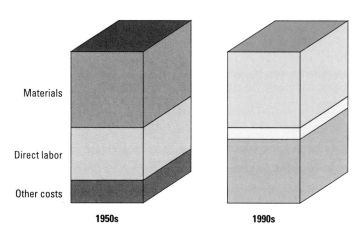

Materials

Direct labor

Other costs

1950s   1990s

Figure 4.2 **Cost profiles are changing**

Yet companies still account for and manage business on the old model, which leads them to charge indirect costs as a proportion of direct costs. Perfect for the 19th century, it leaves the board of a modern business flying blind. By contrast, ABM systems are designed to provide information that shows how indirect costs relate, for example, to products, customers and markets.

CASE STUDY: Chrysler Ditches Labor-rate Costing and Releases Innovation

Bob Lutz, COO of Chrysler, firmly believes that innovation in corporate America is 'imprisoned by the line item'. To Lutz, as to many managers, budgets are tools of repression, rather than innovation. 'What if I've got a market opportunity mid-year. Can I take $1 million out of supplier management and put it into public relations, without a lot of hassle? I don't think so.'

Throughout his long career in the auto industry, Lutz has been frustrated by cost allocations based mainly on direct labor – a system that, he believes, kills many innovative ideas and blinds management to real problems. Take productivity: conventional wisdom held that direct labor hours spent turning out a car indicated productivity. Lutz contended that reducing labor hours per car need not equate with productivity gains – if automation costs surpass labor savings, for example.

Lutz joined Chrysler hoping to try innovations impossible in previous jobs. He wanted to establish a cross-functional, process based platform team for product development. But Chrysler's cost accounting was unable to report process costs or tell whether functions were value adding. About to block the idea – until Lutz insisted on, and received, the CEO's go-ahead – Chrysler instituted activity based costing and budgeting.

Today applied throughout the company, ABM was first used to support the design and manufacture of the Minivan. But when Chrysler introduced its ABM system, opposition and suspicion were rife. Though most operations managers wanted to use activity based data, some were defensive when preliminary reports showed that ABC would uncover waste and inefficiency at Chrysler plants. And the finance team, tied to labor-rate based systems and processes, had a fundamental problem: the numbers used for financial analysis were derived from the same cost data used to calculate external reporting of, for example, profits and taxes.

It was clear that to use ABC as a driving force toward ABM, ownership had to be expanded beyond traditional finance bounds. So James Holden, VP in charge of continuous improvement and the move to process management, and corporate controller James Donlon were given joint responsibility for the system and project team spearheading ABC. The political climate changed once the organization recognized the importance placed on ABM and that it could benefit all areas of the business. Managers began to adopt ABM because they could see for themselves that it really worked. And, as using ABC for decision-making took precedence over the role of costs in external reporting, the finance team could see there were new challenges ahead for them as well.

Essential to this success were Chrysler's ABM training courses. From introductory principles to sophisticated analyses for managers, these courses work so well that suppliers and others enroll. And to sell the concept more widely, the company created a simulation model at the Massachusetts Institute of Technology's Learning Center. Here, managers derive decisions from activity based data and compare results to those obtained from other costing techniques.

Chrysler managers now say that introducing ABM changed their cost system completely. And more, it changed the way decisions are made.

Managers Do Get the Point

The ultimate test of ABM's success is whether managers use it. They'll only do that, of course, if they believe it helps them deliver the results the company's looking for.

ABM's capability is readily demonstrated. For example, efforts to improve margins are among the most sensitive drivers of value in any company, since much of a margin improvement drops to the cash bottom line. Even a 1% margin boost can improve shareholder value by many percentage points. ABM is designed to let managers highlight those activities that combine to create value and those that don't. With cost a key focus in margin management, ABM solves a big part of the value puzzle for them.

But ABM does more than help with managing indirect costs. It offers managers the best way to understand the overall economics of the business. ABM's basic premise – that to be competitive a company needs value based *processes* as well as value based products – was spelled out by Michael Porter when he defined elements of competitive strategy for the new millennium.[1]

'Ultimately, all differences between companies in cost or price derive from the hundreds of activities required to create, produce, sell and deliver their products or services, such as calling on customers, assembling final products and training employees. Cost is generated by performing activities, and cost advantage arises from performing particular activities more efficiently than competitors. Similarly, differentiation arises from both the choice of activities and how they are performed. Activities, then, are the basic units of competitive advantage. Overall advantage or disadvantage results from all a company's activities, not only a few.'

> ABC provides a valuable snapshot of what's right and wrong with business performance in a particular area – but the real gains come with ABM

Managers in companies quick to introduce ABM – like some mentioned earlier – have developed a fresh perspective on its importance. They see it redrawing key finance processes, including planning and budgeting, profitability reporting, investment decisions and – important to them personally – performance management, of which ABM information can form a critical subset. Sooner or later, they see it changing how they themselves manage the business – for the better.

It's Later Than CFOs Think

Every day, multinationals confront the staggering pace of change and growing competition in the global marketplace. One senior executive we interviewed echoes the concerns of CFOs the world over when he says: 'Flexible, low cost entrepreneurial ventures, without the overheads built up by older companies, are taking advantage of new technology to deliver new products and services at speed. Product cycles are shorter and more frequent. Speed or cycle time is the name of the game in virtually every industry'.

With innovation, fast response and cost containment the keys to competitive advantage, periodic one-off ABC exercises are not enough.

They fail to produce warning signals or prompt the right remedial actions: using them to see where it stands, the company will be lucky only to find the competition gaining – most will find it has galloped over the horizon. The wise CFO will consider the ABM option, while there's still time.

GO BEYOND YOUR ABC

Harvard professor Robert Kaplan articulated the basic principles behind ABM in the 1980s (Figure 4.3). Rather than aggregate indirect costs by function, he suggested tracing them to related activities. The idea was to lay bare not only the cost of the company's activities, but how individual products, services, customers and markets consume them – relationships described as *cost drivers.*

Managers like one-off, isolated ABC exercises because they provide a valuable snapshot of what's right and wrong with business performance in a particular area – albeit that they often confirm their worst fears. ABM is more complicated. At minimum, it means analyzing several strands of activity simultaneously to gain a broader picture: a manufacturing facility may involve 100 to 200 detailed activities with as many as 20 to 30 different cost drivers. But the real gains come when ABM begins to steer the evaluation of whole processes, and eventually becomes the enterprise-wide decision support framework.

Get the Most from the Product Portfolio Lifecycle

Perhaps the simplest step up from ABC to ABM is to use it in managing your product portfolio. When companies learn the true cost of their products or services, often as not, they find they're backing the wrong horses. Ascendant customer power makes lifecycle costing of products essential, but most companies lack information to manage this cycle properly. Often, potential product growth is undercut in some areas and product

Figure 4.3 **Basic principles of activity based management**

lines are allowed to decline quicker than necessary, while elsewhere support continues for lines leaking profit on all sides.

By tracking products' progress accurately over time, ABM lifecycle analysis identifies when products stop creating – and start draining – shareholder value. It establishes investment goals and budgets for seven product stages: initial analysis, start-up, entry, growth, maturity, decline and withdrawal (Figure 4.4). It lets the CFO examine activities that support each stage – to help make decisions on, for example, resource deployment, time to market, pricing and marketing.

During *start-up* and *entry* stages, when a product consumes rather than generates cash, it shows where you should focus to minimize negative cash flow through cycle time improvements. It lets you boost a product's *growth* stage through process improvements, and manage its *mature* stage, when investment costs are lower. And by merging current and planned activities, lifecycle costing can budget overall resource requirements – not just for products, but for the entire business.

Speed Time to Market

With speed the name of the competitive game, time to market is critical in any product lifecycle. To show where and how to shorten the cycle, the CFO must know the cost of all resources expended in bringing the product to market – information that ABM lifecycle costing provides.

Gaining a major new account for custom-built products, an automotive supplier looked at start-up and entry activities – engineering changes,

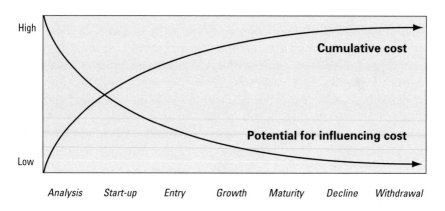

Figure 4.4 **Lifecycle costing of products**

vetting sub-contractors, prototyping, scheduling trial production. While the new customer promised big profits, the company also hoped to ease dependence on one of its long-time customers that seemingly made too many demands to be profitable. ABM analysis surprised management in every respect.

At start-up stage, the costs associated with the new account so far outstripped revenues that some executives wanted to pull out of the contract. But ABM also showed that if the company became more flexible in entry activities, got a better manufacturing resources planning system, and sped time to market, it would profit sooner than expected. And revenues from the long-time customer, ABM revealed, easily offset the account's service activity costs.

Get the Price Right

Another crucial part of managing product lifecycles: setting realistic prices. One company that used activity based analysis to see which products met a 20% profitability objective found 70% fell short, and of those, 20% were *losing* money.

Managers at another company, operating in the regulated US dairy industry, can request only an annual price hike. For years, they got less than they wanted. Analyzing activities gave them evidence to prove to authorities that costs had risen sharply: the company was allowed to price the product more in line with the true outlay.

Select Customers Wisely

With ABM analyses, companies often discover they're spending too much money to keep and serve customers, or market segments, that yield the least revenue or profit. One CEO says: 'I never realized how frequently we reward ourselves for losses. Using ABM, we found that a customer generating $160 million in sales was actually losing money, while one generating $90 million in sales had a 24% profit margin!'.

A consumer products distributor spent many hours in servicing its largest retail customer. The account's apparent contribution to profit was huge and the company continued to pour resources into the relationship, until analysis showed that the retailer cost too much. The distributor had to use unique bar coding on the retailer's products and carry inventory on its books until the retailer sold the product – which increased the company's service activity costs. Realigning the customer profit and cost information revealed a significant loss in shareholder value.

Monitor Broader Performance and Progress

Many companies know their current measurement systems are outmoded. In a recent study, most admit that their systems fail to provide as much as 60% of the data needed for budgeting and reporting. They want a smaller set of broader measures that emphasize innovation, process efficiency, customer satisfaction and value creation – a *dynamic* set of measures that evolves to reflect and inform strategic changes.

ABM is dynamic where ABC is static. It gives CFOs the process and activity detail needed to develop and apply a balanced business scorecard (Chapter 3). It helps them operationalize value strategies by building a bridge between the financials and the performance measurement system.

ABM's view of activities lets operational managers determine how different courses of action will improve shareholder value

Take a company that wants to boost operating cash flow and regards *days of inventory* as a big factor. Using ABM, it can assess activities that affect days of inventory – for example, handling customer returns, reworking and production scheduling – and identify their associated cost drivers, measurable day by day. Now management can see that, in practical operational terms, raising operating cash flow means improving and monitoring not simply days of inventory, but customer satisfaction, first-time quality and sales forecasts.

According to the principles of value based management, value is created or destroyed at the point where decisions are made: any decision based on knowledge of how it will affect shareholder value is the right decision. ABM's view of activities lets *top management* spotlight decision-making points – and lets *operational management* determine how different courses of action will improve value. The underlying variables – the cost drivers – can then be directly related to performance measures to track progress.

A pharmaceuticals manufacturer used ABM to uncover quality control activities related to batches. The company produced over 300 products, many run multiple times annually. For every batch of product it ran – whether a single or a million doses – the company incurred $66,000 in quality control activity (one year, a single site aggregated over $60 million). ABM let the company see how total volume requirements and scheduling profoundly affect the value created by each product line.

TIME TO GRADUATE: PASS THE VALUE CREATION TEST

Often, incremental business actually destroys shareholder value. An activity based *value* management system tells you when that's happening (Figure 4.5). This enhanced system describes the full cost consequences of product, customer and market portfolio decisions, modeling their impact on shareholder value. Besides operating cost drivers, it acknowledges capital drivers implied in the business strategy – and tracks trends in both forms of driver as you implement the strategy.

So ABM can help the CFO to be certain that the business is investing in the right developments to create sustainable shareholder value. The trick is not only to assign revenue costs to activities, but also to examine the capital consumed in the value creation process. How do you go about it? First, agree on the assets and their values needed in the business. Second, identify the capital drivers – the factors that determine how assets are used by the business – that will fairly assign capital values to activities. Then, use the company's cost of capital, consistent with your shareholder value analysis, to convert the capital assignment to a cash cost.

With increasingly globalized operations, and IT overhauls costing

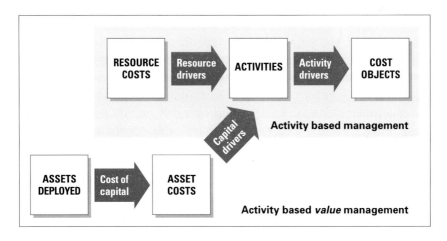

Figure 4.5 **Extending ABM to address value analysis**

upward of $100 million, a single investment mistake can spell disaster. Using ABM readies you for the next major investment proposal to the board: you can demonstrate the shareholder value the investment will create and back your recommendations with rigorous activity based cash flow and benchmark analysis.

The experience of a global financial services institution illustrates the predictive power of ABM in modeling the cash flow effect of investment decisions. Wanting to plan financial instruments for the year 2000, the company developed a state-of-the-art ABM system to analyze which existing instruments created value and which drained resources. Using the system to model processes and activity drivers, it was able to align products and services with its vision of the future.

Deliver an Activity Based Budget

The ideal current budgeting process is done painlessly in 30–45 days. Its detailed information drills down to operational level, rolls up to strategic objectives – a flexible framework that shows how well value strategies are delivered *and* accommodates major strategic change.

In reality, most companies struggle with planning and budgeting. Our Global Benchmarks Alliance survey shows that, on average, leading companies spend three to six months on the budgeting process.[2] Many still base today's figures on last year's plus a percentage, even though rapid change renders this link tenuous. After pouring resources into the exercise, most end up making arbitrary adjustments so the budget makes sense!

Activity based budgeting (ABB) offers an alternative. It links inputs and outputs, to control expenditure and monitor performance. First, look at how strategies will affect key cost drivers during the budget period. Consolidating detailed ABC data into major activity pools, you then project the demand that cost drivers will make on each pool. The projected level of pool activity reflects resources required to meet the plan. *And that's the budget.* Realistic, with startling clarity and detail, and produced in far less time. One transportation company used ABB to improve service to business units *and more than halve its administrative staff* in two years.

Use ABM to uncover where complexity is hindering value creation – and to analyze the impact of proposed improvements

The ABB model sparks valuable debate between parties involved in each activity and their various customers and suppliers, both internal and external. Relating inputs and outputs to the cost of activities educates everyone. Many CFOs are shocked to learn the full cost of processing an invoice – and how this compares to best practice.

The ABB engine lets CFOs do more than calculate future costs based on forecasts of activity consumption. Now, you can play out various scenarios simply by flexing the cost drivers. And validate activity assumptions at the outset. And model the business's future with authority. ABB expresses the numbers in terms that staff, customers, suppliers and investors understand. It produces a well reasoned, credible, achievable budget.

Untangle Complexity

The globalization of operations and consequent jump in mergers and acquisitions dramatically complicates organizations, distracting resources away from their *value creators* – or core competencies – and adding to a sea of inconsistent information based on different assumptions across the business. Chapter 6 explores ways of streamlining organizational structures and processes. As a first step to untangling the web, the CFO can use ABM to design a *complexity audit* that asks questions to uncover where complexity hinders value creation.

- How much product and service variety is there and how much does this cost?

- How do the costs of major activities, cycle times and productivity benchmark against best-in-class companies?

- What are the hidden costs of the organizational and management structure?

- What are the full costs of dealing with external agencies (suppliers, outsourcers, regulators)?

- How complex and costly are the company's decision-making processes?

The audit should highlight opportunities for improving processes – for example, by identifying and investigating non-value adding activity (process duplication and overlaps, downtime, checking, redundancy).

Managers at one company knew that customer demands for special orders were inflating set-up costs, but what could they do about it? They thought they were doing *too many* set-ups. ABM showed that set-ups simply took *too long*. Root cause analysis pinned the blame on lack of training: when workers got up to speed, special orders flowed off the line causing barely a blip in cost.

Using ABM to analyze the impact of proposed improvements can help make sure they achieve real and lasting gains. Cutting out complexity and cost can be a false economy if it compromises another element of the value chain. Using least cost contractors or lower quality raw materials, for example, can lead to more repair, rework, and quality assurance activities later, creating higher overall costs. ABM helps the CFO grasp how common cost drivers link activities in different parts of the value chain, over time.

Complexity audit findings may also lead the CFO to challenge the overall business design. For example, comparing the cost of a process, or its component activities, with the value it creates can help with outsourcing and divestment decisions. Generally, activities that show a cost-to-value ratio of 3:1 or greater are candidates for moving outside the core business.

A global oil company becoming a virtual energy business used ABM to see which activities to outsource. Benchmark analysis showed the company to be world-class in production but ruled out its ever being cost-effective in oil exploration and distribution. The company found itself outperformed by specialist exploration and distribution firms – which willingly bought its capacity in both areas and contracted back services.

Competitive positioning can depend as much on your success in influencing the value chain *outside* the company as on maximizing value creation *within* it. The classic model is the Japanese motor industry, which leverages the competencies of sister companies for mutual gain. These strategic alliances jointly realize a raft of benefits: less risk, lower investment, just-in-time delivery, faster time to market for new products, higher quality components, added flexibility. In short, they sharply enhance shareholder value.

YOUR FIRST JOB: DON'T GO JUMPING OFF THE BOARD

ABM brings proven benefits. How should you proceed toward implementation? A few companies leap into ABM and never look back. They simply throw out traditional cost reporting systems – an experience finance executives describe as the most traumatic of their corporate lives. This corporate equivalent of bungee-jumping is not necessary. It's possible to implement ABM stage by stage: piloting, integrating and embedding (Figure 4.6).

Piloting   As a first step, companies often run ABC as a pilot exercise to meet specific needs – say to check the accuracy of a profitability analysis, or see what areas should be improved in a process under review. Typically, only a few people are involved. Data is re-keyed or manipulated from simple electronic extracts, using cheap software on a stand-alone PC – affecting no other systems. If wrong, the concepts are easily changed. Basically, the business runs on as usual – and *even if the pilot is immensely successful, a company may never move ahead to ABM.*

What's needed is a pilot that convinces the organization to take the plunge. One company's ABM pilot study gained an unprecedented pricing breakthrough. Another's broke the log-jam on the optimal number of components for a major new product. These well orchestrated pilots broadcast benefits throughout the enterprise and had the full backing of senior and middle management.

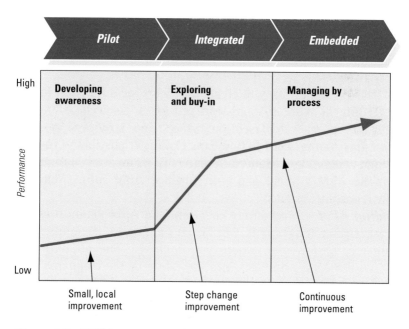

Figure 4.6   **ABM improves performance in stages**

Integrating ABM   If senior managers can see ABM supporting better strategic decision-making, they're more likely to throw their weight behind a move to integrate it company-wide. Their backing is essential to ensure that ABM systems are properly integrated from day one. They must also license the time that will have to be taken to complete more complex cost and management analyses than the business has ever seen before.

One company's pilot set out to compare the performance of manufacturing plants, using a PC in the finance department. Next, one of the plants implemented another version of the analysis system on two of its computers, while several suppliers customized yet more versions on their PCs. The company eventually realized that the only way forward was to link the computers in a network and integrate the data.

Investment at the right level in hardware and software becomes critical. Information systems throughout the business must be capable of handling higher volumes and offering more functionality – interfacing with legacy systems, for example. As ABM systems prove their worth, staff ask for more. They want more frequent updates and wider access to reports. Also some form of enterprise information system (EIS) to let them slice and dice figures on screen. *And* process management information based on key performance measures. *And* information on all products and services to permit multi-dimensional profitability analyses.

> For activity based management to fly, the business as a whole must own it – not just the CFO

The CFO has the opportunity to create a new business function for the care and feeding of ABM systems and processes. As well as finance people, this group must represent key users and providers of ABM information. Integrating ABM fully means making it possible to transfer financial and operational data automatically from core processing systems to the ABM system, and – in finished ABM form – back to appropriate reporting systems.

Embedding ABM   Successfully co-ordinating ABM diagnostics and processes takes you a long way forward from simple cost accounting. But you're still only part way to where you could be. The ultimate goal remains to weave ABM principles into the fabric of the company, such that they *change how the company does business.* For ABM to fly, the business as a whole must own it – not just the CFO.

The critical difference with embedded ABM is *people* – they must be really on board with the systems and processes. You need buy-in not just to get people filling in new *pro formas* and co-operating with new ways of collecting data. People have to be induced to use ABM information to change how they think about the processes they're involved in and, more important, to think how those processes can be improved. For example, most companies have to shift their culture to undertake the cross-functional teamworking ABM calls for throughout the organization. And any management style that blames people for poor performance misses the point of ABM, which is to help them improve their contribution to the business.

Most managers will say that they'd like to take more control over what they're doing; to feel more sure of their ground. Working with embedded ABM is like being able to see an X-ray of any key activity in the body corporate, at any point you want to – before you make an intervention. And that's true not just for senior managers – it offers the prospect of more realistic and effective decision-making *at every level* of the business.

The next section suggests a range of actions that the CFO and board can take – from communication and involvement, to a fundamental shift in their own attitudes and behaviors – to help embed ABM.

PROMOTION AHEAD: KNOCKING DOWN BARRIERS

CFOs embarking on ABM can find themselves on the uncomfortable end of some tough questioning. Not just: 'How do you intend to collect and update data, and maintain the consistency of information across multiple locations?'. But also: 'Why should I change to ABM when my current systems tell me what I want to know?'. Experience drawn from hundreds of projects suggests it's best to tackle issues surrounding implementation as three distinct groups: change management, ABM technical, and systems issues (Figure 4.7). For each group, the trick is to anticipate how the situation will evolve and to view issues not as barriers, but as avenues to explore with others, sharing ideas and experience as you go.

Change Management Issues

ABM gives CFOs a great case to sell. But they must be prepared to handle critical change management issues.

Close the credibility gap Make it a priority to show how the finance function will improve its service to the business through ABM.

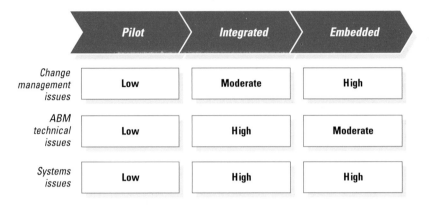

Figure 4.7 **The impact of major issues varies during ABM implementation**

Historically, operational managers have seen finance as blocking new initiatives and generating data useless for decision-making. 'Finance is out of touch with commercial realities. The CFO wants to run the numbers, not help us make them.' The solution is to open up the possibilities of a new type of partnership: working together on ABM, finance and operations can develop a world-class decision support network that lets everyone add value.

Involve all stakeholders – all the time Anyone who feels excluded from the process and its goals will work to thwart ABM. Nurture champions by conducting stakeholder analyses before you begin roll-out. Look at how change will impact on key groups of people and how they're likely to react (Figure 4.8). Then outline precisely what ABM offers each group, over what timeframe. In other words, identify *their* business agenda and build ABM around it.

Marketing managers, for example, often balk at ABM: they've heard it may cut products they think the market needs. One CFO enticed her marketing team to get on board by showing how activity based analysis can make products more marketable *while they're still on the drawing board*. With design determining 85% of product cost, she told them, ABM would help by giving the design team the information it needs to manipulate variables, trading off functionality and quality against cost.

Clear the political deck Promoting a world-class outlook on costs means educating people company-wide to *speak a new language*. Make sure it's intelligible to more than just accounting types, otherwise ABM will look like 'another way finance is trying to control the company'. On the other hand, if the company leaves ABM exclusively to operational management, finance people are likely to fight implementation. In either case, ABM stalls or even fails. Creating cross-functional senior management and project teams is the way to drive apolitical ABM.

Demonstrate, rather than dictate Persuade people that ABM is more than just another management theory. Launch a pilot with enterprise-wide implications to show what it can do.

The CFO of a large consumer products division did just that when management was faced with two costly options to reinforce washing machines for the institutional cleaning market. Hand-picking a project team that fanned out across the division, gathering information and opinions from everyone involved in the process, the CFO gradually taught managers about ABM: how activities are isolated and cost drivers derived. But they still needed convincing on how it could solve their dilemma.

With the pilot up and running on a computer, the CFO ran *what if*

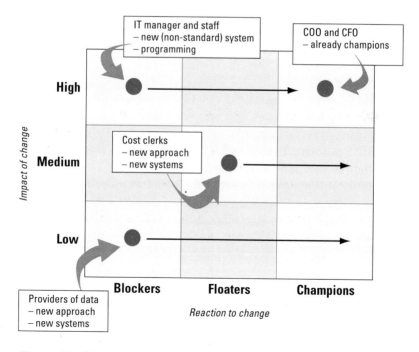

Figure 4.8 **Nurture new champions**

analyses. Option one, using special support bars, required different suppliers and special tooling, set-up and manufacturing operations: higher component costs would raise product price an intolerable 30% at the low end of the market. ABM ruled this out: no positive impact on the bottom line. Option two, using a different metal in standard bars, required overhauling the manufacturing process – a more complex operation which would, again, raise price. But ABM showed that the incremental cost of reconfiguring the factory was offset by production time savings. Confident that option two would marginally improve the picture short-term but have a major impact over the long term, managers returned to their units extolling ABM's virtues.

Train everyone A pilot scores by dramatizing ABM's benefits. But only training – in formal classes, town meetings, institute programs – dramatizes ABM's *process* and how to exploit it. Before roll-out, people need to understand how ABM helps them *and* how it works. It's worth making properly designed training and development available to everyone. Seminars, newsletters, videotapes and other communication media help make the language of ABM second nature.

Deliver on promises Led to expect miracle cures from pilots, managers quickly grow disillusioned. Avoid promising the moon. Use ABM to take on three or fewer pressing *business* problems and broadcast successes before tackling another problem. Let ABM evolve naturally, gaining buy-in as it goes.

Sold on ABM by a magazine article, one CFO set out to win over senior functional and division managers. In a speech, he presented a laundry list of benefits, raising expectations that ABM would cure all their business ills. After taking a year to set up, the pilot delivered far less than promised. Six months later the company abandoned ABM.

Staged benefits will maintain impetus for you and build the business case. As the experience of British Gas Transco confirms, it takes years to create a working ABM system – so relax. Why push when users will pull the process forward?

CASE STUDY: BG Transco Rethinks ABM

British Gas, the privatized UK utility, launched a massive ABC exercise to carve up its $7 billion annual operating costs. In only four months, management identified, by activity, resources relating to each of five business units to provide *core services and products. As part of its resulting restructuring and delayering strategy, it created Transco for the regulated portion of the business.*

Spawned by ABC, Transco relied on annual ABC analyses to substantiate its cost base to the regulator through periods of structural change. But then the regulator proposed significant price cuts: how could Transco maintain acceptable shareholder returns? Senior management now saw ABM as the logical operational cost management and decision support tool to replace foundering 20-year-old systems. Transco set out to implement ABM. It developed an integrated client/server solution across some half-dozen service districts to:

- *analyze alternative strategies to achieve a step change in performance*

- *report service costs*

- *benchmark district activities*

- *set cost performance targets and promote continuous improvement.*

Two years later, the roll-out continues. Some districts wait for the ABM model, while others analyze activities, report service costs, produce performance metrics – but have yet to exploit the information. Despite education, operational managers remain unsure of what's expected of them, what the system should deliver, and when and how to exploit it. Entrenched in a traditional culture with a strong engineering influence, some resist ABM information. Concerned that technology might be an issue, others look at new alternative systems. With limited resources, Transco even briefly considered cutting back the ABM implementation to achieve short-term cost savings.

Jumping into ABM, management's high expectations were destined to trip over change management issues. Experience shows that the key to success is a gradual approach that progressively demonstrates ABM benefits, gains user buy-in and helps articulate what ABM should deliver.

Still determined to succeed with ABM, Transco no longer underestimates the time and effort needed to embed it in the organization. Change management is seen to be as big an issue as systems implementation. The company now focuses on culture and organizational changes at the operational level, working to raise ABM back to the top of management priority and achieve its potential.

ABM Technical Issues

How did a company's ABM system end up detailing 1500 activities and becoming too complex to handle? Clue: the company asked for *everyone's* input. Solution: set the right rules – design a system to include the level of detail needed to manage the company effectively, and no more.

Find the key cost objects   From the start, the CFO must look hard at what dimensions really matter in understanding profitability and resist cluttering the ABM system with extraneous detail. A common temptation is to include many product cost details intended for accounting and statutory controls. With these overlaid by other customer and market profitability dimensions, the system may include tens of thousands of cost objects. When profitability analyses combine the dimensions – product by customer, customer by market channel, product by market – the system gets choked with *millions* of combinations. Hardly viable.

To find strategic direction, even the most complex company with multiple lines of business should focus on major product lines, customer groups and markets. Then, CFOs can use ABM to model specific scenarios in greater detail, as needed.

Craft an activity structure that delivers   ABM systems need an activity structure that shows why costs are generated and which cost objects are related to which. To articulate the activity structure, consider each element of the value chain and component key processes. Then, for each key process, define component activities. Seems straightforward. But often companies misidentify an activity as a *process* – or *component tasks* as activities.

Actually there are trade-offs: it's impossible to analyze all activities as mutually exclusive and collectively exhaustive. One answer is to compile an *activity dictionary* that precisely defines each activity, where it fits in the value chain, and its relationships with cost objects. Once the dictionary is complete, the ABM project team meets with managers, who map into it what their people do and their departmental costs.

Used properly, this exercise gives a schematic for the entire activity cost portion of the ABM system. But, as with cost objects, you must avoid clutter. Eager to accommodate managers' suggestions, you can end up with thousands of activities in the dictionary, necessitating monolithic ABM systems. Don't be too inflexible either. Companies that allow only a handful of activities per function force managers to aggregate activities – distorting what they do to fit the structure. Again, to avoid mistakes either way, focus your conceptual design on major activities strongly related to value creation.

Choose realistic cost drivers   Trying to identify major cost drivers that have a real impact, many companies lose their balance – veering between overly simplistic and intricate choices. Look for drivers that satisfy three criteria: they describe activities' behavior, relate to cost objects and, crucially, can be quantified. Some choose 'the weather' as a cost driver, until they see it's impossible to quantify or relate to cost objects. Keep looking. Realistic cost drivers *may well be* associated with the weather, but they must be broken out individually in relation to specific activities.

Settle on an optimal number of cost drivers, chosen to describe about 80% of incurred costs – then prioritize them, focusing on those that most influence major activities and associated costs. As services become more complex and intertwined with others in bundled offerings, the company needs greater ABM detail to unravel their complexity and improve the cost system's accuracy. An executive developing a high level ABM system at a global financial services concern avoids erring on the side of aggregation for simplicity's sake.

> Focus on realistic cost drivers – those that have a major impact and can be quantified

'Line managers must have access to a level of detail that will allow better decision-making. The right level of detail will either reinforce or be quite different from managers' basic intuition – either way, it allows them to make an informed decision.' But adding cost drivers eventually brings diminishing returns: 200 cost drivers probably provide the same answers as the first 50.

Link ABM into business initiatives   ABM information should be integrated with business initiatives, particularly restructuring and process re-engineering, which change how decisions are made. ABM amply supports initiatives. *Product costing* begins to identify the factors that add complexity and related costs into the business, via either individual product lines or business segments. *Reallocating resources for growth* involves moving beyond restructuring and re-engineering to a concern with growth. ABM *budgeting* uses cost driver information to cut out much of the non-value added time associated with these processes – as well as helping you manage the factors that create value. Supporting initiatives with ABM allows it to permeate day-to-day business routines. Suddenly, everyone starts talking in terms of activities.

Harmonize performance measurement If the company is to manage value, performance measures for virtually every aspect of the business should be aligned with ABM cost information. A major waste disposal and recycling company set out key performance indicators (KPIs) linked to the most important cost drivers. Routinely collected and distributed to plant management throughout the month, KPIs made end-of-month reporting more predictable.

Systems Issues

Elaborate, often PC based systems, developed for external financial reporting and product costing and pricing, litter the business landscape. Deeply rooted in most companies, cost accounting reaches into almost all systems. And it's all the more difficult to promote change since while ABM offers a more precise view of costs, it also complicates cost management. Fortunately for CFOs, they can exploit new and emerging technologies.

Start with low-tech, high impact presentation Most companies already have the technology to promote ABM. It sits on desktops in the form of spreadsheets, databases and modeling tools. Even at the most basic level, technology can be used to foster buy-in by dramatizing ABM's benefits through colorful, high impact graphics. Chrysler took this look-see phase a step further with its simulation model at the Massachusetts Institute of Technology's Learning Center, proving the power of hands-on experience in selling ABM to managers.

Systematize activity based management and, suddenly, everyone starts talking in terms of activities

Plug in ABM and integrate Several inexpensive, PC based ABM software packages, easily set up, lend themselves to early pilots. But the PC approach hamstrings wider ABM applications (Figure 4.9). As one CFO puts it: 'ABM can't be a system until it's systematized'.

Integration can mean setting up numerous interfaces. A typical ABM system interfaces mainly with the general ledger and links to other systems like the order management/billing system for customer, revenue and product shipment information.

For manufacturers, interfacing the ABM and manufacturing systems for billing of materials and process routings data can prove difficult. Manufacturing systems track many complex relationships of parts and processes to products and must be revised frequently to reflect engineering

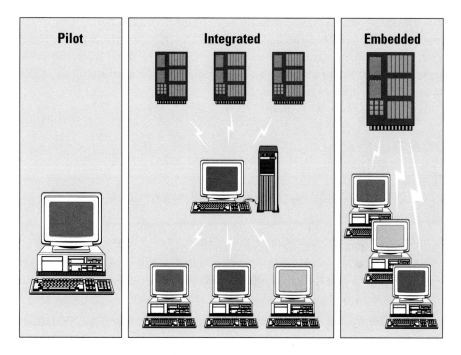

Figure 4.9 **ABM systems: Control the evolution**

changes. ABM exercises can uncover a deal of statistical and cost driver information in upstream business systems – for example, purchase order quantities and part number counts in the purchasing system, engineering hours and resource consumption in the engineering job order collection system, and scrap and rework quantities in the quality systems. Service companies derive parallel information from operational systems which tend to be unique to particular industries: many insurance companies, for example, rely on claims systems.

After identifying 30 data sources, one company elected to automate only 14 high data volume transfers – and manually dispatch the rest. Good practice for effective integration.

Embed ABM when you're ready Fully embedding ABM should reduce interface complexity because it rests on finding an enterprise-wide solution, where much needed data exists in a single repository. But the sheer scope of such an implementation, which involves replacing modules in specific sequence, can mean a lengthy process. Unwilling to go down the embedded route yet, some companies like Iberdrola have concentrated on developing an integrated ABM system using client/server cost and other applications and a data warehouse. This lets them milk the ABM system for information and defer embedding it until confident they fully understand their business needs.

CASE STUDY: Iberdrola Uses ABM to Promote Culture Change

Expecting to create a corporate powerhouse, Spain's two largest privately owned electricity companies combined in 1991. The result was Iberdrola, a vertically integrated generating, distribution and supply company, with eight million customers internationally and a 40% share of the Spanish market. But the merger brought a daunting challenge. Iberdrola would have to reconcile two very different corporate cultures and operating styles to achieve profitable growth and reliable service delivery.

With liberalization of the European electricity market making superior competitive performance essential, the company's 1993 strategic planning exercise committed it to building shareholder value. The company mapped its value chain and began re-engineering processes to yield customer service and cost benefits. A new business management system, built with ABM concepts, established cost management and budgeting processes, as well as objectives and performance measures at business unit level. The management system let Iberdrola analyze profitability by various dimensions, as well as cost drivers, the underlying influences on process cost. The company gained flexibility to play out scenarios and model and track progress of initiatives.

Iberdrola had a long way to go. Legacy systems gave managers financial, materials management and operational data – well suited to the regulated environment – but couldn't integrate it. Unable to understand costs and profitability in the way they needed to meet the demands of the emerging liberalized marketplace, managers could run the business, but not manage it. The company conducted an ABM pilot using ACTIVA cost management software, exploiting the latest client/server and data warehousing technologies.[3]

Convinced of its worth, Iberdrola planned to introduce embedded ABM – replacing all core systems with Oracle, SAP or custom-developed enterprise-

wide software. But the prospect of lengthy implementation of the software platform, and questions about the degree of ABM functionality then available, made the company think again.

Instead, Iberdrola decided to integrate its existing systems using ACTIVA. Now it can take its time to evaluate and implement whatever new systems it chooses. It can also move toward creating an ABM culture, and benefit from integrated activity based information, while keeping its options open on whether or not to evolve to fully embedded ABM.

Even in the best ABM systems, integrating data from legacy systems often proves difficult. Installed piecemeal over a number of years, legacy systems run on many different hardware platforms and involve idiosyncratic, heavily modified software. Data warehousing technology can provide the answer (Chapter 8). A data warehouse pulls information from varied sources into a central location where it can be accessed in a common form. Leading-edge companies are moving to data warehousing to leverage their existing technology investment. Among them, one multinational will capture all information, including activity based data, in a single multi-dimensional repository: the data warehouse will provide on-line access to activity based information that can be sliced and diced to support a myriad of business enquiries.

Heartening news for cost-conscious CFOs: by the time most companies are ready to embed ABM, it's more than likely they'll be able to exploit in-house systems, rather than jump to a new technology (Figure 4.10).

	1990	1995	2000
PC based packages	90%	40%	20%
4GL packages	10%	25%	20%
Client/server based solutions		25%	25%
Embedded general ledger solutions		10%	35%

Figure 4.10   **Share of ABM software market (illustrative data)**

Vendors like SAP and Oracle are enhancing their decision support modules to deliver robust, enterprise-wide ABM. And PC ABM software vendors are developing client/server versions of their software to exploit both the data warehouse and emerging *lean client* hardware (low cost PC-like hardware) to access high capacity servers.

GETTING READY TO MOVE ON

ABM *principles* remain as compelling as ever. This chapter shows that – thanks to pioneering efforts by forward-thinking companies and introduction of new technology solutions – ABM *practice* begins to look similarly attractive. But even now, even when the prospect of success is high, arguing a straight factual case for ABM will not do. CFOs who want to lead ABM must step outside their traditional comfort zone.

Circumstances have to be created where managers can get involved and see examples of ABM in action, so that they themselves will then push for change. If the finance function is to take on the new role of running ABM systems, it may need to overhaul its image within the company. And since culture change is emerging as the key factor in embedding ABM, change management skills will become the order of the day for finance managers.

With all this, and its long-term implications for financial reporting generally, ABM could indeed herald a radical change, not only in the way the CFO and finance function operate, but also the way they're perceived by the rest of the business. With ABM, CFOs can architect their own future, as well as their corporation's.

CFO's CHECKLIST

FOLLOW THE LEAD OF BEST-IN-CLASS PLAYERS Learn from the evolutionary experience of companies that have reaped benefits from ABM. Improve your ability to analyze profitability, manage resources, measure performance.

LAUNCH A PILOT Start out small and let a series of pilot exercises show what ABM can do for a succession of business problems. Chronicle what ABM delivers and foster buy-in by broadcasting successes across the company through every means possible. Achieving staged benefits maintains impetus, builds the business case, and turns users into salespeople for ABM. A small software buy to supplement desktop technology puts you on your way.

CLEAR THE POLITICAL DECK It's easy for operations people to dismiss ABM as just another finance theory – unless they have a hand in designing it. Assemble a cross-functional project team and rally senior management support. Promote the idea that, far from being a way of pointing fingers at poor performance, ABM works to improve all business operations. And start teaching the whole company the language of ABM.

PICK REALISTIC COST DRIVERS Cost drivers describe activities' behavior, relate to cost objects, and can be quantified. Avoid overly simplistic ones that may actually be several lumped together – and intricate ones that miss the point. The aim is to find cost drivers that describe around 80% of incurred costs, then whittle them down to an optimal few that strongly affect major activities and their costs.

CONSIDER A DATA WAREHOUSE Before embedding ABM, first develop an integrated ABM system. Using client/server cost and other applications with a data warehouse is a good option. The data warehouse collects information from multiple sources – including legacy systems on various hardware platforms – and casts it into a common, easily accessed form to feed the ABM system. A data warehouse also improves information for companies ready to embed ABM.

INTEGRATE ABM WITH BUSINESS INITIATIVES One of the best ways to spread ABM thinking is to link ABM to key business initiatives, particularly restructuring and process re-engineering efforts that change the course of decision-making. Help initiatives with product costing, reallocating resources and budgeting. Weave ABM into daily business routines and its language into everyone's daily lives.

HARMONIZE ABM INFORMATION WITH PERFORMANCE MEASURES Promote a consistent approach to managing the business, in pursuit of shareholder value, by linking the ABM and performance measurement systems.

CHAPTER 5
Integrating Financial and Business Risk Management

High-tech leader Vision Systems enjoys a reputation for spectacular innovation and flexible, fast response to the needs of customers in the micro-computing market. But behind the scenes, some projects are less than successful. Products are open to piracy and, beyond litigation arising from infringements of intellectual property rights, risks sometimes come out of left field. Customer credit limits can escalate quickly, making insolvency concerns all too real.

CFO Brad Davis uses financial instruments to hedge foreign exchange and interest rate risks with some success. But management resists attempts to clarify the company's overall risk tolerance. True, shareholders investing in Vision Systems expect to take greater than average risks. Still, a comprehensive risk profile is needed. And since management's highest priority is shareholder value growth, Davis plans to use this lever to convince colleagues. Far from a theoretical exercise, pinning down their risk appetite will help them choose more rationally between competing investment alternatives.

An informal, creative culture is key to the company's success. So persuading people to adopt new risk management disciplines will be a stretch. Davis knows he needs more than the traditional financial skills acquired in his career to date. He needs to implement a culture change and communication program that empowers staff to make decisions within clear boundaries. One that encourages them to anticipate risks – and to share responsibility for actions likely to materially affect the organization as a whole.

What is the CFO's role as business risk manager? As the finance function shifts focus from control to decision support, how can the CFO be sure of anticipating big risks? Looking beyond traditional financial methodologies, this chapter explores how all types of risks, across all business processes, impact on shareholder value. Learn how focusing on risk materiality, rather than source, lets finance professionals support strategic decisions. Blue chips' experiences in treasury risk management illustrate techniques for evaluating risks within an integrated framework. Case studies highlight how a broader, more structured approach to managing business risk boosts financial performance through better policy and decision-making.

A NEW LOOK AT RISK

Notice how risk management has moved up the corporate management agenda? A growing multiplicity of business risks pushes multinationals to find more comprehensive approaches to managing them.

But what is business risk? Risk is a matter of perspective. Finance and operational managers, institutional and speculative investors, all see risk differently. It can mean any impediment, inside or outside the organization, to meeting business objectives. One report concludes: 'Business risk arises as much from the likelihood that something good *won't* happen as it does from the threat that something bad *will* happen'.[1] To plot particular risks, try dividing the population of risks the company is exposed to into five main groups: strategic, financial, operational, commercial and technical risks (Figure 5.1).

Risk groups are not mutually exclusive. For example, human factors – prime drivers of operational risks – are significant in many strategic and financial risks. Also, companies carry their histories with them: a business may have accumulated liabilities or assets, bad or good practices, weak or strong relationships. Consider how past risks influence current exposures

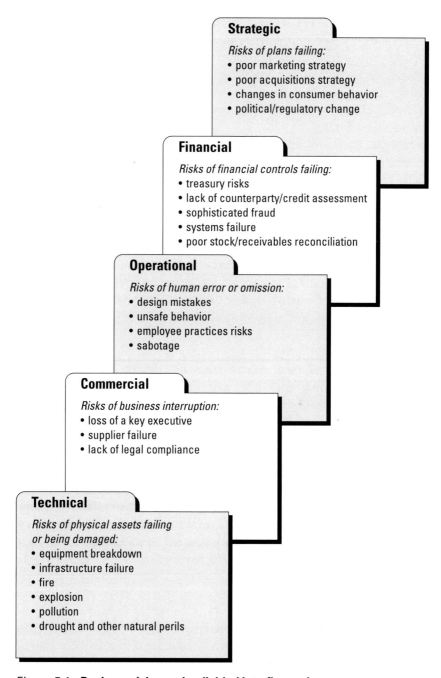

Strategic

Risks of plans failing:
- poor marketing strategy
- poor acquisitions strategy
- changes in consumer behavior
- political/regulatory change

Financial

Risks of financial controls failing:
- treasury risks
- lack of counterparty/credit assessment
- sophisticated fraud
- systems failure
- poor stock/receivables reconciliation

Operational

Risks of human error or omission:
- design mistakes
- unsafe behavior
- employee practices risks
- sabotage

Commercial

Risks of business interruption:
- loss of a key executive
- supplier failure
- lack of legal compliance

Technical

Risks of physical assets failing or being damaged:
- equipment breakdown
- infrastructure failure
- fire
- explosion
- pollution
- drought and other natural perils

Figure 5.1 **Business risks can be divided into five main groups**

– and how risks of all types affect strategic direction and, ultimately, the company's ability to generate shareholder value in future.

Until recently, companies managed risks largely in terms of possible solutions. An insurable risk might be the insurance manager's responsibility. If a risk seemed a financial control matter, the treasurer might deal with it. Risks touching on consumer relations might be managed as part of sales and marketing.

Today, functionally segregating risk management seems dated. The CFOs and other senior executives of many multinationals are learning to take a more integrated view of business risks and business risk management. Why the change?

More and more people study business performance The corporate veil is being drawn away. Banks, investors, community groups, consumers and other stakeholders demand ever more evidence of how a company plans to maintain a strong balance sheet and healthy reputation.

Competitive pressures escalate To make effective, economic use of limited resources, a company puts its capital where its key risks lie. A solid business risk management program lowers the company's exposure to the classes of risk *it is not in business to take* and re-shapes exposure to those it *is* in business to take.

Risk management can create new advantage The *investment community* may favor a stock if it understands the rationale underlying the total risk management effort – believing the company more likely to manage its cost base and produce future cash flows. And *customers* may prefer to do business with a company seen to be managing risks that affect the service they receive, whether corporate reputation, supply line, quality or other risks.

Individual loss or gain can match business loss and gain The personal element remains powerful. Senior executives dread having their names associated with failure. Those whose successful risk-taking brings a string of large gains generally enjoy better career prospects.

Corporate fortunes can reverse overnight In today's technologically advanced world, changes happen so frequently and are communicated so rapidly that, when good or bad news hits the stock market, a company's position can flip-flop almost instantaneously.

Global regulations grow more complex Corporations have increasing obligations to disclose to shareholders which risks they're in business to take, how they're running them, and what they're doing to manage them.

Risk management means dealing with uncertainty. What can go wrong, or fail to go right? How often? What counter-measures exist, or could be installed? How likely are they to be effective? Companies grow large and prosper only by managing huge amounts of risk. Blue chips earn their strong rating because they do manage big risks, successfully and economically. But you can manage only what you know. Switched-on executives ask: 'What about the risks we don't know? Will they harm us or merely consume undue management time?'. Finding the answers takes a keen awareness of *what* risks might arise, *where* and, crucially, *how material* they are to the business.

FOCUS ON MATERIALITY, NOT SOURCE

To manage business risks based on their materiality, the CFO works with the board and senior operating managers to devise an overall risk management strategy and reporting structure. It's vital to look at risk holistically, not pockets of risk measured on different scales.

Map the business impact of each potential risk against its likelihood to get a scale of materiality (Figure 5.2). At one end, *catastrophic* losses are

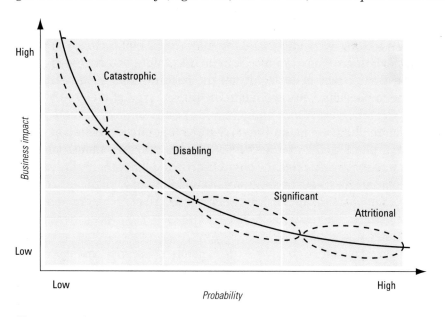

Figure 5.2 **Assessing the materiality of risk**

any failure of business strategy that leaves the organization unable to achieve its objectives: a rare event among larger companies. More common *disabling* events severely hamper the company's strategy for a period of, say, a year. Blue chips with a reputation for being able to manage such losses tend to continue trading as blue chips. Investors understand that life is unpredictable. But for others, a series of disabling events can spell catastrophe: when share price drops progressively, the company becomes vulnerable to takeover, withdrawal of credit facilities, or other constraints that, sooner or later, can cause its downfall.

> A single, relatively minor human error can develop into a multi-billion dollar event, putting an entire corporate reputation at stake

Further along the materiality scale, *significant* losses should be disclosed, but don't seriously impair returns to shareholders – for example, a foreign exchange loss, or use of funds to repair environmental damage. Least material are relatively frequent *attritional* losses, like small damage claims, workers' compensation and safety related losses. Though significant in themselves, these tend to be expense matters for the corporation as a whole.

Clearly, assessing the *business* impact of a risk involves more than simply estimating the immediate *financial* loss. Look at potential short, medium and long-term effects, taking into account all factors and views of all stakeholders. For example, shareholders might be concerned about dividend flow, banks about equity in the business and security of their loans, customers about management integrity.

A single, relatively minor human error or omission can develop into a multi-billion dollar event, putting an entire corporate reputation at stake. Many well publicized corporate losses demonstrate this. Industrial accidents can cost lives, damage the environment and harm the livelihoods of whole communities – leaving the corporation paying for damages, cleanup and compensation to victims. This *ripple* effect from one event to others illustrates the relationship between risks – reinforcing the case for an integrated approach.

How do companies recover? It depends. Research sponsored by Sedgwick Group shows that the impact of a major human factor loss can differ dramatically from one company to another.[2] A study of 15 major corporate incidents – including Pan Am's Lockerbie air crash, Union Carbide's Bhopal gas leak, and the explosion on Occidental's *Piper Alpha*

North Sea oil platform – shows that, irrespective of industry type, companies fall into two distinct groups: *recoverers* and *non-recoverers*. In Figure 5.3, the summarized share price performance for the groups over the 12 months following each incident – with normal share price movements due to market fluctuations and other factors filtered out – is assumed to represent abnormal returns related to the incident.

For *recoverers*, initial loss of shareholder value averages around 5%. But within two months of the incident, shareholder value returns to normal levels and, in some cases, even goes positive. One possible explanation is that, once the immediate scale of the loss becomes known, confidence quickly returns. A second explanation hinges on perceptions of management's ability to deal with the aftermath: paradoxically, such incidents offer management the chance to demonstrate its talent.

In contrast, *non-recoverers* suffer an enduring drop in share price of over 10%. In most of these cases, the incident's potential adverse cash flow impact is enormous. They tend to involve large numbers of fatalities

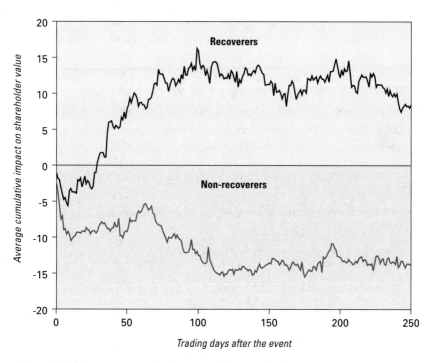

Figure 5.3 **Some companies recover from major losses better than others**
Source: Templeton College

and management is judged responsible, at least partially, for a safety lapse.

Food for thought for CFOs. The researchers attribute the impact of a major corporate incident on shareholder value to two main factors. First, *direct financial consequences* – that is, the effect on future cash flow. The stock market forms a collective opinion and adjusts value accordingly. Second, and more significantly, *management skills*. The stock market re-evaluates the company's management, examining to what extent the loss was attributable to bad management or lack of controls and gaging the effectiveness of management's response.

All this points up important questions.

- *Where would the company be had the loss been avoided?* What the research can't show is the value of the opportunities a company misses while its equity recovers after a major loss. Modeling this would mean factoring the difference between that particular stock and what happened elsewhere in the sector.

- *Have investors already accounted for possible losses?* Accidents in an airline business, serious spillages in a chemicals business, lawsuits in a professional services business – all foreseeable possibilities. Investors, particularly institutions, may price the potential for such loss into the equity.

- *What's the impact on ongoing financial strength?* Beyond market capitalization, a risk event affects the company's solvency and on-going financial strength. Techniques like z-scoring analysis, routinely used in the financial community, can measure relative solvency.

- *Do different investors behave differently?* Examining the nature of the share registry might help explain the share price performance of a *recoverer* following major loss. Early stock selling after the incident may owe largely to the volatile fraction of the share registry – in other words, speculators. But is it also speculators who later *buy* the stock, accounting for the upturn in share price? Or is it institutional investors buying up an underpriced investment?

- *What happens in other loss situations?* Might more lessons be learned by studying the impact of other kinds of human factor losses, such as bad investment decisions or banking losses? What about major losses resulting from natural perils, like hurricanes or drought?

- *How can you measure management quality?* Investors' general view of management's skill in handling risk seems to be crucial to share price performance. But objectively measuring management quality is tough, if not impossible. What *is* clear is that, through the investor relations program, the CFO must communicate evidence of management's capabilities and its risk management approach.

Interestingly, for both *recoverers* and *non-recoverers*, insurance cover seems not to influence restoration of shareholder value. Usually, financial loss is a small part of the value effects of a major corporate incident: many companies seriously question whether to insure for financial loss. What are the benefits to well diversified shareholders who also hold shares in insurance companies? At best, perhaps, a zero-sum game?

The decision of one major multinational to bring the bulk of its insurance exposures in-house illustrates this point. Among factors arguing for self-insurance, the company considered the fairly remote likelihood of certain financial losses – and concluded it could better withstand them than insurers could. But to supplement its expertise, the company does outsource some elements of risk management – relying on the insurance community to provide economies of scale at the *attritional* level, where it can handle large volumes of small claims.

TALKING RISK WITH INVESTORS

Communicating future cash flow assumptions to investors has an important influence on current share price. Companies use sensitivity analysis to judge the potential risk in cash flow assumptions relating to revenues and margins. But the market also judges the risk inherent in the capital investment itself, be it extending the basic business or diversifying, giving investors new risks to contemplate.

Share value performance reflects investors' confidence in management's ability to generate future wealth. Risk contributes to share price volatility, so anything the company does to demonstrate competent risk management should improve its share price. Often, investors look to the quality of the CFO, particularly when a company's facing the unexpected. Arguably, the CFO – at the nerve center of information flows, involved in most major decisions and keeper of the budget – exerts the widest influence in the organization. Frequently it's the CFO who handles investor relations and communications.

Long-term risk figures in computing the weighted average cost of capital (WACC) – one of the drivers of shareholder value (Chapter 2). Lower perceived risk means lower WACC, driving higher value. Since risks vary across countries and business units, CFOs must think through the spread of risks associated with future investments. Cost of capital should reflect inflation expectations in the territory of investment and include a premium to account for any higher political and economic risks.

A UK based conglomerate evaluating an investment project in Brazil adjusted its UK cost of capital to reflect the difference between expected domestic inflation (3.5%) and that in Brazil (24%). To compensate for political and economic risks, the group compared yields on $US denominated bonds in Brazil with yields on similar bonds in the US – suggesting a premium of 9%. These adjustments put the group's cost of capital in Brazil at 45% – dramatically higher than the 11% figure for a UK project with similar business risks. The CFO used this adjusted cost of capital to evaluate cash flows from the project, denominated in Brazilian reals.

> For the corporation's shareholders, risk is good – if managed and exploited for gain

WACC may vary across product groups too – the same conglomerate found differences between 10% and 13%. Overlay such product spread on any geographic spread when evaluating the relative contributions to shareholder value of different investment strategies.

One technique CFOs use to monitor the returns of a particular product division is to examine the risk-adjusted return on capital. Any extraneous (as opposed to systematic) risks that the product division is taking can then be accounted for in the allocation of capital. For instance, a product division taking some relatively exotic risk, such as territorial or political exposure, must pay a premium: its return on capital is diminished compared to other divisions without that exposure.

The free cash flow model discussed in Chapter 2 can be used to quantify how risks affect value at the product, subsidiary or corporate level. Brought together this way, risks previously viewed as incomparable can be evaluated against common criteria. By mapping the relative importance of specific risks to the key value drivers, the CFO can establish a detailed model for judging the effect of risk on shareholder value (Figure 5.4).

Typically, different risks are shown to have different impacts on shareholders. Computing the effects of mitigating those risks lets you show the investment community the benefits of sound risk management. There's

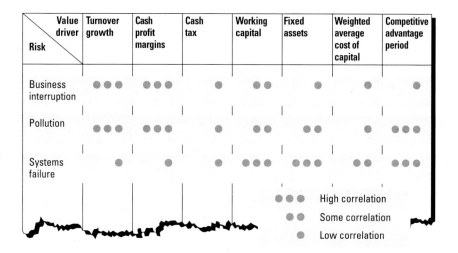

Value driver / Risk	Turnover growth	Cash profit margins	Cash tax	Working capital	Fixed assets	Weighted average cost of capital	Competitive advantage period
Business interruption	●●●	●●●	●	●●	●	●	●
Pollution	●●●	●●●	●	●●	●●	●	●●●
Systems failure	●	●	●	●●●	●●●	●●	●●●

●●● High correlation
●● Some correlation
● Low correlation

Figure 5.4 **Linking risk management to shareholder value**

some evidence that by economically reducing its risk profile, the company bolsters certainty in future cash flows at no additional cost, which should be reflected in determining shareholder value.

IS YOUR BUSINESS HUNGRY FOR RISK?

The link between risk management and shareholder value argues strongly for the CFO taking responsibility for developing an integrated approach. The object of managing business risk is to maximize shareholder value. So risk management, an integral part of the business, should not be isolated from business management.

View the world from a risk perspective, but don't put all your effort into minimizing risk. For shareholders, *risk is good* – if commensurate with an adequate level of return. The CFO must closely link risk management procedures, achievement of corporate goals and reduced volatility of outcomes.

The best CFOs view risk as a business asset to be managed and exploited for gain – turning conventional wisdom on its head. Eliminating risk simultaneously eliminates the opportunity for profit. At the end of the day, risk is all about possible reward. Listing the opportunity potential of risk beside its loss potential (Figure 5.5), the CFO can better judge the

RISK AS AN ASSET	RISK AS A LIABILITY
We must manage risk to	*We must manage risk to*
● seize opportunities	● reduce the possibility of loss
● create value	● protect value
● push to the limits	● stay in control
● beat the competition	● avoid falling behind
● attract investors	● reassure investors

Figure 5.5 **Looking at risk from both sides**

contribution of risk management to corporate strategy and performance over the longer term.

CFO 2000 research highlights risk management as an important issue for CFOs. In certain areas, including financial control and environmental risks, most survey respondents say their companies aim to minimize risks. But in overall business and financial risk management, 20% of CFOs say their companies accept an *above* average degree of risk – nearly matching the 27% whose companies accept *below* average risk.

The toughest question comes when determining the company's risk appetite in specific terms that guide subsequent events. What monies can appropriately be put at risk by taking a particular course of action? For an international products company, comparing past treasury activity with management's appetite for future treasury risk led to new policies and practices.

CASE STUDY: Appetite for Treasury Risk

A products company with research and manufacturing operations in the US, Europe and Japan services customers through a network of more than 90 sales subsidiaries worldwide. It enjoys dominant market share. And continual innovation in its core product area keeps barriers to competition firmly in place. Highly profitable in the past, the company's recent performance has been dented by unexpected losses. In one year, currency transaction loss topped $70 million – a sharp bite out of total profits. Interest rate exposures, too, have been worrying.

Lacking clear policies for hedging these risks, the CFO urged the board to define the company's risk appetite in each treasury activity. The aim was to be risk averse: no more surprises. Performance measures set for treasury managers were linked to agreed risk tolerance limits. For example, the stop loss limit for foreign exchange transaction exposure was set at 2% of forecast group profit: approved investments included forward and spot foreign exchange contracts and currency options. Parameters were set for hedging foreign currency flows on a committed basis. Authority limits were agreed for different levels of transaction.

Implementing risk policy – and adhering to limits imposed by agreed risk appetite – is easier said than done! The company improved the treasury function at the center, with new controls, procedures and systems. All committed foreign exchange flows are netted off centrally and hedged, and forecast foreign exchange flows hedged within approved parameters. But group treasury staff still rely on the operating companies for information on exposure. The long-term plan is to set up regional treasury centers based on the three continental theaters. Shorter term, the treasury team staged a worldwide tour of subsidiaries to present the new policies, gain commitment through involvement, and set up vital communication networks.

Companies decide management's risk appetite in different ways. But the process always involves balancing various factors. Is the risk consistent with the company's current philosophy? With its history of gains and losses? With investors' understanding of how much is at risk? With management's skills and experience? With the business's cash flow, debt position, balance sheet strength – and so on? Again, having an integrated view of risk helps: the CFO should know how much *other* risk the company is exposed to before taking any new risk.

As custodians of shareholders' funds, the CFO and other managers perform broad due diligence. They must ensure that:

- adequate capital is allocated to primary risk areas – that is, risks the company is in business to take

- greater risks bring greater returns – in the ultimate test of risk management, taking a risk should bring future cash flows that exceed the company's cost of capital by a particular benchmark

- the most economic way to manage each risk is considered – for example, the treasurer may choose to deal with foreign currency exposure without using hedging instruments, having weighed associated administrative and other costs against potential rewards.

Bad news sells newspapers. And famous corporate disaster stories could fill this chapter. But gains made through *successful* risk management offer more constructive lessons. The problem is that, in most companies, risk management is a silent partner. Everyone blindly assumes that risk management processes are producing a stability basic to the company's survival and prosperity. So, often, it's hard to identify exactly where effective risk management has produced proper shareholder returns. One exception is financial services.

The financial services industry shows how positive risk management can create and protect shareholder value. Billions of dollars turn over every day in the foreign exchange market, but less than 5% relate to corporations trading goods and services between countries. All other transactions stem from banks and financial institutions trading between themselves in anticipation of making money: they turn foreign exchange hedging instruments into an asset for gain. For every bank that errs by failing to manage the volatility of these instruments, *many more* are making substantial, sustained gains for shareholders.

Managing business risk to produce a return for everyone's benefit takes the discipline of an integrated approach. Consider how one company pulled together its program.

CASE STUDY: Disciplined Risk-taking

A multinational engineering components corporation recently reviewed its risk management philosophy – in particular, its risk-taking stance. This dictated that it put added capital at risk, consistent with its balance sheet strength, operating position and investors' expectations. The corporation opted to end function-by-function risk management activities and, instead, co-ordinate efforts to produce a better overall outcome, in line with its philosophy.

To start, the CEO and CFO sponsored development of a senior level, cross-functional group of risk management practitioners to consider risk in its broadest context. The group brought together perspectives and knowledge of risk in a range of disciplines:

- *treasury (liquidity, foreign exchange, interest rate and credit exposures)*

- *HR (risks related to succession planning, training and development, hiring and firing, and employment practices liability)*

- *sales and marketing (brand name and customer interface risks)*

- *health, safety and environment (plant safety, environmental protection)*

- *production and operations (day-to-day business continuity risks)*

- *group legal (contracts, compliance, legal liability issues)*

- *strategic planning and development (strategic risks, investments and divestments).*

The group reported upward to the executive committee and board, and downward to each product division. Organizing managers from such diverse disciplines was tricky, but minimal infrastructure was required for the change. Adding only some financial and business skills to the existing skills base, the corporation put together a risk management process that business units readily absorbed and converted into meaningful management information on a regular basis.

The change let the corporation better allocate risk costs internally. Now, local managers focus on both minimizing costs where appropriate and allocating more capital where commensurate with the risks being taken. As the international spread of the business exposes it to many different territories and cultures, sustaining such a disciplined effort is particularly important – as is communicating progress to the investment community.

Who has a broad perspective on business risk across the whole corporation? Someone must, and the CFO is ideally situated to be that person. CFOs fulfill responsibilities for tax and treasury, for corporate insurance, and for evaluating capital investment decisions. So they're exposed to techniques for quantifying risks and modeling the effects of risk management actions.

But risk management cannot be the sole domain of one individual or function. Everyone owns it: executives, specialist risk management practitioners and, at their own levels, all managers and employees. As the CFO in the case study showed, establishing, consulting and acting as sponsor for a *risk management forum* is a key step in developing an integrated approach.

MOVING TO INTEGRATED RISK MANAGEMENT

Business risk management mixes a little science with a great deal of philosophy. Formal techniques are becoming established, but this still new discipline remains complex. No single approach suits everyone. Figure 5.6 shows a simple risk management process, with four interlinked phases. It's designed to:

- reinforce the fact that risk management is not only about analytical models and techniques like hedging and insurance, but should fit with corporate strategy and help boost shareholder value

- give a logical sense of order, helping the CFO and risk management forum identify, for each risk, how far current efforts have progressed and what to do next.

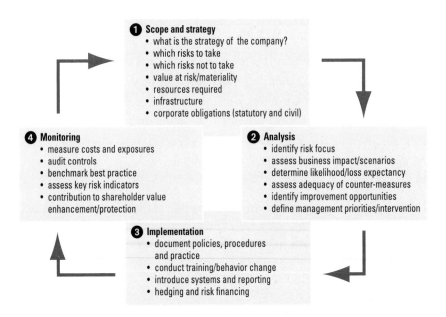

Figure 5.6 **The risk management cycle**

In the s*cope and strategy* phase, the forum gains a high level view of risk management fundamentals. How much and what kind of risk is reasonable for your company to take? What infrastructure and resources must be in place to prevent unreasonable losses?

In the *analysis* phase, explore what changes must be made in light of the agreed risk scope and strategy. Do you fully understand all risks? Are they being managed appropriately? Most companies carefully analyze certain areas, such as credit risk. But other areas – often those related to softer factors, such as loss of reputation – have yet to be considered in depth.

Next, begin *implementation* of improvements. This phase could involve anything from selecting, training and developing staff, to using new or existing financial instruments in new ways. *Monitoring* benefits to the company and shareholders should be an ongoing activity. How do business managers and internal controls contribute to the process? How is the company's overall risk position changing? Should you alter the strategy?

The need to continuously update the risk management process is emphasized in Figure 5.7, which shows a *three-box* analysis of risk. Consider risks relating to (1) existing business, (2) external factors beyond management's immediate control, and (3) planned change programs. Managing these combined types of risk constitutes *dynamic risk management*. For example, suppose that introducing a new product range strains

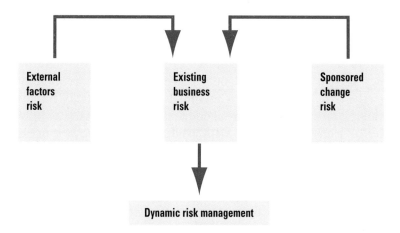

Figure 5.7 **Use the *three-box* analysis to co-ordinate risk and change management**

existing business management. Is the solution to set up a separate, project based management structure for the new business? Or will diverting resources put the existing business at risk? Alternatively, suppose a manufacturing company with most of its capacity in the US builds a new plant in China. What are the political and financial risks to the viability of the business as a whole?

Most key areas of almost all businesses today see internal and external changes come thick and fast. *The inherent nature of the risks involved changes apace.* As risks alter, the CFO must re-assess and adapt the company's risk management approach. In treasury, for example, forward-looking CFOs keep one step ahead of the implications of four major changes.

- **Introduction of the euro** European monetary union may collapse the scale of risk to which multinationals are exposed, simplifying foreign exchange risk management and other market risk practices. This could bring the rationale for many treasuries under scrutiny. Looked at another way – for example, from the perspective of a US parent – a single European currency could create *new* risk issues, exposing companies to different aspects of economic risk and fixed exchange rates.

- **Real Time Gross Settlement (RTGS)** Chances to simplify treasury operations and structure will come when international commercial banks introduce a system of RTGS. If RTGS becomes the standard for intra-day clearing as planned, it will prompt treasuries to improve their liquidity management practices.

- **Automation of treasury operations** Treasury functions' future efficiency and performance will hinge on their using new technology to best effect. With the need to establish separate systems frameworks long gone, next on the agenda are opportunities to fully integrate treasury operations with underlying business process systems.

- **Outsourcing opportunities** Taking advantage of control standards provided by advanced banking systems, many companies now outsource low value added treasury processing activities. On the other hand, treasury can play an important role in co-ordinating and managing risks associated with another new development – shared service centers (Chapter 7).

In a changing environment, risk analysis, improvement and monitoring, linked to review of risk strategy, must be a dynamic, real-time effort – not a conventional annual or semi-annual event. Constantly managing the information derived is a steep new challenge for the CFO of one business undergoing transformation.

CASE STUDY: Transforming the Business, Tracking the Risks

Broken up into five core businesses following privatization and increasing deregulation, a major integrated utility saw its industrial and domestic markets open to competition. Big steps were taken to remain profitable. The transmission business lowered headcount by 40% and cut management layers from 12 to five. At the same time, opening its network to a completely new group of sizeable industrial customers brought all the attendant system and service requirements. Few businesses face a more wrenching transformation: from a relatively bureaucratic monopoly to a responsive, commercial enterprise.

The new, volatile external influences of the regulator and the new demands of industrial customers made business more complex. Contending with both, the board of directors appointed to run the business launched a two-year change management program. Introduce new rules for using the network, reorganize district office and depot facilities, develop new computer systems... the ambitious list of some 400 change projects seemed endless. And topping it was a massive culture change program.

The regulator threatened severe penalties if the company failed to either separate from the parent within two years or meet its obligations to new customers. The whole business would be at risk. Management also had to meet shareholders' demands to see major cost cuts and improved capital productivity.

The board's priorities shifted daily. But the CFO wanted to be in a position to know where the business stood as the change program unfolded. He needed to separate the company's life-threatening risks from those which, though important, were less critical to short-term survival. In such a fast-moving environment, traditional program management disciplines seemed too cumbersome and inflexible. Some projects, such as those dealing with workforce cuts, ran ahead of plan. Others relating to regulatory requirements were in danger of falling behind.

Rather than react, project by project, the CFO took the bull by the horns. He zeroed in on the big issues: defining the boundaries of risk from regulatory, competitive and physical perspectives. What could be the worst thing to happen? How could he manage the regulator's expectations? What contingency plans were needed? The ensuing risk analysis concentrated on material risk. The speed of change and complexity of risk management issues meant using a number of methodologies – including project risk management techniques, business process analysis and scenario modeling of external factors. Analysis done, management ranked the risks.

Critical risks were monitored fortnightly as part of risk mitigation efforts. A key element of this was having independent risk specialists assess the adequacy of management's planned action. The risk analysis was updated constantly: new exposures emerged as critical at each monitoring point and exposures already addressed became less critical.

As the deadline approached for implementing major changes in the sector, management could assess the likelihood of success and the effect of now relatively fewer critical issues – painting the picture with fact and rigorous analysis, rather than intuition.

To understand risk dynamics in fast-moving situations like this, CFOs must understand the change initiatives themselves. Developing *change management* programs, successful companies consider integrating a range of key dimensions, including processes, people, technology, infrastructure, products and markets. And they prioritize change management initiatives to meet corporate objectives in a timely fashion. Developing *risk management* programs, CFOs consider risks in each of the key dimensions, their interdependence and relation to corporate objectives – good tests of a robust risk management approach in a changing environment.

Quantifying Risks

All these techniques and principles point to the need for some degree of quantified analysis of what a risk is worth to the company. Intuition may be management's prerogative but good judgement should be supported by good models. Equally, risk quantification models are *only* models, based on a range of assumptions. Management's experience must complement the technical exercise of quantifying risk.

At the Singapore headquarters of a multinational diversifying into highly competitive markets, the CFO says he 'spends a lot of time educating operating managers from the president down' about how to quantify risk in investment decisions. He comments: 'At first, operating managers resisted because they didn't understand why they had to ask all these additional questions and talk to all these additional people to quantify what they believed they could evaluate using gut feeling. But I argued that their opinions are biased because they're hungry for business. Our risk evaluation is now much better'.

> The chief financial officer should provide Value at Risk measures along with other key business performance indicators

It's relatively easy to produce quantified analyses of many business risks, such as those attached to volatility of foreign exchange, commodity and interest rates. Value at risk (VaR) – usually applied to financial and commodity management practices – is a statistical measure of the maximum expected loss under normal market conditions, over a defined period, within a defined level of probability. A direct measure of potential loss that extends across all types of financial instruments, it provides a common denominator for quantifying different risks.

VaR is based on actual market information, which can be radically different from perceived notions of risk. Some best practice companies develop their own data. Most use widely accepted databases such as JP Morgan's RiskMetrics™. The CFO should provide VaR measures along with other key business performance indicators, such as growth in earnings and cash flow.

VaR can *and should* be applied to all enterprise cash flows subject to financial market risks – not just to financial instruments. For example, many companies originally formulated foreign exchange hedging positions when their international business activity was relatively small and it was appropriate to view currency risk exclusively in terms of their home currency. But too often, companies remain fixated on single currency risks without considering their global exposures, increased revenues and risk appetites.

In such circumstances, one consumer products company with operations in over 100 countries used VaR in setting a currency hedging policy. In evaluating its complete portfolio of operating cash flow currency exposures, the company uses VaR techniques to calculate potential currency losses in normal market conditions. Then it performs stress tests for events such as the Mexican devaluation. The company's exposure portfolio is highly diversified, so the VaR of the portfolio is reduced by the compensating effects of the various currencies. In fact, the company's analysis shows that hedging just one or two exposures would *increase* risk by reducing diversification. So management hedges currency exposures only for specific, exceptionally large projects.

Quantitative and qualitative risks may have an equal business impact – the CFO needs to understand both

VaR can be used to calculate risk-adjusted returns. For example, some organizations (especially in financial services) adjust financial returns for a particular product line or division by the VaR of the underlying cash flows. This lets management weigh rewards against the risks involved.

Although it's necessary to analyze each type of exposure separately, you can gain competitive advantage by understanding how different risks interrelate, how they aggregate to define a company-wide risk profile, and how management's risk appetite changes as the business grows. Here, VaR is a big help. As a component of risk management analysis, VaR supports business strategy and promotes risk improvement initiatives. It assures managers that the actual value at risk is commensurate with what they expect to put at risk and with what shareholders consider reasonable.

Using Judgement and Experience: The Soft Factors

Managers must rely more strongly on their judgement and experience to gage the potential business impact of certain risks. Much harder to quantify, these risks tend to be associated with human behavior: soft risk factors such as inadequate succession planning, poor choice of market or failure of an advertising campaign. They're unlikely to yield an appropriate database permitting use of statistical assessments, like VaR or Monte Carlo simulation – a technique for determining the probability that particular events will arise over particular time horizons. So you'll need to decide on another measure, for use in so-called *qualitative analysis*.

Figure 5.8 contrasts some of the relatively quantifiable risk factors with softer factors that – even though they may have an equal business impact – tend to be less well understood. CFOs and their peers may have to

RISK FACTORS	
Hard	**Soft**
Foreign exchange rates	Inadequate succession planning
Commodity prices	Culture change
Equity prices	Misleading/fraudulent conduct
Interest rates	Illegal trading
Attritional losses (eg employers' liability)	Corporate reputation and goodwill
Customer complaints	Inadequate training and development
Time cycles for assembly	Poor IT strategy
Changes in consumer behavior	Customer/supplier relationships
Systems failure	Employment practices
Earthquake	Advisory mistakes/omissions

Figure 5.8   **How good is your understanding of risks, across the spectrum?**

carefully consider these and many other qualitative risks in day-to-day running of the business.

One large multinational improved succession planning after a senior management investigation showed that its biggest risk was having a high profile CEO with no apparent internal successor. Interviews with the CEO's immediate subordinates, non-executive directors and representatives of the investment community made it clear that he controlled all crucial stakeholder relationships: with banks, customers and managers in the corporation. Overwhelmingly, institutional analysts indicated that – because he was not immediately replaceable – the loss of the CEO would be catastrophic for the business. Absence of one individual could irreparably damage market capitalization.

As sponsor of the risk management forum, bringing together the full spectrum of business risks, the CFO has two key challenges.

Align risk management techniques   To look at an aggregate risk position for the company – how much risk of all types the various businesses and functions take collectively – the CFO must ensure that comparable models are used to analyze risks. Finance may provide the most appropriate benchmark. For example, VaR modeling could become the centerpiece of the company's overall analysis framework. When particular forms of risk are found not to fit well within the VaR model, including those needing a more qualitative approach, the CFO should work with practitioners to come up with something reasonably close.

Establish a shared language   What people want to talk about varies between groups like treasury ('value at risk'), health and safety ('accident rates per employee'), sales and marketing ('risks to sales volumes') and legal ('judgements' and 'awards'). Since risk management messages are the subject of both external and internal communication, the most appropriate language will be based on common, finance and business vocabulary. Forum members will likely need some training and development. The CFO can act as arbiter and influencer in converting to the new vocabulary, helping to ensure that it's one everybody understands, relates to and uses. Don't let technicians and risk management practitioners fill the heads of business managers with jargon!

Developing a Risk Management Culture

CFO 2000 survey results put cultural risks in perspective: they pose the biggest potential barrier to delivering value from business restructuring initiatives and the second biggest barrier to delivering value from mergers and acquisitions.

Something important for the CFO to consider is the *level of risk awareness among management.* Do key business managers make good decisions about risk? You can give them policies and techniques to help, but when under pressure, what attitudes and instincts do they fall back on? How will the individual manager come to a conclusion about whether, on balance, a particular risk is the right one to take? Evidence from successful companies shows that developing a healthy risk management culture is more about helping managers help themselves than coming up with a rigid set of rules and procedures. Setting clear expectations of risk disciplines within an *empowered* culture, these companies create a more unified decision-making process for consistent risk management.

Think of the various aspects of culture. Our book *The Paradox Principles* defines organizational culture as having six characteristics on two levels:

1) *values* and *beliefs* – the essence, and underpinnings, of culture

2) *climate*, *norms*, *symbols* and *philosophy* – cultural artefacts and manifestations.[3]

The process of defining your risk philosophy, defining the risk management functions and establishing risk controls is merely the *hardwiring*. At best, it influences some of the level two cultural characteristics. What most genuinely influences people's behavior is the organization's deeply seated values and beliefs. The role of senior executives is to set the tone – and encourage the rest of the organization to absorb it.

Risk management is most effective when the corporate culture encourages every individual to play a balanced role. They should be aware of risks and bring significant risk issues to management's attention – and *simultaneously* be entrepreneurial and innovative when risk offers an opportunity for substantial rewards.

Any culture that punishes or ignores 'bad news' inhibits communication that's vital if the company is to anticipate and deal with the unexpected. Senior executives must see that it's necessary to receive news of potential threats and judge, in each case, whether that's a risk they're in business to take.

A good example of empowerment is the decentralized treasury risk management at a multinational diversified conglomerate, headquartered in Europe. With 1400 subsidiaries and operations in manufacturing and construction, global turnover is some $70 billion. The group is heavily decentralized in its management approach – finance functions, including treasury, corporate finance and accounting activities, are set up as separate businesses, supporting each country's management. Thirteen treasury units around the world operate as profit centers and reflect local needs, taking treasury positions based on conditions in their own environment. Country management teams are encouraged to manage their own risks, providing information to form a corporate-wide overview when needed.

> Risk management is most effective when the corporate culture encourages every individual to play a balanced role

The success of this operation springs from letting local management make local decisions and, where necessary, learn from their mistakes. Financial decisions are taken in tandem with business decisions, supporting the group's integrated risk management philosophy. Corporate cash pooling arrangements are in place, available *as an option* to treasury units, who are encouraged to exploit the most competitive banking arrangements available on the market.

How do you know you have a supportive environment for risk

management? When people at all levels in the organization think and behave in characteristic ways.

- **No excuses** They each take active responsibility for managing some risk. Risks are identified – and apologies are unnecessary.

- **No complaining** They accept that sometimes bad things happen. And good things don't.

- **No cover ups** They're truthful and candid. They promptly communicate all issues that need to be addressed. Asking for help is not seen as a weakness.

- **No blind spots** They understand that risks are opportunities. Aware of potential losses, they also look for potential rewards.

So a healthy risk culture encourages rapid, decisive action. It feeds off honest assessments of risk, timely information on materiality, effective communication within and outside the company, and a generally positive approach that treats risk as an asset – to be exploited rather than avoided.

BEST PRACTICE OR BEST BALANCE?

Is it possible to define best practice business risk management? Probably, best practice reflects the most appropriate balance between, on one hand, the underlying exposures that a particular corporation takes and, on the other, its risk control and counter-measures. What, for instance, is best practice in managing risks associated with succession planning? Naturally, the answer varies from case to case, depending on the company's current business cycle, position in its sector, underlying management quality, existing succession planning processes and so on.

A more useful aspiration may be *best balance* in business risk management programs. Rather than aim for a standard set by external third parties, who may not have your company's own best interests in mind, try to examine each set of potential risks, rewards and compromises objectively. One step toward setting performance benchmarks is to decide internally what managers consider an appropriate balance of risk and reward. You might take the views of third-party advisors on which techniques to use and what peer group companies are doing. Of course, you also could conduct an external survey of peer group companies to learn the philosophy and behavior of management in similar businesses or those with similar values, nationally and internationally.

Whatever standards you set, measuring performance is central to sustaining effective risk management policies and strategies. How else do you know whether the risk management approach adds value? Check out the cost saving opportunities that may arise from better allocating capital and resource to risk management. And ask whether *more* capital and resource should go to managing certain risks, relative to the other risks the business is taking at a particular point in its cycle.

Before setting up a performance measurement system for risk management, ask yourself the following questions.

- What are the critical functions and tasks we want to influence – and so must measure?

- Against what benchmark do we want to measure ourselves?

- What are the targets, against the benchmark, we aim to achieve?

- Are systems and data available to monitor performance?

Our international study of corporate treasury control and performance standards illustrates why it's worth benchmarking the performance of risk management processes with external data.[4] The study shows group treasurers assuming a much broader role as financial risk managers, responsible for activities such as tax, pension fund management and insurance, as well as traditional treasury activities. Treasury risk management approaches vary widely: 66% of respondents actively manage underlying business risks (implying that treasuries *add value* by applying their skills to manage risk), 28% take a fully hedged approach (that is, *eliminate* risk), and 1% take on risk unrelated to any underlying business exposure (that is, *speculate*). Across all companies and territories, a major focus is on using derivative products to manage core treasury risks. But only 40% of corporations apply formal control parameters, such as limit controls, to these activities.

> Measuring performance is vital – how else do you know whether the risk management approach is adding value?

What studies like this show, above all, is the importance of *profile*. Far too many boards of directors do not approve treasury policy. And in even more companies executive management takes a haphazard approach to monitoring risk policies and controls. When fund managers in one institution reviewed their controls over derivative trading, they asked the director in charge of derivatives: 'Who authorizes the deals? Who values positions? Who does the deals?'. To each question, the director replied: 'I do'. Recognizing this arrangement as unacceptable, they agreed to introduce periodic external valuation and sign-off of all deals by the deputy managing director. In this and many other risk improvement stories, success hinges on getting the attention of a broader group of senior managers and generating more internal discussion on a fuller range of risks.

One leading manufacturer of aero-engines with an innovative, well developed treasury identified the full spectrum of financial risks. Beyond standard derivatives for forward exchange contracts or interest rate swaps, it used creative solutions – such as hedging for differential inflation on long-term aero-engine contracts sold in foreign currencies with long lead times. *The board was deeply involved in making decisions for international financial hedging and integrating it with the business risk.* Capital was allocated to treasury activity in the same way capital was allocated to normal business projects, providing the basis for comparative investment decisions. Most companies do this subconsciously but in this case it was done deliberately, through a formal investment appraisal and capital management process, led at board level.

> The CFO is in the strongest position to integrate business risk management processes throughout the corporation

As most multinationals adopt enterprise-wide risk management policies for operating companies to follow, they learn that they must spend more time managing a dynamic business risk profile. Developing appropriate risk management policies across the organization is an important step *in the short term*. But business risk management requires *continuous* vigilance and attention from the board and executive management. Of course, being a senior executive means balancing matters of greater urgency and those needing long-term attention. There's no easy solution. But as our research shows, the big test is to examine how a company – particularly the CFO – would handle a crisis if it hit.

Take time out of a busy schedule to ask: 'What happens if all this goes wrong? What would be the effect on our shareholders? What would the banks think?'. As the lightning rod for risk management issues, the CFO has the chance to be the key sponsor of this kind of scenario analysis.

Make time, too, for integrating information flows to support centralized risk policy making and devolved decision-making. When the organization consistently speaks with a common vocabulary on business risk matters, the CFO and risk management forum can make the best possible judgements on behalf of shareholders about risks that may have competing priorities internally. The CFO is then in the best position to receive that information, balance it up, provide a consolidated view and promote the business risk management process throughout the company.

CFO's CHECKLIST

DEVELOP A STRATEGY FOR MANAGING BUSINESS RISK Which risks are you in business to take? Which risks are you not in business to take? Which risks would investors expect you to take? Which would be unanticipated? What is the allocation of resource?

CREATE AN AWARENESS OF MATERIAL RISKS – YOUR VALUE AT RISK Evaluate the potential impact of all risks on the business, in the short, medium and long term.

REMEMBER YOUR RISK PROFILE CHANGES AS THE BUSINESS AND EXTERNAL ENVIRONMENT CHANGES Use the *three-box* approach to consider (1) the dynamic impact of your internal change programs, (2) potential external influences outside your control, as well as (3) ongoing risks of doing existing business.

DEFINE YOUR CORPORATION'S RISK APPETITE Treat risk as an asset. Consider taking more risk (and reward) in areas that fall within your tolerance limits. Where risks exceed your appetite, look for innovative solutions.

CONSIDER SHAREHOLDERS' NEEDS Link risk performance measures to both corporate objectives and shareholder value drivers. Communicate the quality of your risk management: perceptions will influence share price performance and may even reduce the ultimate measure of risk – your cost of capital.

DEVELOP AND IMPLEMENT A RISK MANAGEMENT FRAMEWORK The framework should be used as both a communication tool and a risk improvement tool. It should clearly articulate your risk management policies, what risks you are prepared to take, and your plans for risk improvement. The better you are at risk management, the greater your ability to make risk an opportunity. The weaker you are at risk management, the greater your preoccupation with controlling and avoiding risk.

USE A RISK MANAGEMENT FORUM TO BRING TOGETHER EXECUTIVES WITH KEY RISK RESPONSIBILITIES Remember the importance of developing a common risk language. Communicate decision-making parameters to management and provide training.

CREATE A CULTURE THAT EMPOWERS EVERYONE TO MANAGE BUSINESS RISK At the same time, ensure that you have a sponsor at board level, who has overall responsibility for integrating and co-ordinating your risk management program. Typically, this is the CFO.

BENCHMARK YOUR TREASURY AND OTHER RISK MANAGEMENT PRACTICES Performance in this fast-developing field can vary wildly from company to company. This area is not well researched and there is as much to learn from the success stories as from the better publicized disasters. Monitor what you're doing. Measure what risk management practices and processes contribute to shareholders.

CHAPTER 6
RE-SHAPING THE BUSINESS FROM A VALUE PERSPECTIVE

Phil Brown, until recently the CFO of World Food Industries, is on his way to his first board meeting as executive chairman. His thoughts flash over the business changes he's set in motion. Only three years ago, World Food was suffering a slow, inexorable decline in share performance – despite brand strength in more than 90 countries and being a household name in the US since the 1920s.

Known for breaking down old boundaries, Brown's first moves as CFO had seemed bold and, to some, foolhardy. In retrospect, they appear brilliant. Today, finance is a worldwide support function. Three shared service centers support operations in three continents. With one center already outsourced, the other two prepare for this fundamental change. And the finance function has become the Trojan horse for such restructuring. Finance's formula is now being applied to strategic marketing and manufacturing decisions – ending country based management that had sub-optimized global brand performance. As World Food recaptures market share, it sees a corporate culture beginning to emerge that transcends geographic frontiers.

The sole item on today's board meeting agenda: Operation Streamline. The goal is to merge Asia Pacific marketing operations, and outsource the

> *highly fragmented primary food manufacturing operations to one site in Manila, using a third-party provider eager to sign a ten-year contract as a strategic alliance partner. High risk moves like these could shorten Brown's term as chairman... but the business case promises unprecedented returns for World Food's shareholders.*

The organizational structures of many global corporations remain an accident of history and slow to react to new competitive pressures. This chapter invites you to re-examine your business design. It argues that knowing *how* and *where* value is created or destroyed enables the CFO and management team to make the right structural decisions. How else can you see what to keep in the core, what to outsource, what gaps must be filled, and where value win–wins might lie for strategic partners? Managing value performance within networks of suppliers, business partners, intermediaries and customers becomes the *glue* that holds the new, more virtual organization together.

Your two-fold challenge is to *streamline the organization's core* to activities that form the engine-room of value creation and *expand the organization's reach*, through others, to better serve customers worldwide. Describing how multinationals cut complexity from operations to strengthen their competitive position, this chapter shows how you can redesign and align the finance function with changes in the organization – or, better, put finance in the vanguard of structural changes to benefit the business as a whole.

LINKING ORGANIZATION DESIGN TO SHAREHOLDER VALUE

Corporate structures are changing shape. The traditional model in which corporations maintain clearly delineated relationships with suppliers, contractors and customers is breaking down. And as distinctions between entities blur, so it becomes more important to manage skillfully the interfaces between them.

Today's organizations must hone their own competitive machines *and* co-operate across complex networks that add value for end customers. Even fierce rivals are now compelled to work together in key areas of their business, while competing in others for a share of the total value created. Witness the computer industry's collaboration on *open* architectures.

Powerful market forces drive companies to organize themselves – and the way they do business – in new, less rigid ways.

Globalization Competitive advantage often comes from cutting time to market or production cost. Companies are partnering with other organizations to improve their coverage of international markets and to take advantage of lower labor and delivery costs in certain countries.

Innovation As advances in technology cause the *death of distance*, organizations interact globally. And as the hyper-pace of development demands that companies bring new technologies to market fast, so developers use others to manufacture and distribute product.

> To make the right structural decisions, you need to know how and where shareholder value is created or destroyed

This lets them hit the market while it's still hot: they gain the agility they need to make money *and* stay focused on their core skill of product development.

Speed Businesses now run at warp speeds, expecting immediate responses – anywhere, anytime. Finding business allies who offer quick access to capabilities it would take years to develop yourself is an overwhelming force for creating virtual organization structures.

Personalization Customers get what they want or go elsewhere – a fact that persuades more and more companies to work together on integrated solutions. Many of today's PCs, for example, include components put together to the specification of the individual consumer – and often, the component manufacturers are better known than the integrator.

Micro-competition Markets are opening to small, flexible, innovative entrants. To survive, these companies cannot work alone – they need a network, often including larger players who have the muscle to help them meet demand for their services. Again, IT shows the way, with creative powerhouses working alongside industry giants. *In the market for ideas, everyone is equal.*

Costs To remain competitive, companies constantly explore ways to optimize efficiency of functions such as finance, IT and facilities. They use international shared service centers, outsourcing and other strategies to cut costs to levels that, until recently, they could only dream of.

Under strain from these forces, corporate structures – built up over time in response to customers' needs and the organization's growing capability to deliver – are being radically reassessed. How do multinationals re-design at macro-process level – so called *Big-R Re-engineering* – to enhance shareholder value? The answer lies in learning the value created or destroyed by individual processes and capabilities (Chapter 2). You must analyze and confront the true drivers of value – then, based on this understanding, revamp your organization design.

- *Where should the organization enhance its capability?* Successful companies compete by creating value through inherent competencies – in other words, by having access to knowledge and skills that competitors lack and customers value highly. Analyzing these areas points to the organization's core capabilities.

- *Where should the organization seek cost advantage?* In areas where competitors hold similar capabilities or where others can supply greater capabilities, the only real source of competitive advantage – no matter how fundamental the area – is cost. Analyzing these areas points to where rationalization, shared services or outsourcing can create competitive value.

- *Where should the organization expand its scope?* The need for rapid global growth to keep pace with developing market opportunities robs many companies of the time to build new capabilities from scratch. Analyzing these areas points to options for forming strategic alliances.

These are the issues that will dominate the change programs of the future. In the face of ever more complex and far-reaching market forces, CFOs will turn their attention to streamlining business processes to maximize their organizations' capabilities to create shareholder value. And, more and more, they'll look to changes across multiple organizations – re-shaping the value creation of entire global networks, if not whole industries.

STREAMLINING: PEELING TO THE CORE OF VALUE CREATION

To clearly see – and yield most from – the company's vital value creating activities, CFOs must answer basic questions.

- Who are your company's customers?

- Who are your suppliers for the future – and how can you establish strategic vendor relationships?

- How can you drive out complexity and cost from core processes?

- What non-core processes should you outsource – and how?

Rediscover Your Customers

Essentially there are two ways to add value to a business: reduce the amount of cash flowing out or increase the amount coming in. Cut costs or boost revenues. The value you can add by cost reduction is mathematically limited to 100% of current costs. In practice, savings rarely top 40%. But revenues, in theory, can grow almost without limit. Customers – the source of revenue – get harder to find as markets mature around the world. So the goal becomes maximizing profitability from *existing* customers by gaining a bigger share of their spend.

Many companies have access to a wealth of customer information: customer numbers can run into millions with wide geographic coverage. And as one CFO says: 'It's a sin to have information but not use it'. With new technologies like data warehousing making it possible to put integrated information at the fingertips of managers across the enterprise (Chapter 8), the challenge has shifted from gathering facts to *making them work for the business.*

Tesco, a major UK supermarket chain, introduced its Clubcard for customers. Benefits to card holders – any customer who wants to join – include rewards in the form of coupons, based on how much they spend. The scheme, on the face of it aimed purely at customer loyalty, was initially derided by some competitors. But the real advantages lie in using the customer database that the Clubcard supports: for the first time, the retailer can target consumers' individual needs over the longer term, in a mass market. For example, regular buyers of, say, pet food can be identified and offered tailored incentives.

A thorough understanding of the nature of the customer base should be the crucial, first building block in a company's organization design. For example, a worldwide brewing company recognizes two customer types: on-trade (bars, pubs, clubs) and off-trade (supermarkets and other retail intermediaries). Traditionally, drinks manufacturers oriented customer management toward the on-trade. But recently, off-trade – with markedly different consumer profiles – has grown in relative importance. The brewing company caters for each market through variations in product packaging. And it has separately restructured and re-engineered customer service processes around off-trade needs, both in front-office sales operations and, unusually, way upstream in back office and production. For the brewer, this approach to channel marketing is one way to focus an otherwise complex and disparate customer base.

Move from Purchasing to Partnership

Typically, purchases account for between 50% and 60% of a corporation's expenditure. CFOs who release strategic purchasing power to achieve full value procurement can gain big rewards. In many corporations, the average purchase transaction involves $500 or less in goods and services but costs as much as $100 to process!

In world-class procurement, purchasing decisions are based on criteria directly linked to the corporation's long-term strategic goals. Such decisions can be made only when the right information, in the right places, is assembled in the right way.

One corporation had 86,000 supplier records. Analysis showed that it actually dealt with only 20,000 suppliers. But even these created huge amounts of bureaucracy and cost. By searching supplier databases, the corporation discovered that different parts of the business were using large numbers of suppliers for common purchases. Causing unnecessary complexity, this also added work downstream in accounts payable – clogging up processing and making it difficult to complete first-time document matches.

Exploding populations of suppliers afflict many industries. Using simple, computer based analytical techniques, companies have been able to cut supplier numbers by up to 80% – especially those with fragmented, division based structures and relatively unsophisticated vendor management. The corporation in the example rationalized its list of 20,000 suppliers after installing Procurement Analysis Workbench™ – a decision support system exploiting data warehousing technology.[1] Using it to take large aggregates of data from disparate sources, including accounts payable, purchasing and inventory, the corporation built a truly relational procurement database covering three dimensions:

- *suppliers* – who they are, who owns them, what their corporate affiliations are, where they're located, how much is spent with each

- *buyers* – which business units or divisions are buyers, which countries they're in, how much each buying unit spends

- *materials and services* – what's being purchased, which supply markets are involved, how much is spent on each commodity type.

Using information from the database to reduce supplier numbers, the corporation at the same time shrank the volume of work – and unit costs dropped dramatically. The information also helped managers to identify and develop their most important buying relationships (Figure 6.1). Consequent total value added was significant. The corporation could attach less importance to purchase price alone, pay more attention to the needs of product designers and operations planners, and fill critical gaps in manufacturing technologies and plant capacity.

By establishing strategic partnerships with suppliers, leading

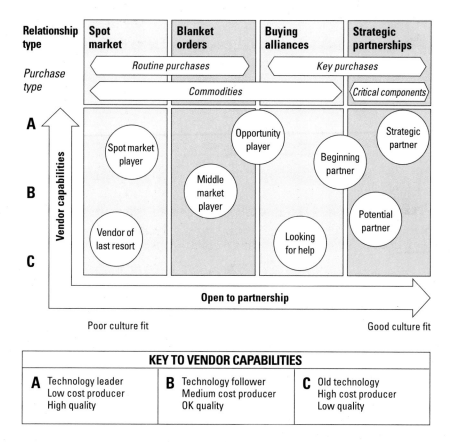

Figure 6.1 **Establishing strategic vendor relationships**

corporations like this are building increasingly sophisticated operational networks, linking internal and external sources of competitive advantage.

Cut Complexity and Cost from Core Processes

Combating complexity is a major challenge in managing high performance companies to achieve superior results. As businesses become more successful, as change accelerates unrelentingly, things grow more complicated day by day. For management confronted with too many choices, too little time, the tendency is to burden processes with bureaucracy – workarounds, special cases, temporary fixes. How do you recognize when the business is getting unnecessarily complex? How do you know whether the decisions and actions you take to cope are for the best?

Consider six sources of complexity:

- *customers* – the more you have, the more widely scattered, the more diverse their needs

- *suppliers* – the more you have, the greater the duplication of services, the more complicated the contractual arrangements

- *geographic spread* – the more dispersed your markets and operational locations, the more intricate the legal structures, the more extensive the supporting infrastructure, the more complex the fiscal arrangements

- *products and services* – the greater the variety, the faster the pace of technological change, the longer the supply chain, the higher the inventory

- *management organization* – the more layers, the bigger the volumes of complex information, the less flexibility

- *people* – the more employees, the more time and effort needed to organize and manage them, the more traditionally entrenched the culture.

When the *total quality movement* defined sources of waste in corporations (waiting time, transportation, preparation for work...), its followers identified generic responses aimed at eliminating waste (automate, raise productivity...). What might be the equivalents for a corporate *anti-complexity movement*? At the core of successful companies, a few simple ideas and capabilities are at work – it's by focusing on these that they know what business they're really in.

Five generic responses to complexity:

- **choose** – identify the few things you do well and concentrate on them

- **combine** – put together simple, repeatable steps to create solutions for complex business problems

- **co-ordinate** – use information, procedures and team roles to integrate activities across the enterprise

- **conform** – stick to a stable blueprint to regulate the pace of organizational, cultural and business process change

- **charge** – if complexity is forced on you by others, charge them for it.

Our *CFO 2000* survey reveals a clear agenda for driving out complexity and cost from finance processes: 70% of CFOs report that they're under pressure to cut costs and 68% that they've restructured the finance function in the last three years in response to changes in the business-wide organization.

It seems that CFOs regard technology as the major enabler of change – likely to remain true for most companies for some time to come (Figure 6.2). The survey results indicate that *simplification* and *rationalization* programs may be reaching maturity, as CFOs complete the first wave of reducing numbers of sites, products, customers and suppliers. But these, too, will probably remain hot issues, as decision support techniques improve – for example, expanded use of activity based management (Chapter 4) to identify sources of profitability – and as the organizational trends of streamlining and creation of virtual networks develop. In fact, the survey shows that, in many companies, organization, people and culture issues are already important as levers for change.

Spotlighting organizational change, the survey also asked CFOs about their biggest challenges in delivering value from mergers, acquisitions and business restructuring. Respondents put *tracking results against expectations* near the top of the list. But more important for most CFOs are the difficulties of managing *cultural risks* and achieving *integration* of organizational elements. The move in favor of alliances and partnerships should de-emphasize culture and integration problems by letting organizations join forces in pursuit of value without compelling them to merge.

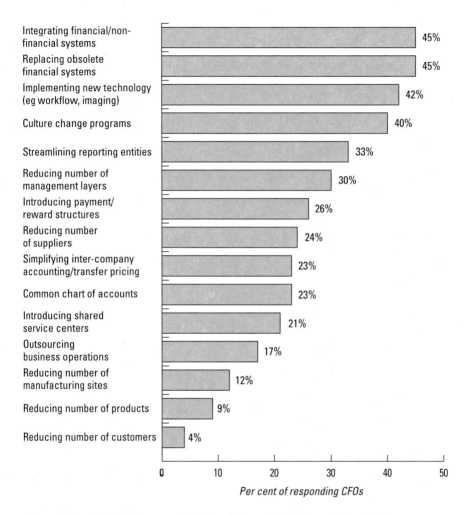

Figure 6.2 ***CFO 2000*** **survey: Which of these initiatives will be highly important to your business over the next three years?**

Outsource for All-round World-class Capability

Few companies can achieve world-class capability in every facet of their business. Through outsourcing, you can focus the business on what it does best while accessing the capabilities of others who are world class in what you regard as non-core. The outsourcing trend is intensifying as companies gain better understanding of their core competencies, pursue shareholder value improvements, and develop a service culture in support functions. In the late 1990s, outsourcing as a world market is growing by around 20% a year.

The scope of outsourcing has evolved from simple activities like security and catering to processes fundamental to mainstream operations, as well as complete back-office departments (Figure 6.3). Few major companies today view IT management, finance operations and supporting administrative processes as among their core competencies for the future.

As activities being outsourced get bigger, more complex and more closely related to the success of the business, managing outsourcing is itself fast becoming a core competence. Clearly, the benefits must be weighed against the risks. Consider the case of a utility that outsourced a substantial chunk of its high volume, relatively low value added,

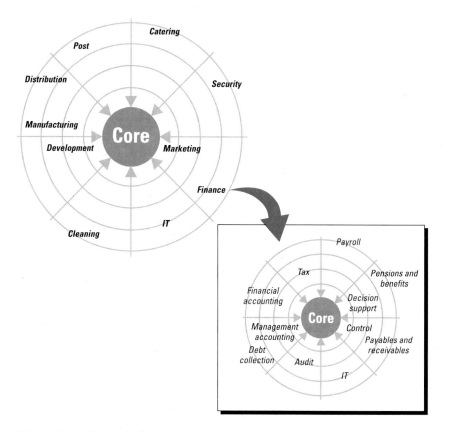

Figure 6.3   **The evolution of outsourcing toward the core**

distribution maintenance activity. It appeared to be taking a big risk: customer service, if not continuity of supply, was the top priority. Finding the potential supplier market immature, the utility worked with strategic partners to stimulate its development.

CASE STUDY: The Onion Strategy

Since privatization and flotation, an integrated water utility serving more than 1.5 million consumers had shown one of the best share price performances in its industry peer group. Management presents the stock market with the clear impression of a strong, well balanced team, blending industry expertise with commercial experience.

The group's strategy concentrates on the core of the business: management of water resources and treatment, customer service, and process and information technology. But the strategy – known by managers as the onion strategy *– has implications for the business as a whole. It involves* peeling away the outer layers: the water distribution maintenance, support and admin*istrative functions. Vital to its success is technology that lets the group properly manage water and sewage treatment and pipeline assets, while reducing risk.*

The key step for management was defining the real core: activities in*dispensable to providing a quality water and sewerage service.* Non-essential *activities could then be moved beyond the core, as* outbusinesses. *These were developed either independently (for example, a pipeline maintenance company was set up) or through strategic joint ventures (for example, for engineering services). The ultimate goal was for outbusinesses to become commercially viable in their own right and – when appropriate – be handed over to an outsource supplier, downsized, or even closed.*

To decide what should be inside the core, and what outside, management relied on an activity analysis of the various business units. More than 130 distinct activities were aggregated into 40 main business areas. Each area's approximate operating costs were calculated. And each was then evaluated as high, medium or low risk against three parameters.

- Service standards   *Consequences of failure were categorized. Catastrophic failure could lead to adverse health implications and media exposure. Minor breaches of regulations could lead to court censure or a tolerable lowering of standards.*

- Technology   *Activities needing little or low technology were classed as low risk. Risks were high where inadequate, or unproved leading-edge, technology is used.*

- Operating cost efficiency   *Finding enough suppliers for the specialist services required in this new outsourcing market was difficult. As the market matures, competition is expected to drive down costs.*

Using a points system, each business area was given a total score for risk. When scores were plotted against costs, just over half the 40 areas were deemed non-essential – that is, high cost, low risk. These areas accounted for 65% of existing operations employees: candidates for the outbusinesses.

Today, the core of the streamlined business contains largely management activities. A critical component is a re-shaped procurement function, equipped with new front-line skills for contracting goods and services from outsourced suppliers at lowest possible cost.

In most corporations, the CFO is well placed to take an objective view of the potential risks and rewards of the overall outsourcing strategy. And to ensure that its economics are managed effectively from the outset. Experience shows that the toughest challenges for buyers of outsourcing services are:

- *identifying what to outsource* – what should be *in* and what should be *out*?

- *choosing the right supplier* – this is a marriage, so the partnership should be long-term, with mutual rewards

- *establishing service levels* – baseline them, measure them, and agree targets for both *tangible* cost reductions and *intangible* quality improvements

- *coping with change* – business conditions, both internal and external, may prompt you to renegotiate, so make contracts flexible and conduct thorough, ongoing risk assessments.

EXPANDING VALUE CREATION BEYOND THE CORE: THE VIRTUAL ORGANIZATION

As divisions between countries and regional markets become less distinct, and sometimes disappear altogether, multinationals adjust to the emergence of a truly global marketplace. Rapid growth of Southeast Asian economies, opening markets such as China and Eastern Europe, development of a single European market – all contribute to the period of unprecedented change that's shaping the competitive world of the 21st century.

The advances in computer and communications technology that helped create this change are also stimulating more efficient, *intercontinental* support systems. Opportunities for common product development, integrated business systems and supply chains, and more competitive pricing are among the benefits for companies responding to the globalization challenge.

Pressed to find new ways of doing business on a world stage, companies are having to expand the scope of their thinking at the same time as reducing the complexity of existing operations. They're having to review and redesign costly, unconnected organizational structures, often too cumbersome to provide platforms for growth. What might the results look like?

The following case study offers one answer.

CASE STUDY: Telefonica Spreads Its Net

In the mid-1980s, Telefonica was like other European telecommunications utilities. As a government controlled entity, the Spanish company enjoyed a monopoly in its domestic market and it is the first to admit that its performance left much to be desired.

But then, Telefonica adopted the challenging vision of becoming the dominant pan-American telecommunications operator: the company took an aggressive international expansion strategy to investors in London in 1985 and in New York two years later.

Since 1991 Telefonica has been able to pour investment funds of more than $3.5 billion into an expansion program in South America, where it's now the largest foreign telecommunications company. Revenues in the region have *grown by 27% to $2.45 billion. The company's aggregate value has increased ahead of managers' forecasts to $6.4 billion, with $2.5 billion of unrealized capital gains.*

How did Telefonica's managers pull off this feat? With the market attaching high risk premiums to investment in South American countries – many reputed to carry chronic debt, hyperinflation and underdeveloped infrastructure – how did they carry conviction with stockholders?

Three features characterize their approach.

- *By constructing a network of alliances and joint ventures with local and foreign telecommunications companies, they offset their own exposure to risk. They use free cash flow analytical techniques to place a value on each alliance partner.*

- *They have established an international subsidiary whose corporate goal is to maximize Telefonica's market value – developing investment opportunities in foreign markets, with a focus on South America, and integrating management of the operating companies. They and their alliance partners use this as a means of gaining easy access to international capital markets.*

- *Telefonica exploits the competitive advantage created by the various partners coming together, by leveraging off their combined core competencies. Each partner takes sole responsibility for delivering specific shared services into the alliance, based on who can achieve the highest standard of performance.*

Director of investor relations Francisco Blanco Bermudez says: 'Throughout the investment appraisal process we constantly examine the strategic risks and factor these into our economic analysis. We analyze our competitors' position pre-deal and post-deal to determine how competitive advantage may change, how the various players will react to each scenario, and the upside and downside to our own game plan. Then, when we're questioned by the investment community, we can place before them solid reasoning behind the big decisions we're making'.

At first, Bermudez admits, it wasn't all plain sailing. 'As we began to win more and more bids, both our competitors and their advisors complained that we'd paid grossly over the odds in these deals. We maintain that this was due to differences in perceived risks and returns in their own valuation models. Because we were "new boys on the block", people listened to what they were saying, temporarily decreasing our credit rating.

'But it didn't take too long before our results began to justify our original statements and our credit rating bounced back. We take this as an expression of confidence in our ability to deliver the objectives of each investment proposition we seek backing for.'

Breakthrough Alliances and Networks

We define the virtual company as one that co-ordinates economic activity to deliver products or services to its customers using resources outside traditional organizational boundaries. In effect, it's a network of companies working together – all willing to give up part of their control to create value that none of them could achieve alone.

What makes a virtual organization thrive?

- **Excellence**   Because each company brings its core competence to the effort, it's possible to form a *best-of-everything* organization – all functions and processes world class.

- **Technology**   Information networks help far-flung enterprises co-operate at all stages in a venture.

- **Opportunism**   In the new organizational model, partnerships are less rule-bound, more geared to timely action. Companies band together to exploit a particular market opportunity – and often as not become separate again once the need evaporates.

- **Trust**   Far more reliant on one another than ever before, participating companies share a sense of *co-destiny*, inspiring high quality collaboration.

Tempted to think these are just buzzwords? A recent survey of FTSE 100 companies shows a rise of 55% in the number of formal equity alliances in the past five years – and of more than 200% in the number of co-operative agreements to share technology, or develop it in partnership, in the past decade. Major corporations now publicly declare their aim to become virtual or nearly so. For example, British Airways' stated intention to focus on *transporting passengers and cargo* means it needs to own only its route structure, brand and yield management system: almost everything else can be leased or bought in.

So why are corporations reducing their own resources and relying instead on quick access to collaborative networks? Gaining scale without mass, they're able to buy the best services, whenever and wherever they need them. Figure 6.4 illustrates the sort of alliances that can be built up outside the core – with specialists in design and logistics, for example – and criteria to evaluate their strategic contribution. As a senior executive at one global corporation says: 'Collaborative networks deliver better products, higher quality, improved time to market and higher returns to the bottom line. They leverage the strengths of each link in the value chain, improve efficiencies, reduce expenses and focus on the inter-operability of processes and supporting systems'.

CFOs who champion virtual organization structures – and the rest of their management teams with them – must be prepared to learn new

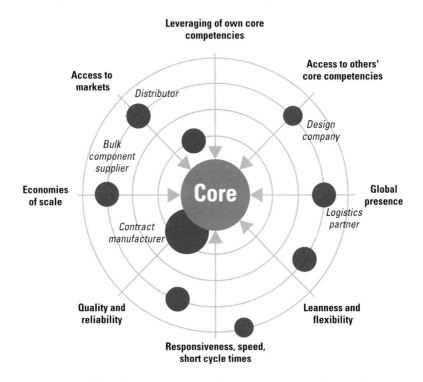

Figure 6.4 **What does the network bring to your virtual organization?**

skills. Without the convenience of having your own resources at hand all the time, you need to develop new types of relationships with partners with compatible goals and values. You need to negotiate win–win arrangements that strike the right balance between freedom and control. Aim to:

- identify, and form a mutual understanding of, actual and target core competencies – use this to trigger joint learning and management development

- build a management infrastructure that supports knowledge sharing, communication and joint working by dispersed teams

- measure and monitor the hard facts of business performance *and the soft facts* that indicate qualitative improvements in services and people's skills and attitudes – too many contracts hinge on technical conformance rather than on developing a robust relationship.

Gluing It All Together: The Business Control Center

Our discussions with CFOs often lead to the same question: is there an optimal model for organizing business operations in the new order of the global marketplace? Perhaps. Envision a single streamlined company, geared for a single, transnational marketplace. Constantly innovative, it's determined to keep a clear focus on customers and avoid obstacles of bureaucracy, hierarchy and overhead. This virtual organization comprises a *business control center (BCC)*, served by a closely knit but flexible network of partners, who produce, distribute and sell the products it develops (Figure 6.5).

The BCC does only what it's really good at:

- introduces competitive new products and services

- develops brands

- exploits technology, know-how, brands and other intellectual property via license fees

- manages the financial strategy, including risk, cash flow and tax.

Outside the BCC, innovative structures serve to streamline specific operations. *Manufacturing* and *distribution* are outsourced to specialist contractors, remunerated on a toll manufacture or cost-plus basis. The

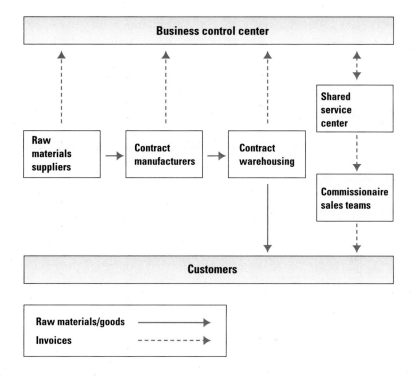

Figure 6.5 **A streamlined business control center structure**

BCC passes output from its product development activities to the contract manufacturers: since the BCC retains title to both raw materials and goods, these contractors (or franchisees) receive a service fee and avoid manufacturing royalty payments. They transfer finished goods to the contract distribution structure. Holding inventories in its own name in contract warehousing, the BCC makes *sales* to customers market-wide through the agency of local commissionaires, remunerated on a commission basis. *Back-office functions* are performed by a shared service center.

This network may include BCC-owned operating units – using intra-group contractual arrangements – with or without external contractors. Whatever the mix, the BCC delivers its products and services with the appearance, from an *economic* standpoint, of a single entity. By concentrating commercial risks, such as inventory, within the BCC, the CFO can affect the incidence of profit in the overall organization and, in turn, its tax burden. For example, since contract sales teams never take title to the goods, revenues are reflected in the results of the BCC: you can reward them with low compensation, commensurate with their low risks and limited operations, leaving the bulk of profit in the BCC's home territory. If this is a relatively low tax jurisdiction, your net overall tax liability could be much less than in a comparable, conventionally structured business.

But potential tax advantages are unlikely to be the prime reason for such restructuring. As corporate centers for operations across regional or global markets emerge in the US, Europe, Asia and elsewhere, it's clear that broad benefits are promised. Improved cash flow, reduced capital expenditure, better customer service and more productive use of assets leading to lower unit costs are among gains made by multinationals implementing BCC structure components – as the following examples show.

Streamlining sales operations using commissionaires With a contract sales operation, the BCC as principal supplier sells to customers throughout the market in the name of local commissionaires (Figure 6.6).

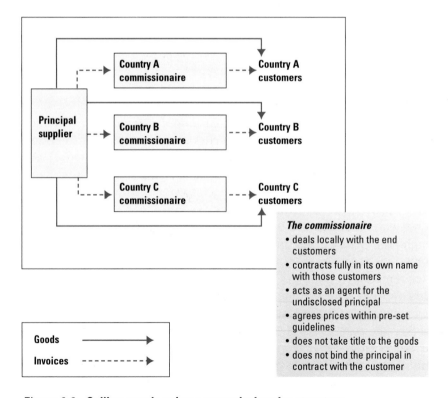

Figure 6.6 **Selling goods using a commissionaire structure**

Initially conceived as a way of creating a single selling company for the single European market, commissionaire structures have more recently been implemented in other regions, including the Pacific Rim and Latin America.

Taking the place in the supply chain traditionally held by buy–sell distributors, commissionaires end the need to determine transfer prices on inter-company product sales – and the chore of documenting and justifying them. An added attraction is that customers usually remain unaware of the existence of the structure, allowing for flexibility in implementation. For example, commissionaire arrangements can be introduced solely for new product lines – and with little, if any, disruption to working relationships between existing local sales teams and customers. In general, the costs of converting buy–sell operations to commissionaire status are mainly those of one-off physical reorganization and changes to financial systems. Normally, they're far outweighed by the benefits, including improved logistics and inventory controls, and reductions in costly country management and back-office infrastructure.

> CFOs are most clearly seen as change leaders when they take on the challenge of re-shaping business structures for optimal value creation

A US based manufacturing group grappled with a complex question: how to structure a $600 million marketing and distribution joint venture with a European manufacturer of complementary products. The answer lay in creating a commissionaire company in the Netherlands, with branches in all of the two groups' European territories. In each territory, each group's existing sales company still made its own sales but through the local commissionaire. Providing one outlet for the two product types, commissionaires boosted sales of both. All that needed dividing up was the small amount of commission: profit on sales continued to go to the relevant sales company. This simple arrangement sidestepped the difficult, time-consuming work of establishing a legal structure for the joint venture. And it let both parties avoid capital gains and other tax liabilities – and utilize brought-forward losses in their sales companies to offset tax liabilities on profits.

Streamlining back-office services using shared economic interest groups Putting *selling* under a spotlight almost invariably sheds light on opportunities for reducing duplicated *back-office* financial and administrative activities. One increasingly popular way is bringing together processes in a shared service center, to capture economies of scale and improve service across business units and geographies (Chapter 7).

The structural housing for shared services could be a group company, taxed on a cost-plus basis. In Europe, a European Economic Interest Grouping (EEIG) can be formed under EU law. EEIGs are fiscally transparent vehicles with legal personality, formed by companies as cost sharing partnerships. Designed to ease cross-border activity through a common structure that's flexible and inexpensive to establish, EEIGs allow members to retain their economic and legal independence. Traditionally set up by unconnected parties, EEIGs are now being applied to intra-group situations too. Depending on the activities it undertakes, there may be no requirement for the EEIG to earn a mark-up on cost for tax purposes: absence of the profit motive could save tax, as well as helping to secure the support of the entities it serves. *Non-EU companies may also be able to participate in an EEIG* through service or association agreements and other techniques.

By linking a shared service center and commissionaire structure – as the company in the next case study discovered – all invoicing can be taken over centrally, as well as major elements of the financial reporting requirements of the various sales teams.

CASE STUDY: Starting a Streamlined Business from Scratch

When a leading US pharmaceuticals group refocused on its core activities and sold off its medical appliances division, the buyer gained a problem. Although the division comprised a manufacturing plant selling products to sales companies in both the US and Europe, only the US sales operations were included in the acquisition. The new parent company could share the European facilities for one year, but then was on its own for personnel, premises and systems.

Viewing it as a greenfield situation, the company evaluated conventional operating structures like buy–sell. But it realized that all it actually needed in Europe was sales people: local faces doing business with local customers. The solution: use an existing US base to act as a principal selling through a newly formed pan-European network of commissionaires. An unexpected bonus was that inventory and receivables retained in the US could be used as collateral against new loans, driving down borrowing costs.

The company also created a shared service center in the UK to handle European back-office functions, including invoicing and accounting. Designing common systems tested its skills and resolve: each country had its own rules for record keeping, covering VAT returns, corporate income tax returns and retaining documents for accounting – not to mention the challenges of working in more than ten languages.

Helped by the relative ease of building its virtual structure rather than having to convert to it, the company was quickly positioned to take advantage of its acquisition. Today, with the new systems well embedded, the commissionaires do what they do best – arrange sales locally – supported by a shared infra-structure. And the parent enjoys the fruits of a streamlined business.

GLOBAL MANAGEMENT AND THE ROLE OF FINANCE

CFOs are most clearly seen as change leaders when they take on the challenge of re-shaping business structures for optimal value creation. Finance professionals tend to be the people who design and manage the systems used for business planning and control: they should be among the first consulted when major structural changes are proposed.

One of the world's largest oil companies, with a turnover of $69.7 billion, operating profits of $6.5 billion and 53,000 employees, BP offers a telling example of how the finance function can play a pivotal role in the move toward a virtual organization. In common with many companies in the early 1990s, BP's financial performance suffered as a result of the recession, compounded by a drop in oil prices. In 1992, the company's share price had fallen to £1.84. But over the next four years, it out-performed the industry and saw the price soar to some £7.00.

How did BP achieve the transformation?

CASE STUDY: BP Re-shapes for the Future

To regain its position as an industry leader, BP had to make significant advances. Big cuts in operating cost, improved returns, reduced debt and a major program to divest non-core operations all contributed to the turnaround. But above all,

BP decided to focus on its core hydrocarbon operations, spanning six continents and organized primarily as three distinct businesses.

- Upstream *(BP Exploration) – finding, developing, and producing oil and gas.*

- Downstream *(BP Oil) – refining and marketing.*

- Chemicals *(BP Chemicals) – manufacturing and marketing petro-chemicals.*

Each business has its own core processes, driven by market forces, and its own supporting infrastructure. BP still sees opportunities for improving performance within each business. But it believes the big leap going forward will be to exploit competitive advantage and generate shareholder value by cutting across existing organizational barriers and across national boundaries.

BP's philosophy is to react quickly and with agility to external market pressures. At relatively short notice, the company may wish to scale up operations in certain parts of the world and scale down operations in others. Such flexibility requires a low fixed-cost base and recognition that doing business in different countries and cultures demands different strategies. For example, in mature markets such as Germany, the pressure is to re-shape the existing infrastructure. In immature, high growth markets such as Poland and Venezuela, the infrastructure can be built from scratch with the flexibility of business partnering in a greenfield situation.

Prepared to change its organizational shape to reach this goal, BP is now becoming a federation of high performance units integrated under the BP brand. Factors critical to getting there include continued best-in-class financial performance, highly skilled teams with a focus on core competencies and, above all, radically different streamlined processes.

Implementation is built on a highly flexible organizational approach, coupled with an extensive network of external partnerships. Change on this scale calls for unprecedented management skills and agility.

Structural Vision

The original BP organization was built like a pyramid: a strategic apex and an operating core, linked through a middle management buttressed by manage-

ment support and technical infrastructure services. Undergoing major change during the early 1990s, BP developed a flatter structure that let decision-making take place further down the organization, but remained very much functionally based. More recently, the company announced that it's to be run as a federation of smaller, flexible business units, based on asset grouping and co-ordinated through a streamlined corporate center.

Performance out in the businesses is now more transparent: new business unit managers will report directly to the group executive committee, in-centivized in a contract to perform to profit, return and cash flow criteria. One data flow from these business units to the center will permit reconstitution into statutory accounts for legal purposes.

In the next stage, the organization will be trimmed to an hourglass shape: a more tightly defined strategic apex and operating core, with a much slimmer middle-management connection (Figure 6.7). Management support and technical infrastructure will be detached into free-standing virtual entities, some set up as separate companies and shared with other oil majors, others possibly turned over to external outsourcers.

BP's vision retains critical processes as the sole preserve of the company (for example, managing external relations, business partners and resource integration), while other processes are shared within the energy industry or delivered in partnership with key suppliers (for example, transport, procurement and finance). The strategic processes in the structural apex (for example, balancing geopolitical risk and assessing market demand) act to integrate the

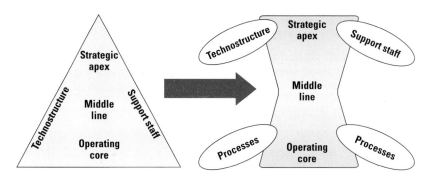

Figure 6.7 **BP's structural vision**

one BP brand. The operational processes in the core are being decentralized – and managed and measured according to value added criteria. The biggest changes will be in middle management (streamlined for control and co-ordination only) and management support infrastructure (project focused, knowledge based and concentrated through shared services).

Barriers to Change

Top management at BP believes that overcoming barriers means having the will to start and the willingness to take hard decisions. Without question, overcoming the huge barriers ahead for BP will depend on strong leadership with a focus on clear goals. High on BP's agenda since the early 1990s – and likely to remain there for some time – is cultural change: managing behavioral issues and attitudes across existing power structures, addressing individuals' fear of change, and overcoming nationalistic views.

Managing the journey through the complexity and diversity of the existing organization requires a single-minded approach from a dedicated project team drawn from management at various levels in all three major businesses around the world. Despite BP's strong track record in managing projects to time, scope and budget, the senior managers involved remain preoccupied with overcoming cultural resistance flowing from not invented here attitudes. This project team based structure keeps senior players in touch with the sharp end of the business.

Making the Results Stick

BP sees implementation as a journey over more than five years. Delivery comprises several shorter steps. Having clarified the strategic vision, processes need to be simplified and standardized to drive out unnecessary diversity. In parallel, behaviors must be re-shaped around new groups, entities, services and external partnership arrangements. All this change has to be reinforced with a new organization infrastructure, sometimes based on shared services and arm's length supplier contracts. A new information architecture is to be built – leaner and meaner, focused on measures that really do tell the CEO if the strategy is working and provide early warnings of the risks of failure.

Close partnering with all stakeholders is essential. New partnering skills are being developed in areas beyond current boundaries – with suppliers, retailers, competitors and energy generators. For example, BP's strategic joint venture with Mobil for downstream oil in Europe should lead to major benefits for shareholders of both companies.

The organization will flex according to market requirements but be held together by:

- corporate parenting – *from critical senior appointments to capital allocations and incentives based on shareholder value improvement*

- sharing – *disseminating best practice and knowledge, and internal trading based on common interests*

- common values – *customer focus, coupled with a bias to collaborate and consistent treatment of external partners.*

The Role of Corporate Finance

Finance plays a pivotal role in the implementation. BP is now acknowledged as a partner in a world-class accounting service based on shared accounting and delivery, and outsourcing through external service providers. Much of the costly transaction processing that clutters today's operation is being obliterated (Figure 6.8). Increasingly, transaction processing will be built on trust – assuming things are right first time. Systems should handle routine transactions without manual intervention, which should minimize checking. BP and its new accounting service providers should work together to drive down costs: the balance of staff effort should shift radically from transaction processing and control to decision support.

Integration of the accounting and control process takes place, country by country, in three steps – consolidate, simplify, standardize. *A three-year effort, it will lead to greater efficiency through upscaling. It represents a quick win in the total change journey: achieving the overall BP vision, based on a fundamental, ongoing review of the relative value of critical business processes.*

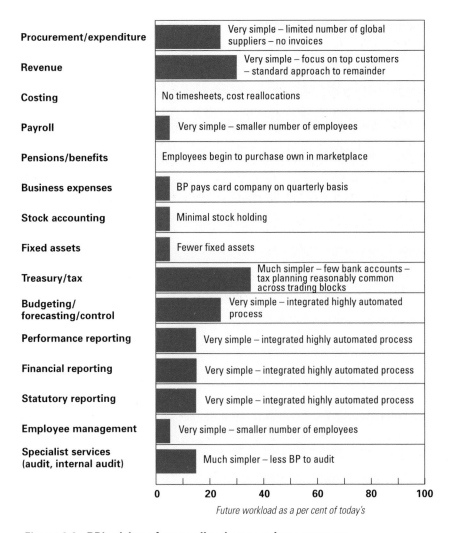

Procurement/expenditure — Very simple – limited number of global suppliers – no invoices

Revenue — Very simple – focus on top customers – standard approach to remainder

Costing — No timesheets, cost reallocations

Payroll — Very simple – smaller number of employees

Pensions/benefits — Employees begin to purchase own in marketplace

Business expenses — BP pays card company on quarterly basis

Stock accounting — Minimal stock holding

Fixed assets — Fewer fixed assets

Treasury/tax — Much simpler – few bank accounts – tax planning reasonably common across trading blocks

Budgeting/forecasting/control — Very simple – integrated highly automated process

Performance reporting — Very simple – integrated highly automated process

Financial reporting — Very simple – integrated highly automated process

Statutory reporting — Very simple – integrated highly automated process

Employee management — Very simple – smaller number of employees

Specialist services (audit, internal audit) — Much simpler – less BP to audit

0 20 40 60 80 100

Future workload as a per cent of today's

Figure 6.8 **BP's vision of streamlined accounting processes**

Clearly, with their pervasive power, the CFO and finance function can be key enablers of business restructuring. And the BP case study shows how the finance organization itself can serve as a role model for introducing world-class practices in the rest of the business. Finance – *the Trojan horse for change* – can lead the charge, knock down old organizational barriers, introduce fundamental new ways of doing business, and pave the way for enterprise-wide improvements with new systems.

To fulfill their role, CFOs must stay one step ahead of opportunities for re-shaping business processes and structures – and their implications for technology, people and culture. For example, to ensure that you help *reduce* complexity through implementing change (rather than inadvertently add to it), be prepared to redesign and *replace* old measurement systems (rather than try to superimpose the new on the old). An outsourcing environment needs less internal information on detailed operating performance, since the suppliers provide this: what's required instead is a new set of metrics critical for the financial success of contract performance. CFOs, in their role as risk managers, should also proactively identify and use new risk measures to manage the operational consequences of shared or outsourced activities.

CFO's CHECKLIST

AIM FOR ALL-ROUND WORLD-CLASS CAPABILITY Shrink your business to the size of its core *and* expand to cover the globe. Being world class in everything may be impossible on your own: future competitive success depends on staying highly focused on what you do best and teaming with networks of similarly focused partners.

RETHINK YOUR BUSINESS DESIGN Where value is being created, look for opportunities to streamline processes by cutting out unnecessary complexity and cost. Where value is being destroyed, look for opportunities for sharing, outsourcing, joint venture or disposal.

DISCOVER WHICH OF YOUR RELATIONSHIPS REALLY CONTRIBUTE VALUE Find ways of maximizing income from your existing customers by increasing your share of their spend. Map vendor capabilities to partnership potential: establish strategic relationships with your most important suppliers.

CREATE A WORLDWIDE NETWORK OF ALLIANCES Break out of your organizational box: the changed nature of global competition and co-operation calls for a change of mindset. Flexibility, fresh thinking, resourcefulness – bring these to the table when preparing to build and manage a value creating network of organizations.

MANAGE THE FULL REACH OF YOUR ORGANIZATION, NOT JUST THE CORE Consider the costs and benefits of intra-group or external contract manufacturing, distribution and sales operations. Where feasible, set up shared services for back-office functions and seek tax-saving opportunities from economic interest groups. Try envisioning your virtual organization using the *business control center* concept.

TURN YOUR FINANCE FUNCTION INTO A TROJAN HORSE FOR CHANGE Use finance as a role model for the rest of the business. Introduce world-class financial practices across the corporation, breaking down business unit, geographic and hierarchical divisions.

One of the shared services success stories in the US: the finance function at Healthwise Inc. For nearly five years, a dedicated center has performed transaction processing and accounting for operational units nationwide, cutting costs by nearly half. Service level agreements between the center and its internal customers, just updated, reflect enhanced expectations of performance. Now, Healthwise is expanding the center's scope to include its South American operations.

When the US moved to shared services, Healthwise decided against creating an equivalent center for its substantial European business: the required investment seemed to outweigh benefits. In particular, costly, unreliable telecommunications in certain countries ruled out shared processing across borders. Today, CFO for Europe Claire Levitt sees a different picture. Preparing to exploit the latest technology to introduce shared financial services in the region, she knows Healthwise will gain a chance to move ahead of the competition. Indeed, only once they can quickly analyze information from multiple countries will her finance professionals be able to help manage the pan-European customers on whom the future of the business depends.

Levitt is determined to identify and circumvent the myriad barriers

173

to shared services. Central staff must work with diverse languages and cultures, but Healthwise already has recruited highly skilled, multilingual people in several territories. Local tax and legal issues must be confronted – she's begun mapping ways round them. And while the reorganization will take careful project management, it's less of a concern now, considering recent transformations achieved in the corporation. Surveying these complexities, Levitt must convince colleagues it'll be worth the effort. She must craft a compelling business case – the sort of exercise she does well.

Why devote a whole chapter to sharing services? Often cited as a source of major cost savings and service enhancements in financial and other support processes, the shared services concept is already well known. But research shows that *actual* achievements in implementing shared service centers fall short of *perceived* progress. To narrow the gap, CFOs need to know this chapter's answers to key questions. How do shared services differ from other forms of finance streamlining? What lessons can be learned from finance functions getting the most out of implementation? What are the critical success factors?

With guiding principles for delivering shared service center benefits, quantitative and qualitative, the chapter draws on the practical experience of major corporations. It separates the realities from the myths surrounding the difficult – but far from impossible – task of sharing services across businesses and geographies with multiple languages, currencies and cultures. And it explores the challenges for corporations moving toward global shared services, showing how strategies like developing service level agreements can drive continuous performance improvement.

WHY INVEST IN SHARED SERVICES?

As many large multinational corporations introduce shared services, many *more* review closely the possibility of doing so. Their straightforward intention is to streamline non-customer facing business support processes, managing and operating them within one or more centers. Flying in the face of conventional wisdom, a few have begun sharing *front-line*, marketing and other services. For instance, Hewlett-Packard's European Customer Support Center provides multilingual telephone assistance to 19 countries. All shared service centers depend heavily on effective systems and telecommunications. Even in an advanced region like Europe, only recent technology improvements allow corporations *practical, cost-effective* ways of centralizing common activities traditionally performed at several locations. What's prompting them to make the investment?

A shared service center represents a big step toward providing lowest cost services to business units (Figure 7.1). Before making this move, companies often simplify or standardize relevant processes within the units. Itself a form of *internal outsourcing*, shared services may lead to or be superseded by full-blown outsourcing using a third-party provider. Sometimes companies jump more than one step up the escalator and then work backward. For instance, one major multinational plans to move selected finance activities to an outsourced center before looking for ways to simplify and standardize – sharing with the external supplier the risks and rewards of doing so.

Each step brings more benefits. But each step also means wider change in the organization and taller barriers to be overcome.

Simplify – do things better, country by country   This approach involves basic business process re-engineering within each country and subsidiary to eliminate non-value adding activities and develop local solutions to improve performance. Some corporations achieve cost savings around 30% by simplifying.

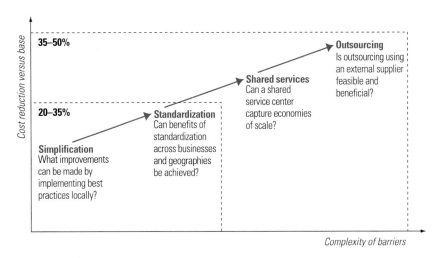

Figure 7.1   **An escalator of change to world-class performance**

Standardize – do things in a similar way in all countries   The next option is for operating units, across national borders, to implement common systems and use consistent charts of account. Best practices demonstrated in any one unit are extended to the others. Beyond further reductions in costs and complexity, the company gains the ability to compare data across companies in different countries.

Share services – bring together resources and processes to achieve economies of scale   Here, processes are moved from the business units to a dedicated center that provides services on a national, regional or even global basis. Going further than the previously established practice of using a single *data* center, this concept brings together the people and facilities involved. Reorganization eliminates many duplicated costs – the center both exploits economies of scale and frees business units to refocus on higher value adding tasks. The CFO of a US based multinational comments: 'We can streamline the process dramatically and remove big chunks of cost by having heavy mechanization. We get higher quality transactions with fewer errors. It's a home run all the way round'.

Outsource – use an external service provider   Certain processes may be best managed by third-party outsourcers who combine minimal cost with maximum service. Now widely used for functions like facilities management and IT, outsourcing is increasingly considered for aspects of non-core business processes. For example, an external supplier provides tax compliance services for BP, along with elements of the group's accounting processes in Europe and South America. In the US, more than three-quarters of *Fortune* 500 companies are undertaking outsourcing initiatives involving business support services.

In any one circumstance, there may be a point at which the costs offset the attractions of moving to a higher step. Shared services may not be suitable for all finance processes in all companies. For example, some CFOs decide to centralize accounts payable activities, but leave order management with the business units to allow for local differences in the way they handle customers. Some use a shared service center for treasury risk management, but leave cash collection decentralized.

Similarly, outsourcing works for only some non-core processes. One Japanese finance director regards his staff as the 'brains' for the CEO and senior management, and says he 'could not conceive of outsourcing their services'. Often, corporations hesitate to run the risks associated with outsourcing: they fear losing control, or getting locked into using a single supplier, particularly in functional areas where, as yet, few suppliers operate.

In deciding whether to outsource processes *internally* or *externally*, consider five issues.

- Does the company philosophy incline you to keep direct control, rather than cede it to an outsider?

- How rapidly do you want to move? Implementation may be achieved in a shorter timeframe using an external supplier, especially if other initiatives compete for internal resources.

- Can your team make the change itself? Honestly appraise your track record in internal re-engineering and restructuring – do you actually deliver benefits as and when expected?

- How do people feel about each alternative and its implications – for example, for their career paths? Could external outsourcing cause industrial relations problems?

- Can your systems be segregated easily to permit external outsourcing?

The logical progression shown in Figure 7.1 scarcely suggests the full power of sharing services. While some CFOs may be surprised at the potential savings (and often, these alone prove enough to justify moving to shared services), the center must do more than drive down costs. What differentiates shared services from merely consolidating functions is the internal *supplier–customer relationship* that develops between the center and the business units it serves. In the most successful corporations, the shared service center handles activities on behalf of the business units, both efficiently and in ways that *better meet their needs*. The center actively manages the supplier–customer relationship: it establishes, and aligns its competencies with, the expectations of internal customers who, in turn, provide continuous performance feedback.

In short, business units hand over activities to the center *in return for* higher levels of service. The center gives operating managers more timely, consistent information, combined across multiple legal entities, for better decision-making. It opens their eyes to a true view of global customer and product profitability – a bracing, sometimes shocking, reality check. With altered perspectives, line managers often develop sharper analytical skills and greater sensitivity to market shifts. And the center's there to back them up – swiftly responding to support changes in the underlying business. Sharing expertise, support and best practice, the center breaks down cultural, divisional and functional borders.

It is these cumulative gains, quantitative and qualitative, that make sharing services an exciting breakthrough. In finance and other service areas, it answers the conundrum of how to cut costs and, at the same time, enhance value to the business. And it can deliver prompt results, as the CFO of one US company demonstrated in a two-year change project.

CASE STUDY: Supporting Business Strategy

In the early 1990s, executives at a major US foods company looked into the future and saw dark clouds on the horizon. Expanding through mergers and acquisitions, bringing new brands into the fold, the company's growth spawned disorganization in the finance function. Multiple processes, a patchwork of systems and a fragmented infrastructure supported largely autonomous business units. Problems in assimilating newly bought entities made pursuing the growth strategy more costly. With razor thin margins in its businesses, particularly the grocery division, extra costs threatened the company's competitive position. Something had to be done.

The executives knew that to continue growing through mergers and acquisitions, the company must reduce back-office costs drastically. It must abandon business as usual and push massive change through the finance function – fundamentally rethinking the processes, structure, culture, systems and facilities of each business unit. Chosen to architect and lead the change, the CFO prepared to do more than simplify and standardize processes. He opted for sharing finance processes across business units, helping the company to:

- *capitalize on recent mergers and acquisitions by marshaling scarce functional and technical skills across the organization*

- *share process and technology-specific best practices over the various businesses.*

The CFO's vision was a company-wide, financial shared service center, designed to achieve economies of scale through high volume transaction processing and to focus on serving customers in the business units. Two years later, the fully operational center generates cost savings that fuel added mergers and acquisitions growth. The CFO and his staff continue to score firsts at the company – including a single, streamlined procurement process, linked to the end-to-end revenue process, and a state-of-the-art, enterprise-wide client/server system. Shared services also engendered a new culture in the finance function, rewarding center staff based on performance measures and incentives in line with the service level agreement with the business units.

Now, managers in the revenue-producing side of the business view shared services staff as true partners who boost their effectiveness. They rely on the center to bring welcome input to decisions on value strategies, for example for product mixes and marketing.

Successfully implementing shared services across the US foods company demanded that the CFO get several things right:

- assemble a compelling case for change and communicate it effectively throughout the organization

- sell the idea that a single process could satisfy 90% of the needs of the various business units

- focus on people issues – selecting and training center staff, building target skills requirements, and designing and encouraging the appropriate culture change

- introduce systems and facilities solutions in a methodical, integrated manner, taking account of needed enabling technologies.

Later parts of this chapter look more closely at such success factors, managed in the case study in a relatively quick approach. But, in general, the shared service center remains an emerging reality. Other companies make progress following different routes that can take some interesting twists and turns.

WHO'S (REALLY) DOING WHAT? AND WHERE?

Multinational corporations restructure in three broadly different ways to accommodate sharing of financial or other services (Figure 7.2).

Set up a single center for all operating units This most ambitious option involves sharing services *globally* across the entire corporation.

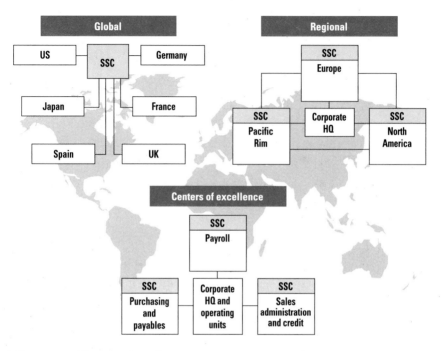

Figure 7.2 **Three options for introducing shared service centers (SSCs) into the corporate structure**

The structure allows greatest scope to exploit economies of scale, and simplify and standardize processes. But processes must be designed to meet the varying requirements of the operating units. The center must contend with global tax and regulatory issues, and needs fully integrated systems. Defining the skill sets of center staff may prove complicated.

Set up a center for each geographic region In a more readily achievable option, individual centers serve only operating units within their own *region*. Each designs processes in line with local requirements, addresses regional tax and regulatory issues, and accommodates cultural nuances and language differences with relative ease.

Set up a center for each process or combination of related processes Performing particular activities on behalf of all operating units, these *centers of excellence* encourage the development of functional specialists. Process design can concentrate on individual functional areas, possibly at the expense of integration. Because of their global reach, the centers' ability to capture economies of scale may be countered at least partially by the impact of tax and regulatory issues. Fully integrated systems may not be mandatory.

No best practice model exists. The choice of structure depends on the corporation's circumstances, its overall business and marketing strategies, and the nature of any other enterprise-wide initiatives. Many adopt a synthesis of the structure options. They might, for example, use regional centers built to a global blueprint, with common processes, systems configurations and other design features. This approach suits one large consumer products company, moving to share financial services in every region as it restructures the business to face global markets. With similar aims, another multinational began separate projects for three regional shared service centers, but quickly recognizing the synergies to be gained, combined them under one global design team with representatives from all territories.

> Recognizing major potential to cut costs and improve performance, multinational corporations are investing heavily in shared services

Taking a *phased* approach, many multinationals standardize processes, procedures and policies within each major business unit, in readiness for moving later to a shared service center. Some begin by setting up a center to serve business units in one country or region, intending to go further once the value of sharing is proved or more preparatory work completed. Then, they extend the scope of sharing to include more processes or geographies in the same or additional centers. For companies with numerous products and lines of business, phasing can be an effective way of dealing with the complexity and politics surrounding a large-scale shared services project.

The CFO of a US company says: 'We did our first centralization of accounting activities ten years ago, and have gradually been centralizing more and more. Our objective, really, is to centralize as much of the core transaction activities as we possibly can, so that finance people who remain in our facilities can focus more on business issues and a lot less on supervising a staff of clerks'.

In Europe, a company creating a financial shared service center for more than 20 countries is managing the task by including subsets of countries in four waves, spread over four years. Last to come in scope will be those countries where the relatively poor infrastructure and local business practices pose special difficulties (in certain areas, most suppliers still request payment in cash!).

181

The prospect of *virtual* shared service centers presents yet more possibilities. Shared processes need not reside in one physical location, some senior executives argue. They could be the responsibility of appropriately skilled people anywhere in the business, all using the same systems and under the same management. Introducing such sharing could cause less upheaval, allowing local staff to remain in place. More difficult would be the practicalities of disconnecting them from their existing operations, to form new, remote connections with their counterparts in other business units.

Some corporations have adopted solutions that approach virtuality. For example, a company based in Southeast Asia had trouble standardizing the finance processes of its diversified businesses. Instead, it set up 'centers' of expertise for treasury, tax, legal and accounting – in the form of specialists who go out and help business units achieve their local functional goals. (Cutting costs is not an issue for this company's finance function, according to the CFO.)

Although multinational corporations invest heavily in shared services – recognizing major potential to cut costs and improve performance – the focus remains on the finance process arena. Pursuing opportunities in other service areas, such as HR, project management, internal audit and R&D, is relatively rare. And even in finance processes, *perceived progress outstrips implemented reality*. Most initiatives are still in their early stages.

We surveyed 11 major corporations today actively pursuing financial shared services initiatives (Figure 7.3). While nine already share services across businesses within a country, only two do so across multiple countries within a region. Five more have begun implementing their regional centers or plan to start shortly. As yet, none of the companies runs live with a shared service center structured on a center of excellence, or a global (or enterprise-wide), basis – though most aim to move to one of these structures in future.

BUILDING THE BUSINESS CASE

Whatever the approach employed, before implementing shared services the CFO must develop a comprehensive business case, setting out the business issues to be addressed, and the costs and benefits of the proposed solution.

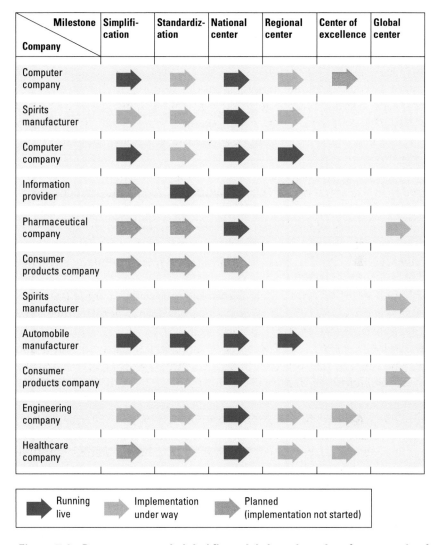

Figure 7.3 **Progress toward global financial shared services for a sample of major corporations**

While some corporations may emphasize benefits of *cost reduction and economies of scale* over those of *performance and information improvement* – particularly where there's been little previous functional re-engineering – any well built business case will feature elements of both. Figure 7.4 summarizes an example, from a major healthcare company

Business issues

■ Financial systems unable to support evolving market requirements

■ Multiple systems/interfaces and complexity add cost

■ Inconsistent data across countries

■ Management information only available with significant manual intervention

■ Inconsistent processes which are not best practice

■ Complex inter-company pricing structure which is expensive to administer and vulnerable to transfer pricing investigation

Shared service center (SSC) business case contents

■ Executive summary

■ Scope

■ Constraints

■ Current situation and business issues

■ Vision for European finance processes

   - Acquire goods and services

   - General accounting

   - Planning, budgeting and forecasting

■ Resource requirements

■ People skill requirements

■ Proposed SSC structure

■ Commissionaire tax structures

■ Systems and technology

■ Location

■ Implementation plan

■ Costs

■ Benefits

Benefits

■ Simplification of European business structure

■ Cost reduction

■ Improved management information

■ Soft benefits excluded from financial justification

	$m pa
■ Tangible benefits	
- Sales and marketing data: gross profit increase	2
- Improved marketing and R&D productivity	1
- Improved productivity in logistics	1
- Other productivity gains	2
	$6m

Financial case

■ Capital costs	$11m
■ Revenue costs	$14m
■ Cumulative NPV	$28m
■ Payback period	3 years
■ Internal rate of return (after tax)	30%
■ Headcount reduction	250 to 115 (including 25 in the SSC)

Figure 7.4 **The case for change in a multinational healthcare company (illustrative data)**

with multiple production and selling entities in Europe. To add benefits in the region, the company proposed to link a financial shared service center to commissionaire structures (Chapter 6) – streamlining selling operations to eliminate complex transfer pricing arrangements and reduce risks of investigation by local tax authorities.

In some situations, introducing shared services may be seen as a *strategic imperative*, essential to survival of the business. For example, one company has been willing to accept a marginal rate of return from shared services: industry pressures forced it to go that route, or quit the business. Another, in contrast, expects shared services to provide a platform for rapid growth in Europe, without setting up substantial local infrastructures (especially in nations like Germany and France, where finance and administration employment costs can be twice those of lower cost nations).

Broad business benefits like these help the case for a shared services project, giving it a greater chance of success. The stronger the case for change, the more likely it is to receive needed management support. In one multinational, the CEO decided on shared services solely to lower headcount in finance – the project now flounders, without a sponsor to keep it moving forward. Anticipated after-tax return on an investment in shared services may vary between about 5% and 30%, depending on the circumstances.

To better understand strategic challenges facing the corporation, the CFO should consider how ready it is to do business on a more global basis.

- How are your *markets and customers* evolving? Can you satisfy their emerging requirements?

- Do your locally developed *processes* stand up to best practice?

- Do your *systems* provide the functionality and data you need to manage the business across national and regional borders?

- Do you need a more consistent approach to developing your *people and culture* in order to support the changing needs of the business?

- Will the local and regional variations in your *products and services* remain cost effective in the face of increasing global competition?

- Are significant business, political or other situations developing inside or outside the organization that you should be using as *catalysts for change*?

- Are you making effective use of your purchasing power with *suppliers*?

- Does your management *structure* help or hinder achievement of business objectives?

Using a diagnostic tool[1], you can rate *first* where the business is now, across these variables, and *second* where it must be in, say, the next five years to sustain competitive success. The bigger the gap, the more radical the solution needed.

Plotting results for its European operations, a US-owned consumer products company could see where and why it needs to change the business to cope with expected demands (Figure 7.5). By 2000, more than 50% of the company's turnover will likely be with retail customers who have the capacity to co-ordinate buys from multiple countries. Country specific processes are a long way from best practice and must be standardized across the region. Current locally based, customer facing systems lack the functionality to support cross-border selling and involve significant manual data analysis to keep track of total sales to major groups. The company needs high quality people across the business to provide consistent customer service – yet today's operating staff remain too locally focused. And the organizational structure, emphasizing local management control with little regional co-ordination, inhibits introducing best practices.

In a series of workshops, executives at the company considered potential initiatives that align with the development needs they'd uncovered. The outcome of their discussions: a business case detailing the benefits of global business process integration over all divisions and geographies. Financial shared service centers in both Europe and North America, with common systems support, will act as key enablers – as well as bringing savings in headcount and logistics.

Beyond spelling out the strategic and operational impact of shared services, a corporation's business case should demonstrate the likely contribution to shareholder value. It's worth pointing out that compared to similar sized investments in market expansion or acquisition activities, a shared services project inherently may pose far less risk in terms of cash flow variability.

Benchmarking can help create a mandate for change within the organization. One CFO describes how, with 'a double-digit margin and growth at double-digit rates', he'd found it hard to motivate finance

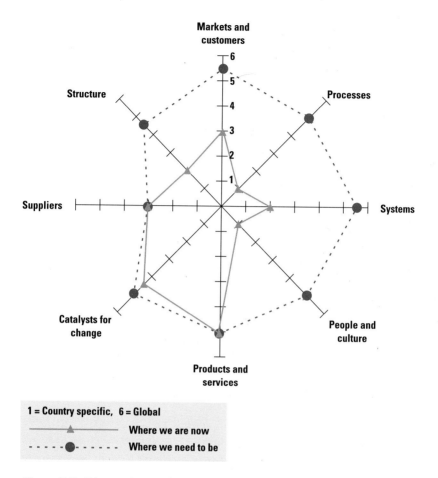

Figure 7.5 **Diagnosing major opportunities for finance function re-engineering**

people to *control* support costs, let alone *cut* them in response to pressure from operating companies. Benchmarking studies let him demonstrate the rationale for moving to shared services.

'When we looked at what other companies were doing, the finance people couldn't argue,' he says. 'In the past, they all wanted to run a full shop. We suggested that running payrolls is essential but not very gratifying. So let somebody else do it. Outsource it within the company and treat it as a service function. We are gradually going around the world with that and have had dramatic results. Finance activities used to cost 2.8% of sales. Now we've cut that in half, which is worth about $250 million a year.'

Building consensus around the need for shared services, benchmarking can also identify best practices useful for setting benefit targets and designing ways to achieve them. For the company in the next case study, reviewing best practices helped create a vision of the shared service center that today runs its procurement process.

CASE STUDY: Shaping up for Best Practice Procurement

In 1995, a manufacturer of paper products in the US and Canada decided to revamp its procurement organization to promote strategic sourcing. Gaining leverage in its supplier relationships would ensure faster delivery and better quality of procured products. The company could shorten product cycle times and offer better quality in its final products.

Ready to sharply improve its competitive position and performance in its various markets, the company reviewed best practices for procurement. It set out a vision including enterprise-wide co-ordinated buying from assessed and certified suppliers, along with centralized invoice and payment processing, and procurement card roll-out and support.

Weighing options for how to adopt best practices, the company concluded that a center performing procurement for all business units would save over $20 million annually. Significantly lowering costs in the personnel and systems areas, it also would eliminate many non-value adding activities.

Now running live, the company's shared service center relies on a newly designed procurement process, along with integrated systems, financial EDI capability, new training and development programs, and self-empowered work teams.

This company and others grapple with the same complications in setting up a shared service center. The cross-border reorganization involved forces companies to think through more than the design of relevant processes. What are the changes implied for the organizational structure, people and culture, technology and facilities? How does central sharing of services affect current solutions to tax and regulatory issues?

For shared services to deliver the full benefits expected – and to avoid potential pitfalls – CFOs must consider each of these *building blocks* (Figure 7.6), on its own and in relation to the others. And *then* they revalidate the business case to guarantee its viability.

Even with a robust business case, a shared services solution might be rejected. Perhaps the business units' processing requirements differ greatly or their varying levels of profitability leave some unable to afford a given level of service. Wholly *qualitative* reasons for rejecting shared services might include lack of support from top management. If and when a proposal to share services warrants approval, the challenge becomes to avoid many barriers that still could bar the way.

FINDING YOUR WAY AROUND THE BARRIERS

Obstacles to introducing shared services are legion. Some barriers have fallen in recent years, thanks to advancing technologies in many parts of the world, and to new and evolving geopolitical structures, such as the EU and North American Free Trade Area. But a host of barriers remain: hard problems, like meeting legal and regulatory requirements in different countries, and softer issues, like people and cultural difficulties.

The good news is that none is insurmountable. Persistent and re-sourceful, many multinational corporations find effective work-around

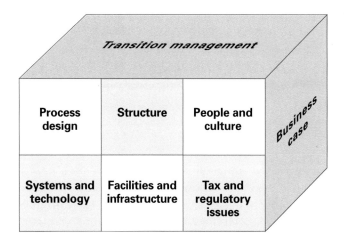

Figure 7.6 **The shared services *building blocks***

strategies, even in traditionally problematic regions like Europe and the Pacific Rim. The tried and tested course is to weigh carefully the costs of overcoming any barriers against the benefits to be derived – and to be sure that implementation plans are flexible enough to allow for the unexpected as the project proceeds.

This measured response implies what CFOs know from hard experience. It takes careful planning to anticipate, prevent or overcome difficulties. And no matter how carefully planned the move to shared services, completely unforeseen difficulties arise.

Shared services success stories suggest some principles to guide CFOs in assembling the six *building blocks*.

1 Choose Which Services You Will – and Will Not – Include

Deciding which processes to include in a shared service center, and which to exclude, can prove difficult. Figure 7.7 shows one way to start defining the scope of sharing, and gives examples for services in finance and tax. *Strategic* processes that add highest value and represent core competencies are likely to remain local. At the other end of the scale, *generic* processes that add least value and are purely transactional can be moved to a shared service center or possibly outsourced. These categories are relatively easy to identify. For most CFOs, the challenge lies in showing how bringing *middle ground* activities within the center's scope will add incremental value to the corporation.

What can be shared in theory is very different from what will be feasible and cost effective in practice. When the CFO examines the list of candidate processes for redesign, against the other five shared services building blocks, a whole new set of considerations arises. Different selections may need to be made for different businesses or geographic territories. For example, the center might perform a particular process on behalf of only *some* business units, excluding those with complex or unusual requirements, or across only *some* regions, excluding those that pose thorny local tax issues.

Using a shared service center allows operating unit finance teams to play a bigger role in the business

One corporate CFO says: 'We operate with a matrix structure: product and geographic. We have shared services in finance, accounting, tax, treasury and human resources. I decide if we go toward shared services depending on the size of the country, the structure we have locally and

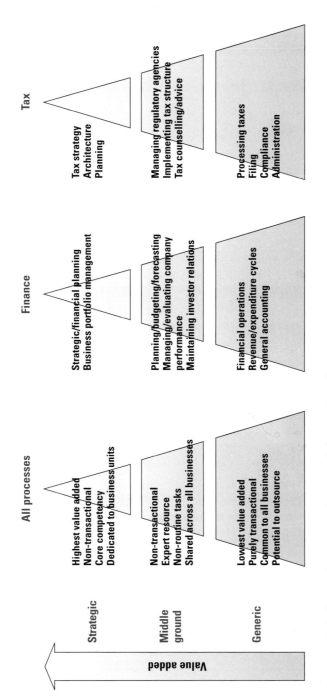

Figure 7.7 **Defining the potential scope of a shared service center**

the business activity'. Using shared service centers lets country CFOs play an increased role in the business, he adds – with a focus on local financing, bank and investor relations, and decision support.

2 Boost Productivity through Self-empowered Work Teams

Before choosing the most appropriate shared services *organizational structure* from the options described (global, regional, centers of excellence, or some variant), CFOs find it useful to visit other companies implementing initiatives of comparable scope. This prime learning exercise offers the chance to examine how these companies are using the *reporting structure* to determine the status of their shared service centers (profit center, cost center, legal entity, economic interest group, subsidiary, or joint venture). Another factor to check is the way they've designed the *operating structure* of each center (self-empowered work teams, or something else).

Experience suggests that – if the culture supports it – the best way to organize shared services staff is in work teams operating under a low span of management control. Energized by new responsibilities and authority, these self-empowered teams usually develop a strong sense of loyalty and pride that translates into higher productivity. But for some companies, this arrangement is a fundamental change: predictably, staff will be anxious and resist the idea, unless properly prepared for their new roles. The following case study shows how people in one general accounting department will be helped through the transformation.

CASE STUDY: Phasing in Self-empowered Work Teams

For the general accounting staff at one major corporation, shared services means liberation and growth, minus many of the fears that come with learning new roles. Previously organized in several slow-moving, bureaucratic, hierarchically structured groups, staff are being prepared to run their global shared service center as smaller, self-empowered work teams. Their goal? Quicker decision-making and faster action.

To give people time to get comfortable with the required new ways of working, restructuring within the center is planned over three distinct phases (see Figure 7.8).

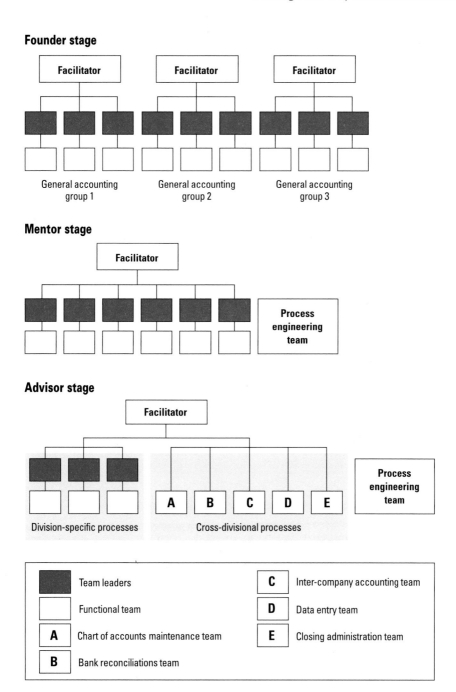

Figure 7.8 **Moving to new ways of working**

The founder stage *begins on day one in the life of the shared service center. Though people work in modified teams, these still have a relatively traditional structure. The nine accounting teams form three groups, each founded by a facilitator who determines the staffing mix and manages the teams' boundaries. Each team is supervised day to day by a team leader who reports to the group facilitator.*

About two years after the center goes live, when the teams are operating efficiently and people are more empowered, they are ready to move to the mentor stage. *The accounting groups consolidate into six teams, organized along business lines – reducing headcount by nearly 30%, from 70 to 50. Three team leaders from the first stage and two facilitators form a team of process engineers, serving as internal consultants responsible for continuous performance improvement. The one remaining facilitator mentors all teams and has overall responsibility for the department.*

When the shared service center has been running five years, it should have reached the advisor stage. *Three more team leaders become process engineers. Division-specific tasks, such as closing, are handled by three teams of accountants; within each, a team leader serves as liaison to the division. Generic, cross-divisional tasks, such as inter-company accounting and bank reconciliations, are handled by a group of accountants and associates. Total headcount is down to about 40. One facilitator advises and sponsors the whole department.*

3 Manage the Impact on Culture

Introducing shared financial or other services may provoke objections – some rational, others irrational – from many areas of the business (Figure 7.9). To give the implementation the best chance of success, the CFO must anticipate these fears and ensure that they're addressed as soon as possible. Two of the most common reasons for failed shared services projects are *not communicating with stakeholders early enough* and *underestimating the impact of shared services on the corporate culture.*

Resistance to change can be overcome through only one means: a strong mandate from the key players. From the outset, successful CFOs cultivate buy-in and then maintain it in every way possible. Ongoing

Shared services staff

- My job will be less interesting
- My job will be less secure
- I might have to move
- What's in it for me?
- I'll lose contact with the business

Core business staff

- I'm worried about my job security
- What is my new role?
- I'll be pigeon-holed
- This is change for the sake of change

Business unit manager

- I don't need this change and disruption
- This will disrupt my staff and reduce morale
- Am I now just operational?
- I'm going to lose some key staff
- This seems just like the centralization
  of the 1970s
- I'll lose flexibility

Figure 7.9 **Key stakeholders may resist a move to shared services**

communication of the business case helps with this. The CFO should clearly demonstrate the added value a shared service center creates for the business, both directly (cost savings, higher productivity, *right first time* focus, better managed assets and liabilities) and indirectly, via the business units (resolving problems, smoother response to changing business needs, improved information, easier data access and transfer).

Even a very strong case for shared services, fully communicated, is just the starting point. Extracts from interviews illustrate CFOs' attitudes to breaking down cultural resistance to shared services.

Work to change people... 'The lessons we have learned are, one, it takes longer than you think and, two, there is always a sense of parochialism when you change these things in a company that's both international and domestic. It's worth the effort when you're through it all but may not seem so in the middle. Training is the key. Technical training and also group cultural change: getting the group ready to accept change, on not just a division-by-division basis but a company-wide basis. You need to give people an understanding of where you're coming from and why you're doing these things. And the more time you spend doing that up front, the easier the change is accepted down the organization later on.'

...Or accept that people won't change 'In centralizing some European treasury activities, we are taking away certain tasks that are typical of a local treasurer. I encountered resistance in one country and it stopped only two years later with the departure of the person. Learning from my mistake, I would first try to assess thoroughly the degree of the local financial manager's acceptance of the overall financial strategy. But if the person is convinced you're taking away something essential in his or her job profile, we have to part ways quickly.'

4 Link Process Improvements to Standardized Systems Software

What kind of technology is needed to share services? Generally, an integrated, enterprise-wide systems software solution works best because having one system is a key enabler for many process-related best practices (Chapter 8). In our survey of 11 major corporations implementing financial shared services, ten chose an integrated package solution. Implementing new systems often takes a substantial up-front capital investment. But the systems software choice can account for big cost savings in the long term (three to four years), by efficiently running redesigned processes and cutting both personnel and duplicate systems maintenance costs.

Whatever solution the corporation favors, take no decision to invest in standard software *without* considering seriously whether shared services are appropriate. This only *sounds* obvious. Some companies are well down the road to integrated package roll-out before recognizing that they also should have been pursuing opportunities to improve the efficiency and effectiveness of processes. Shared services should have a major impact on the software selected and the design and implementation program.

Two alternatives for rolling out the systems software solution involve a trade-off between speed and organizational disruption. Roll-out can be:

- staged in parallel with implementing shared services – this approach entails sweeping change across the organization and requires excellent project management skills

- part of preparing for shared services – standardizing all business units on one system before moving redesigned processes to a shared service center is easier and less risky, but takes longer and may prove impractical from a business case standpoint.

A leading multinational implementing enterprise-wide financial shared services in parallel with SAP offers an object lesson on a common pitfall. Avoid underestimating the extent to which enabling technologies, such as imaging, scanning and workflow, may be needed – in addition to standard software. Though unanticipated at the outset of the project, enabling technology is now a major part of the company's systems design.

The multinational in this case study is using its new center for shared European accounting services linked to a new SAP system as a model for wider improvements in the business. Experiencing the full potential of the shared services approach after a five-month implementation program, the corporation has accepted the system as its standard and is creating centers for other processes and regions.

CASE STUDY: Opening the Door for Enterprise-wide Gains

After years of continuous growth, the PC division of a large computer manufacturer faced increasing market pressure, threatening its profitability. With prices in the PC market generally fixed by the market leader, the division's one option was to scale back its cost base to maintain margins.

Analysis showed that the division had multiple information systems across Europe, the various technologies inflating development, licensing and maintenance costs. Staff in several sites supporting the division's accounting activities added to the outlay.

The remedy, management saw, was a central system for all business activities in the region, supported by a single accounting group in continental Europe. The PC division picked SAP as a tightly integrated technology that could meet the needs of multinational operations and eliminate time-consuming reconciliation processes. It quickly opted to install SAP's finance, manufacturing, and sales and distribution modules in one go.

With all accounting processes completely redesigned, activities surrounding fiscal close, revenue accounting, inter-company accounting and accounts receivable were moved to the shared service center. Now, a core group of five staff supports the accounting activities of 27 countries.

The project hinged on setting up a single chart of accounts and common business practices across all the European subsidiaries – a feat in itself, because the division was also re-engineering its business process to eliminate local inventory, transitioning to a direct ship, plant-to-customer model. But what seemed harder was grasping how the project changed people's roles and responsibilities.

Shared services altered the accounting function's relationship with local country management. The central group now controls the general ledger – and countries that once owned it became users of the information it provides. Introducing an integrated system also did away with many clerical roles, since transactions flow in real time between the sales, manufacturing and finance systems. What's more, integrated SAP puts up-to-date financial information into the hands of a much broader audience. For example, sales representatives can monitor net operating revenues, margins and allowances daily.

Redesigning the organization and deploying systems took about five months, including user acceptance testing and conversion. And the project has been deemed a great success. Making large strides in improving its margins in Europe, the PC division is today extending the model to the US and Asia Pacific regions.

Always a proponent of the shared services approach, the corporation only *now sees its full potential. Using the PC division's principles, it recently set up a center to perform fiscal closing activities for all European business units. And it has accepted the base system configuration developed by the division as the corporate standard, to be followed by all other business units installing SAP.*

Though hardly a cure-all, shared services let the PC division end duplication and gain economies of scale. And it has freed country finance personnel to focus on value added business analysis and other activities, rather than pure accounting. The division's management shepherded this project, involving all affected stakeholders throughout, to retrieve the business's viability.

5 Find the Right Home for Shared Services Staff

Cost, an important consideration in choosing a location for a shared service center, is but one of many. In certain regions, the quality of the telecommunications and infrastructure at the physical site may pose concerns. Qualitative factors, too, often have a significant effect on site selection: to staff in the business units, the process can seem arbitrary. Here, as at every step, the CFO must work hard to communicate the decision effectively and retain stakeholder buy-in.

The first decision is whether to house the shared service center in an existing (*brownfield*) site or move to a new (*greenfield*) site. This decision takes into account four HR considerations:

- staff morale

- severance and relocation costs

- retaining key employees (some might be unwilling to move to a new site)

- the need to create a reasonably self-contained culture in the center, while locating it so that staff still feel connected to the wider enterprise.

In selecting a location, the CFO may want to screen choices against common shortlist criteria: second-tier considerations should help with the final decision (Figure 7.10). Strike a balance between *economic* and *practical* criteria. And take time to *learn from others' experience* before making a decision: some benefits and drawbacks of a particular site may become clear only after a center is established.

Shortlist	Final selection
Social labor climate Availability of language skills Country/region investment incentives Relative cost of labor Proximity to major highways and airports Proximity to other business units Quality and proximity of schools	Lease considerations Square footage Cost per square foot Security Parking Number of restaurants Access to public transport

Figure 7.10 **Factors affecting selection of a shared services facility**

6 Assess Tax and Regulatory Issues, Country by Country

Various legal and regulatory requirements that relate to performing finance processes outside the territory in which business is being transacted can affect shared service center operations. These raise some issues likely to affect *all* finance processes run out of a center serving multiple countries. Such issues include data retention, national tax administration, workers' issues, and the location and format of books and records. Others will affect only *specific* finance processes. For example, charts of account and financial reporting issues will affect general accounting; those to do with electronic interchange of data or the form and content of inter-party documentation will affect expenditure and revenue cycles.

Countries in every region present a range of significant tax and regulatory issues. But in this complex, fast-developing area, our ongoing research points up that, wherever companies are in the world, they can find ways to work around any difficulties. Success depends on hard effort and a willingness to break new ground. It means understanding both what the latest regulations *say* and how they might be applied. A legal requirement to maintain books and records within a particular country may, in practice, be enforced *always* (as in certain South American countries) or *never* (as in certain European countries). Electronic storage of documents may (Sweden) or may not (South Africa) prove negotiable with local tax authorities.

> The shared services approach delivers value only if the center and business units develop the right partnership behavior

GETTING THE MOST FROM THE NEW ORGANIZATION

One thing must be clear by now. Introducing shared services means complex change – for any organization. Making the transition depends on a skillful combination of management techniques: change management, project management and risk management. An all too common mistake is reducing the attention and resources devoted to managing the initiative once the implementation phase is complete. The CFO must remain alert to as many critical success factors in the phases *after* implementation as in those *preceding* it (Figure 7.11).

The shared services approach might make perfectly good sense to everyone involved. They may be eager to adopt it. But it delivers anticipated value to the business *only if* the center and business units develop the right partnership behavior. As already noted, to achieve customer satisfaction and cost effectiveness, staff at the center establish and align their competencies with internal customers' expectations. Arrangements like service level agreements lay out robust, clear rules that detail and

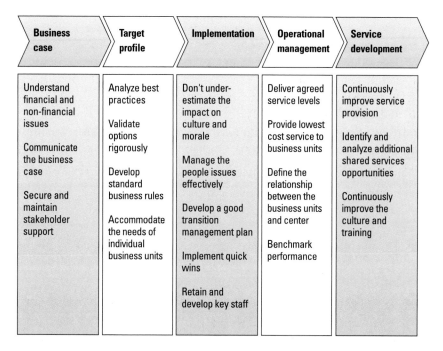

Business case	Target profile	Implementation	Operational management	Service development
Understand financial and non-financial issues	Analyze best practices	Don't under-estimate the impact on culture and morale	Deliver agreed service levels	Continuously improve service provision
Communicate the business case	Validate options rigorously	Manage the people issues effectively	Provide lowest cost service to business units	Identify and analyze additional shared services opportunities
Secure and maintain stakeholder support	Develop standard business rules	Develop a good transition management plan	Define the relationship between the business units and center	Continuously improve the culture and training
	Accommodate the needs of individual business units	Implement quick wins	Benchmark performance	
		Retain and develop key staff		

Figure 7.11 **Critical success factors in the lifecycle of a shared services project**

guide the relationship between the parties. These agreements define and document the cost, quality and specification of all services the center provides. The best include hard measures (speed of processing, number of errors), as well as softer gages of the service level (responsiveness of center staff when dealing with customer queries).

Some companies find other, less formal ways of managing the partnership. One has a *shared services charter*, linked to a problem resolution process used only when customers believe the center's service standards have dropped below agreed levels. Whatever the nature of the partnership agreement, be sure to involve center and business unit staff in designing it from the start. Both parties must see their views represented, if they're to rely on it as a workable tool. Keep it clear and straight-forward. A too complex agreement, if it is administered at all, takes up undue management time.

Partnership agreements lend working structure. But other strategies also help get the most out of the new organization:

- encourage the shared service center to strive for provision of lowest cost service – center staff should aim at matching the *market* cost of services available to the business units

- review and update performance measures, and agree on stretch targets to encourage improvement

- benchmark performance frequently against the agreed targets, the external marketplace and the baseline set by the business case

- seize opportunities to streamline the process flow between business units and the center.

Finally, consider whether implementation may have paved the way for a wider range of financial or other shared services aimed at supporting the business units. At the US foods company in the case study that started this chapter, the CFO capitalizes on his success with financial shared services. He seeks opportunities to add business units, processes and geographic regions to the scope of sharing, which ultimately may expand to include some supply chain functions, such as order management.

CFO's CHECKLIST

DIAGNOSE THE OPPORTUNITIES FOR YOUR CORPORATION   Use the diagnostic approach described in this chapter to consider where you are now, compared with where you need to be for future competitive success. Identify which business issues the corporation must confront in terms of its *structure, markets and customers, processes, people and culture, products and services, suppliers, systems* and any *catalysts for change.*

STEP ON AN ESCALATOR OF CHANGE TO WORLD-CLASS PERFORM-ANCE   Identify finance processes that, consolidated in a shared service center, would capture economies of scale. Think about whether the corporation can move straight to a shared services approach or first needs to simplify or standardize processes.

THINK THROUGH AND COMMUNICATE THE BUSINESS CASE   To gain maximum support from senior colleagues, express the business case in terms of contribution to shareholder value. Remember, the business case forms the baseline against which everyone will judge the benefits: make clear what the shared service center offers all stakeholders.

PIECE TOGETHER THE SHARED SERVICES BUILDING BLOCKS   In planning and managing implementation, focus on each of the *building blocks* – and their interdependencies – to maximize benefits and avoid potential barriers. To gain tax advantages, consider housing the shared service center in an economic interest group, or combining it with a commissionaire sales structure.

CONSIDER QUALITATIVE AS WELL AS QUANTITATIVE BENEFITS Softer benefits may not figure in the financial justification for moving to shared services, but will be important in shaping the right culture. For example, introducing shared services can trigger new learning and behavior, making the finance function a training ground for skilled business managers.

ENCOURAGE A SERVICE MENTALITY Establish the expectations of the center's internal customers and ensure that the center has the capabilities to meet them. Make sure a service level agreement, or equivalent, defines and documents the cost, quality and specification of all services provided. Encourage business units to provide feedback on performance to ensure that the center achieves both cost effectiveness and customer satisfaction.

GO LIVE – AND THEN PLAN YOUR ENCORE Successfully operating a shared service center takes effective, ongoing management of the supplier–customer relationship. Continuously review and improve partnership agreements. Measure the benefits achieved through introducing the center. Identify and analyze new opportunities for expanding the scope of shared services or moving to external outsourcing.

CHAPTER 8
STEPPING UP DECISION SUPPORT WITH SYSTEMS CHANGE

As CFO of a rapidly expanding US company, Jon Wilmot knows the pressure of systems change. Eight years ago, he managed a buy-out of regional competitors. Now, international growth promises to make that exercise seem child's play. After sourcing components from Thai and Korean suppliers for years, the company is negotiating acquisitions in both countries. At the same time, the new Sino-US trade agreement has cleared the way to building a plant in China – a move that should sharply boost the company's margins. Sure of closing all three deals, the CEO and COO already agree on how to rationalize production. They aim to consolidate product lines in the Korean and Thai plants within a year and open a production facility in China soon after.

The knock-on effects will mean wholesale re-engineering throughout the company – processes, structures, systems. And Wilmot is gearing up to drive the change. But the systems area worries him. He's confident that the technology exists to let the company work across continents with different languages, laws, currencies and cultures. But he knows selecting it means confronting a staggering array of options in hardware and software. Say he wants to replace a raft of inherited 'legacy' systems with one that's 'enterprise-wide' – how can he anticipate what that will do to productivity levels during the transition? Could it even wipe out the margin advantage altogether? And there's another nightmare for Wilmot, scarier than the rest. With a seven or eight-figure outlay just for the basics, this is a decision he has only one chance to get right.

Companies everywhere are spending millions on new business systems. But who's ensuring that these giant investment decisions link to business goals? Or that the implications for people running and working in the business are fully thought through? Or that control over lease–purchase choices, for example, and over implementation itself, is in the right hands? This chapter shows how CFOs can establish themselves as prime movers of large-scale systems change.

The opportunity – and challenge – center on the fact that IT now penetrates deep inside organizations. Decisions about how to select, install and use technology are at once more important, more complex and more risky than anything previous generations had to face. This all makes systems scarier than ever. But CFOs *can* approach them with something like confidence – if armed with a properly integrated business and technology perspective. This chapter helps by surveying core systems and decision support tools designed to make sure IT delivers, not just information, but *the information your company needs to compete.* It also lays out the groundwork for successful systems change, including what's needed to tackle the people, culture and organizational issues that make or break implementations.

SIX PLUS ONE STEPS TO SYSTEMS CHANGE

CFOs need not become technical wizards to understand what new technology offers them and their organizations. And for the CFO who wants to pursue the role of corporate architect, major systems change is an ideal arena in which to take the lead.

But where to start? Experience suggests putting yourself and your corporation through a six-step program:

- know why new systems are needed
- make a business case for specific changes
- start re-engineering underlying processes

- survey the technology options

- select the most appropriate software package

- implement the new processes and systems

...plus the one step that almost (but not quite) goes without saying...

- manage the change.

This chapter's discussion – and practical case studies – are structured around helping the CFO to set up and follow just such a program.

KNOW WHY NEW SYSTEMS ARE NEEDED

The search is on for technology that can support critical business decisions by providing accurate, easily accessed information – *on a company-wide basis.* But for around 30 years now, companies have been content to weave new systems into the fabric of their businesses bit by bit. Why is everyone suddenly going for wholesale change?

The Global Clock Is Ticking

Companies throughout the world are facing a trio of pressing problems that only new technology can solve.

The year 2000 throws up a one-off need, now widely recognized. Unable to register dates beyond 1999, computer systems are being reworked or replaced. And with computer technology affecting virtually every aspect of modern business, from production planning to salary payment to building security, companies must resolve this issue in time – or confront chaos. With estimates of the likely total cost running at up to $600 billion, it seems buying new systems is generally proving less expensive than modifying existing ones.

European monetary union is also on the horizon. Global businesses must consider how to cope with introduction of a single euro currency, the uncertain impact of which poses a greater systems challenge than the known year 2000 requirements.

Even without these two incentives, companies would have been, and are being, forced into systems change anyway.

Legacy systems are the ungainly composites of old and new IT solutions that most companies get by with day to day but which are beginning seriously to impede competitive developments, particularly in areas like communication and new international ventures. A hangover from the piecemeal approach that characterized the first three decades of computer development, a legacy system is in reality an agglomeration of smaller systems, often still isolated by function.

The ramifications of retaining legacy systems are many. Such integration as exists is achieved through costly interfaces. Data, even within function, is often inconsistent. Maintenance consumes most of the IT budget – giving US companies, for example, an average 34-month systems development backlog. With different sites and functions running exclusive configurations, common software decisions are largely ruled out, as are links with suppliers' and customers' systems. Again, adapting existing systems usually proves cost-prohibitive, so companies are having to replace them.

To achieve the shareholder value agenda, the CFO must empower people through improved availability of information

New-model Competition Is Coming

More companies are shifting from function-oriented to process-oriented business. Not long ago, only pioneering multinationals like BP and Bristol-Myers Squibb seemed concerned with breaking down organizational and geographic boundaries to find competitive advantage. But the trend is becoming a juggernaut, particularly as companies go global. And small wonder. The horizontal, cross-functional business model lets a company track costs better, hone the supply chain, speed time to market, adjust quicker to market shifts, and improve customer service in line with changing expectations.

In adopting the process model, it's wise for the CFO to take opportunities to re-shape the organization before implementing systems change. Chapters 6 and 7 show how CFOs, as business partners:

- simplify processes throughout the organization

- standardize processes across diverse business units

- integrate processes both within the organization and with those of external organizations, including customers and suppliers.

These changes are an essential jumping-off point for choosing new systems. Companies have ignored basic business processes because it costs money to fix them. But it's worth it. Moving to streamlined, common processes, the CFO can focus on how to minimize low value adding activities – for example, through shared services or outsourcing. For many companies, integrated, globally distributed systems – capable of meeting emerging process and information needs – become key (Figure 8.1).

People Need Better Information Now

With processes becoming streamlined for value creation, a new priority for CFOs is empowering people through improved availability of information. Managers and key employees demand easy, real-time access to detailed, quality information, including combined financial and operational data. Senior management, too, needs better information, including

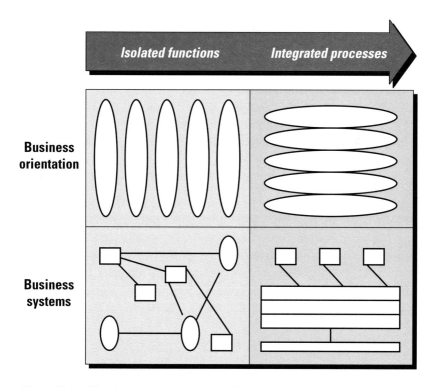

Figure 8.1 **Aligning new processes and systems**

external data on suppliers, customers, competitors, regulators and world economies.

The CFO's first task – again in partnership with the business – is to distill from a sea of data, the information needed to support good decision-making at all levels. The next is to find management systems and technology tools that will deliver the information in the right format, on demand – and not just to one function or site but *to the whole enterprise.*

Companies are making increasing use of new, high level management systems.

- ***Value based management systems*** Linked to shareholder value, cash flow is critical. Value based management (Chapter 2) is about linking operational performance to drivers of shareholder value and is fast becoming one of the CFO's most important roles.

- ***Performance management systems*** What gets measured gets managed, gets done. Performance management (Chapter 3) helps the company move from narrow financial measures to a balanced set of measures that weigh everyone's performance against the business strategies.

- ***Activity based management systems*** Used *ad hoc* for costing, pricing and profitability analyses, activity based costing (ABC) lets the CFO identify those products and services that create value – and drill down to find root causes of failure in any that don't. ABC becomes ABM (Chapter 4) when embedded in decision-making processes to provide a realistic cost framework company-wide.

CFOs looking for new hardware and software tools to enable such management systems find a host of them appearing. *Enterprise systems* store the company's data in a single repository, so it's much easier to access than data in non-integrated systems. *Data warehouses* extract data from both enterprise and legacy systems – and combine and enhance it to produce information unavailable from any one source. With data warehousing, companies create and use large databases with speed and flexibility. *Decision support systems* offer robust analysis capabilities that enable managers to drill down instantly within any system to information with which they can model business scenarios. They let the finance function analyze the heart of the business to take the guesswork out of decision-making.

Gaining a better understanding of technology options – dealt with in more detail later in this chapter – the CFO can highlight how changing the company's systems will markedly advance the business.

MAKE A CASE FOR THE CHANGES

It's important that not just senior managers, but all managers in the business, get a chance to see and agree on the relative value of any systems changes being pursued: after all, it's they who will have to work to deliver the benefits. So before making recommendations, the CFO will want to consult colleagues to find out and consider what opportunities change would open up.

Then comes the essential step of preparing a value proposition for each of the recommended changes – predicting the impacts on the business, positive and negative. It's hardly an exact science, but the CFO must nevertheless ensure that the analysis behind each proposition is thorough and that assumptions are challenged.

Quantifying *benefits* is most readily done by putting a value on the potential success of the *business driver* for a suggested change. Suppose an automotive company's design engineers want improved systems in order to exchange information more easily with manufacturing engineers based in another country. The telling benefits would arise, not so much from saving costs of, for example, travel and faxing, as from the company's ability to speed new model to market times relative to competitors.

> Systems change without process change is pointless – the question for the CFO is how much to re-engineer before selecting a system and how much to re-engineer after

Often, *costs* or other reasons to avoid change are easier to quantify. Tangible costs – hardware, software licenses, training courses and the like – are obviously the least variable. Intangible costs – for example, those associated with the learning curves employees go through on new systems, and consequent disruption to customers – are harder to pin down. So they're usually given only a cursory glance. In fact, of course, it's just such variable, potentially large costs, that tend to cause budget over-runs.

The CFO should also draw up a risk profile for each suggested change. What might be the net long-term effect on the business if new technology fails to deliver to specification? As Chapter 5 shows, each company has its own definition of acceptable risk, depending on its strengths and prospects: the real hazard is unrecognized, unmanaged risk. So in arguing for change, CFOs make a balanced case by anticipating all associated risks.

START RE-ENGINEERING PROCESSES

Systems change without process change is pointless. Companies up-grading their IT gain new capabilities *only if* they reorganize to take advantage of it. But a surprising number of companies make the mistake of overlaying technology 'fixes' on inefficient business processes. So their 'new' systems simply fossilize existing processes and infrastructure. The company is left unable to segregate non-value adding tasks. It remains boxed into old territorial or functional systems solutions, incapable of coping with rapid change.

Process re-engineering in itself brings huge cost savings and com-petitive flexibility. The question is how much to re-engineer *before* selecting a system and how much to re-engineer *after*.

Considering each re-engineering opportunity alongside the company's strategic goals narrows the software solution options. For example, if a company has manufacturing and distribution operations in several countries, but wants to shift production to one low cost site, it must define a global supply chain. It considers only software options that support this scenario – a non-negotiable requirement.

When it comes to *detailed* process re-engineering, it may be best to have a particular software package – or at least a subset of them – in mind. There are several that offer a process-oriented approach. Using one as a prototype – a vehicle for demonstrating the art of the possible – avoids the risk of designing a process that the company is then unable to implement because the software needed is not available. Even with enterprise solutions, companies often rework processes to fit the package.

One multinational amalgamated ten regional centers into a single shared service center. For a while, the plan was to adopt the detailed processes used by the best of the ten as a model for the new center. The alternative was to review off-the-shelf packages, choose the best-of-breed among them, and then design processes around it. The company finally decided to go for the package option because, by doing so, it gained access not just to its own best practice but to world-class best practices.

Using this approach of exploiting new software to improve processes, the US food products company in the following case study revamped its business.

CASE STUDY: Keebler Does It the Sensible Way

In the early 1990s, America's second largest cookie and cracker manufacturer, the Keebler Company, faced growing competition from market-dominant Nabisco. Behind the scenes, Keebler's business systems – based on 20-year-old mainframe technology – struggled to support a nationwide sales network of 36 offices and 2500 people, plus 70 distribution centers, 14 shipping departments and 13 plants. Without shared databases, managers found accessing information was not only slow and difficult but the data used was sometimes inconsistent.

But then Keebler began a change in strategic direction. It called on management to take an integrated view of the supply chain and customer service activities, which would mean producing state-of-the-art information. The company launched a major re-engineering of manufacturing, distribution and sales operations – at the same time as introducing new enterprise-wide IT systems based on software packages from SAP and Manugistics.

As re-engineering and systems implementation neared completion, Keebler reorganized, focusing its business on the core cookie and cracker product lines and divesting its salty snack and frozen foods operations.

Managers began making decisions using the new, fully integrated systems. Covering finance, manufacturing, sales, inventory management, distribution and HR, the systems yielded the same on-line, real-time information to everyone. The budget review rolled out to plants and sales offices let managers review their cost variances anytime, without waiting for month-end reports. Now, month-end budget/actual reports are generated only on request: most managers use on-line information.

Senior management has a truer picture of outstanding receivables, product costs by plant, and the company's financial standing. The tight integration of the software lets those people initially coding transactions assume a new degree of control. That in turn has sharply reduced the burden on the finance function's transaction processing staff, who now spend more time analyzing financial results.

Today, the company has improved its competitive position, enjoying strong growth in profits and increased market share. Despite the project's high price tag, Keebler has found the results well worth the investment. Its new strategic direction has the support, both of a strong IT infrastructure based on world-class integrated software, and of re-engineered processes, creating a more efficient operating environment across the supply chain.

Keebler believes its success stems largely from the sensible nature of its approach: it broadly *laid out how the business had to change and began with process re-engineering – but then for* detailed *process design, exploited best practices contained in packaged software.*

SURVEY THE TECHNOLOGY OPTIONS

This is where the CFO must do some homework. If you want to make informed choices and plot a logical course, you have to develop your understanding of what's involved in the various technology options – the main ones being:

- enterprise systems
- best-of-breed systems
- decision support systems
- data warehousing.

Beyond these, be prepared also to look into key components of supporting infrastructure – including:

- electronic commerce
- workflow technology.

Enterprise Systems

Built for flexibility and robustness, enterprise systems are capable of running processes across the entire company. Their seamless design reduces time spent maintaining and upgrading separate systems and interfaces, freeing IT specialists for higher value adding work on strategic initiatives. The most advanced enterprise systems take in other new technologies, like bar-coding, data warehousing and electronic commerce, to streamline processes. Most important, by making processes visible across the enterprise, they can remove organizational, geographic and political barriers.

Most companies favor a single-vendor package of enterprise solutions for a range of transaction processing needs – bringing the advantages of simplicity, integration, and one contact point for sales and support. Vendors whose packages provide greatest functional coverage include SAP, Baan, Oracle and PeopleSoft (Figure 8.2).

Although today's enterprise systems offer generic processes suited to most industry sectors, they often meet no more than 70% of a company's total functional requirements. In an increasingly competitive market, enterprise solutions will continue extending deeper into business processes – and wider across new processes not yet covered. But as the market

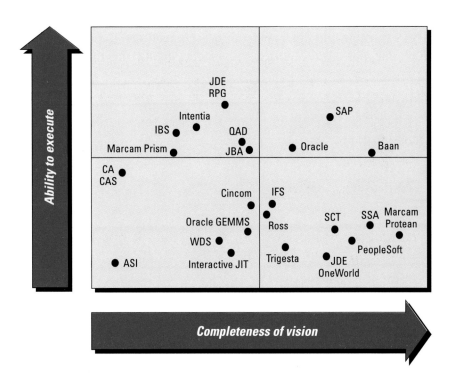

Figure 8.2 **Enterprise system vendors**
Source: Gartner Group

stands now, companies generally need to rely on a combination of vendors for a complete business solution (Figure 8.3). CFOs should consider the best-of-breed option – finding the best-fit solution for each particular function, integrated to span the business – particularly where their companies have unique business needs or core processes that demand the most robust systems available.

Best-of-breed Systems

Some best-of-breed vendors focus on specific *business process segments.* For example, several provide only client/server accounting software. They pour their resources into world-class general ledger, accounts payable and receivable, fixed assets and other financial function modules. Such financial vendors include Coda, Computron, Hyperion, FlexiInternational and SQL Financials.

Others focus on *cross-industry functional niches.* For example, Hyperion leads in the critical financial consolidations market segment, with SAS Institute and others emerging as competitors. Hyperion's Pillar product line has also captured mindshare among the many finance

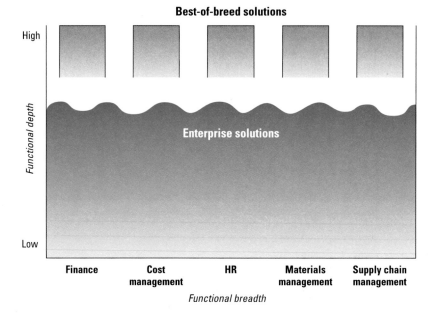

Figure 8.3 **Choosing core systems**

executives eager to revamp their budgeting processes. Other specialist solutions are available for operational functions – like demand planning, order configuration and production – that may not be well covered by enterprise systems.

Decision Support Systems

Enterprise and best-of-breed processing systems contain basic information to support decision-making: compared with legacy systems, they give management better reports with which to run day-to-day operations. But, although leading enterprise vendors are improving their decision support modules, these systems still fall short when managers need high level analysis and modeling capabilities. To fill the gap, other vendors have created information access and decision support systems (DSSs).

Employing user-friendly, business (rather than technical) language, these query based systems let managers quickly and readily interrogate data from numerous sources – whether enterprise, best-of-breed or legacy systems. DSSs integrate financial and non-financial, as well as internal and external, information. They are particularly good at helping you maneuver around competitors when fast response is key. The platform for powerful modeling techniques, including regression and trend analysis, they offer unparalleled flexibility to test scenarios and anticipate the effects of various business moves.

So while a DSS lets one manager drill down from a drop in monthly results to spot ten lost orders, for example, other managers may be modeling what introducing a new customer service will cost – and still others anticipating the effects of a strike at a plant.

DSSs are generally characterized as either *managed query* tools or *on-line analytical processing (OLAP)* tools. Often, companies use both. Managed query tools let users query data in relational databases and other legacy systems (without needing any technical knowledge of those databases or systems), and produce reports suitable for distribution to various groups in the business. Leading managed query tools include Impromptu from Cognos and Business Objects from Business Objects Inc. OLAP tools offer more sophisticated analytical capabilities, such as drilling, trend analysis, *snapshots* and *what if* analyses. Leading

> A decision support system lets business managers quickly and readily interrogate data from numerous sources

examples are DSS Agent from MicroStrategy Inc, Decision Suite from Information Advantage, Express from Oracle, Essbase from Arbor Software and Holos from Holos Systems.

Used cost-effectively, DSSs can give you extra time to plan migration to an enterprise solution. For example, if legacy systems remain adequate for transaction processing, DSS tools can extend their useful life. Without programming, they let managers explore non-integrated systems, overcoming data inconsistencies, to access real-time business information.

Data Warehousing

Analysts currently spend more time collecting and verifying data than analyzing it and making decisions. Data warehousing turns this situation on its head.

Many companies use the analytical power of decision support systems alone. But high level DSS tools are only as good as the underlying data. That's why *many more* companies choose to combine DSSs with a data warehouse, which extends the information base by extracting and *enhancing* data from existing processing systems (Figure 8.4). Companies yet to move to the enterprise model gain most, but even enterprise systems can benefit.

A major technological breakthrough, data warehousing lets companies build, maintain and manage large databases – and query them in minutes, not hours. A data warehouse converts data from all sources to a common format, and manipulates and presents it in the form most useful to managers and other users.

> This major technological breakthrough puts competitive intelligence at the fingertips of users, across the enterprise

Greater than the sum of its parts, the data warehouse consolidates and enriches data to create information unavailable from any single source. It puts vital competitive intelligence and improved decision support information at users' fingertips, across the company.

When Seagram – the subject of the next case study – found its financial reporting process was being described by staff and customers as 'cumbersome, multi-layered and bureaucratic', the company responded quickly. Adding financial reporting to its radical change agenda, it chose a data warehouse as the best vehicle to transform the process.

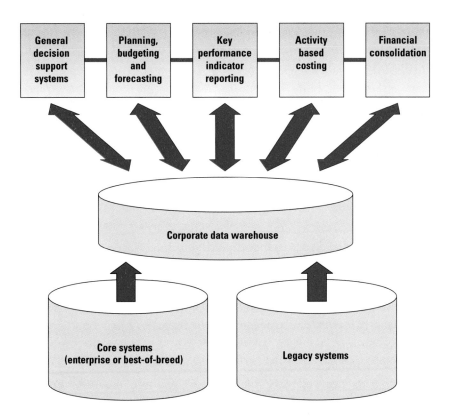

Figure 8.4 **A data warehouse feeds linked analysis and reporting applications, giving users access to enhanced information**

CASE STUDY: Seagram's Data Warehouse Streamlines Financial Reporting

Re-engineering its global beverages businesses, the $11 billion Seagram Company found many projects competing for the same human resources. Responding to a strong business case, senior management decided to give priority to automating and standardizing the worldwide financial reporting process. A project team working to a two-year timeframe is making good progress, thanks to solid management support, an effective implementation process, tight teamwork – and the right technology. Key to the latter is a newly created data warehouse.

Seagram's formerly complex financial reporting process saw its 70-odd business units take 30 days to get reports to the CEO's office. Each business unit had to close its general ledger, extract data, perform currency exchange conversions and create corporate reports – then review, reconcile and analyze them, adding off-line entries, before sending them to the next level for review (Figure 8.5a).

Accounting practices showed marked inconsistencies. Many business units failed to adhere to the standard platform for finance: most made off-line adjustments for corporate reports. Methods used to map the chart of accounts to standard corporate reports also differed from one unit to the next. And multiple, identical review and reconciliation processes were performed manually at various levels across the organization.

Before implementing dramatic change, the project team focused on quick wins. Asking business units to halve reporting time to 15 days, the team took steps to make information transparent, implementing a spreadsheet driven, flash report system, which all businesses and finance staff can access. Seagram also replaced the mid-year budget review with more timely quarterly forecasts, and developed a standard customer profitability analysis.

Well within its two-year schedule, the company now has a design that standardizes accounting and report generation. In the new process, a data pipeline *directs data from the business unit's general ledger to a data warehouse with a multi-dimensional database. From here, key financial data can be*

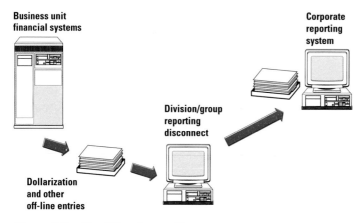

Figure 8.5a **Traditional reporting process**

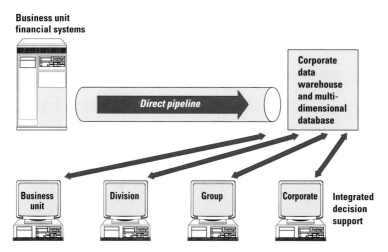

Figure 8.5b **Automated, standardized reporting process**

accessed for management reporting and analysis (Figure 8.5b).

Three sites have already gone live. Agreeing to supply consistent reports on a common platform and end off-line adjustments, each business unit need only close its general ledger. Accuracy and integrity are validated automatically as data is transmitted. The data warehouse and multi-dimensional database perform all currency conversions, reconciliations, consolidations and reporting.

Meantime, Seagram is on track for broad benefits – among them tighter controls, a new information culture, and a faster, more effective way not only to create reports but to implement changes.

Electronic Commerce

CFOs wanting to get the most from new systems may need to evaluate and enhance components of supporting infrastructure, like electronic commerce. Using computer and telecommunications networks to conduct and manage transactions, both internal and external, electronic commerce offers big benefits – for example, helping companies to win new customers, cut inventory costs, shorten procurement and product development cycles, and improve communication with business partners, banks and regulators.

The popularity of electronic data interchange (EDI) in the 1980s set the stage for dealing with customers and suppliers electronically. Today's companies rapidly adopt Internet and Intranet vehicles for electronic commerce. Vendors are developing Web-enabled applications for the virtual organization, giving suppliers, customers, employees and financial institutions real-time access to company systems.

Key issues remain to be resolved. Security prompts short-term concerns – although it's now safer to use a credit card number on the Internet than over the telephone. Some worry about the cost of doing business on the Internet. But with continued influx of technology based communication products and vendors, the market is sure to mature.

Workflow Technology

Another enabler of electronic communication, workflow systems can automatically deliver the right information to the right people at the right time – strengthening links between everyone involved in particular processes, including suppliers. Making processes more visible, workflow can also help you to continuously examine and redefine the business.

Workflow systems originally emerged from imaging technology, which created, processed and stored electronic documents – greatly benefiting paper-intensive industries like insurance (claims handling) and banking (credit and loan applications). This technology automated manual processes, but stopped short of actually *improving* the processes. In contrast, workflow means changing processes – in other words, changing how people do their jobs – from start to finish. A workflow system monitors and validates processes by measuring how work is being done against company policies and procedures: modifications are judged against the same measures.

Imagine a company's purchasing cycle – with all the requests, approvals, checks, invoices and payments that create a margin for error and delays. Now consider some of the ways a workflow system can reduce costly disruption and improve service levels:

- *replacing paper with electronic documents* – standardized electronic forms contain the intelligence to ensure that data is complete, as it is entered

- *routing documents electronically to predefined recipients* – purchase orders are automatically sent to the purchasing department

- *enforcing rules on who can grant authorization and under what circumstances* – the system even determines who can approve requests if someone is unavailable or fails to respond by a set time

- *eliminating written signatures* – electronic signatures or PINs speed approved electronic communication with vendors

- *monitoring the process* – management can see how many purchasing requests are being processed and how long it takes

- *extending workflow architecture to vendors* – purchase orders pass directly to vendors' inventory, shipping and billing systems, and invoices enter the company via a similar electronic path.

CHOOSE BETWEEN SOFTWARE SOLUTIONS

Most battles between customized and packaged software solutions were settled in the mid-1980s. Today, only companies with highly specialized requirements write custom systems. Effectively outsourcing part of a company's application development function, packaged solutions offer broad functionality, yet usually need only minor modification to match specific business needs.

But does *packaged* spell easy choice for the CFO? Far from it. In the heated application software market, vendors come and go. Some who were dominant ten years ago now hang by the thread of legacy business, while niche software houses enter the market daily. Industry analysts foresee more massive change over coming years. Widespread consolidation is expected, alongside further growth fueled by enabling technologies like the Internet. According to one forecast, the client/server enterprise applications market total will be worth nearly $19 billion by 2000, based on a cumulative annual growth rate of 37%.

All this adds to the pressure on CFOs to select wisely. And that means being very clear about the basics. To look for the best software solutions, you need to consider three things:

- what opportunities exist

- how to exploit them for competitive advantage

- the costs and benefits of each possible solution.

At the *opportunities* level, most CFOs come up with similar shopping lists. They want seamless integration between modules, because they want data the business can depend on to improve decision-making. They want standard products that offer robust, enterprise-wide functionality, and as little proprietary technology as possible. And they want considerably faster, easier access to data than in the past. Essentially, they're after systems that leave the company unconstrained today and empowered for the future.

But companies differ widely on the other two considerations – for example, in what they regard as 'efficient' for their purposes. In evaluating software, it's possible to take a traditional, market-led or proof-of-concept approach (Figure 8.6).

In *traditional* software evaluation, the company looks at every vendor offering the basic functionality needed and rates each one in turn. This generally takes six to nine months, elicits superficial responses from the many vendors queried, and ties up considerable resources. Meanwhile, the company waits.

A company taking the *market-led* route adopts the same software its major competitors use, on the assumption that 'they can't all have been wrong'. Done in anything from two hours to two months, this faster but riskier approach sidesteps mapping software to business and technical needs. The company fails to assess whether the chosen package offers

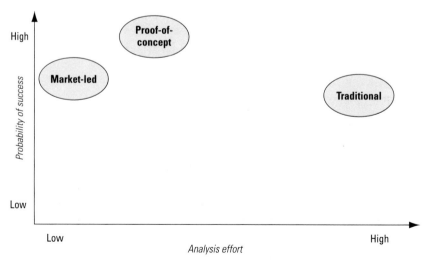

Figure 8.6 **Companies take different approaches to evaluating software packages**

point solutions – those needed to fill particular functionality gaps, which may represent opportunities for competitive advantage.

Proof-of-concept evaluation means using experts to do a first pass of candidate products – then assessing just a small number in full to find the best fit. This middle course should take two to three months, and lets the company make a more sure-footed move.

The experience of CFOs using the proof-of-concept approach to select software packages suggests several guidelines.

Form an evaluation team Bring together key players as an evaluation team, including representatives from business units, plus corporate and external specialists in areas like supply chain, IT, finance and HR.

Detail your needs List the high level business and technical needs against which the team will rate software products. This exercise also helps you identify functionality gaps in enterprise and best-of-breed systems – and the added point solution software components that can fill them. Documenting requirements for *standard* procedures wastes time: most vendors cover them. Instead, identify *unique* requirements – perhaps a special discounting method on payment, or other factors that help differentiate the company in the market.

Establish a shortlist of vendors Consider each vendor's track record, and their current and future capabilities. Do they have solid experience with companies of comparable size and complexity? Do they have a reputation for providing robust functionality that meets companies' needs? Are they well established, with a sustaining client base which suggests they will be in business well beyond the period of time that you will need them? Are they flexible enough to work in partnership with the company over the longer term? A good test: are they willing to enhance the package for the company and support enhancements in future releases? If different vendors offer roughly the same functionality, think about their *culture*. Which vendors best reflect your company's own style of working and are likely to interact well with staff?

> Chief financial officers want systems that leave the corporation unconstrained today and empowered for the future

Hold scripted software demonstrations Invite shortlisted vendors to show their products' capabilities to the evaluation team and principal users. Such pre-prepared demonstrations also let vendors attempt to build rapport with their prospective customers. Spend ample time allowing vendors to run the company's data through their systems and play back business scenarios. How will they handle high volume input? Can staff in a remote office occasionally approve an invoice, for example, without involving the company in buying a complete system just for them?

Draft an implementation plan   Determine the level of involvement needed from key players, the timeframe to complete the project, and its approximate cost. In later stages of the project, the evaluation team should refine this high level plan to include detail on, for example, specific tasks, deliverables and resource needs.

Finalize the business case   Based on information gathered in preceding stages, you can now finalize a strong business case for change. Paradoxically, this is a point at which many CFOs hesitate. Anxious about making the right choices, they want to wait for the next wave of technology. But things move so fast in this marketplace that the picture will alter no matter what you do. The best advice is to avoid spending too much time deciding. Plant a stake in the ground and go forward.

Sign the contracts   Spell out all terms of agreement with vendor partners *at the outset*. That includes who's in charge of what areas, how people will be tasked and directed, who can actually make changes, basic reporting mechanisms needed, the single point of contact, who gets what monies, and how fees and project capital expenses will be handled. Specify roles for replacing

> Things move so fast in the software market that the best advice is to avoid spending too much time deciding

any vendor who leaves: otherwise remaining vendors will have a big problem and the company an even bigger one. Vendors too should spell out how they'll deliver and handle any problems that arise. Note what constitutes a material change and who can evaluate the impact of changes on the partnership.

If vendors promise systems that bring a competitive edge, the CFO may structure the deal so that the company pays only as the systems generate a certain income stream, thus sharing with vendors the risks and rewards of producing a solution they'll ultimately take to market. The agreement – written and signed as a legal document – steers the partnership through fair weather and foul.

Using proof-of-concept software evaluation to marshal resources and avoid errors, a world-renowned US company primed itself, in just four months, to re-engineer processes and implement new systems.

CASE STUDY: Fast-forward Package Selection

A West coast based consumer products company had always achieved at least 20% profitability growth. But new revenue competition threatened to slow it down. An added worry was that operating units – with different processes and systems – acted as independent entities. Luckily, they seemed buoyed by their expanding international market and willing to work together. All freely admitted that processes and systems were so archaic that re-engineering was bound to enhance revenue and cut costs.

The corporate CFO, the CIO, and operating unit leaders developed a strategy, setting the scope to include warehousing, order management, distribution and finance. They decided they needed to go for an enterprise system, augmented by point solutions for warehousing and for demand and transportation planning.

An evaluation team promptly limited software selection to four enterprise vendors: the company's current supplier and three market leaders. Each business unit determined its unique requirements – ignoring those common to most consumer products companies. As a first step toward standardizing processes and systems company-wide, the team analyzed these requirements and combined them into one comprehensive list. Based on this list, vendors prepared scripted demo presentations. Meanwhile, team members weighted require-ments and evaluation criteria. Beyond functional fit, they looked at factors like vendor stability, cultural fit, software and vendor flexibility, ease of implementation, compatible point solutions – and, finally, cost.

During vendors' demonstrations, evaluation team members independently scored their capability to meet requirements. Afterward, a panel of experts was called on to answer any remaining questions, but to avoid favoring any particular software. The team's recommended solution: Oracle as the enterprise vendor, McHugh Freeman as the warehousing vendor, and Manugistics for demand and transportation planning.

While management negotiated contracts, the evaluation team targeted a limited number of processes for major re-engineering using the packaged software as an enabling tool. The team drew up a plan detailing, function by function, assigned-by-name resources for tasks in each phase of implementa-tion – including a pilot to increase user buy-in and roll-out speed. Estimates were based on appropriate metrics and actual process and system information. And the team developed a change management plan in tandem with the implementation plan.

PLAN FOR IMPLEMENTATION AND SUCCESS

An effective evaluation process raises everyone's sights and galvanizes the project – providing a strong basis for building and maintaining momentum through the remaining stages. What does successful planning and implementation take? Many companies use consultants extensively at this point on the grounds that they implement systems every day, while the company does it once a decade. As with vendors, it's clearly important to partner with consultants the company can rely on and work alongside comfortably over time.

With or without external help, you need to develop a detailed implementation plan – the crucial blueprint for all that's to follow. Aiming to minimize disruption to the business, the key is to plan work in short phases that yield maximum benefits. Avoid tackling too much at a time.

Even with the best planning in the world, of course, things can still go wrong. If CFOs knew everything that would prove difficult in large-scale systems change *going in*, fewer would proceed. But some problems are predictable and merit avoidance planning.

Watch for missed deadlines   Adequate time for planning and competent project management are needed to prevent the missed deadlines that so often signal when a large-scale effort is going off-track.

Avoid part-time input   Running a 100-person project is certainly ten times more complex than running a ten-person project. And it demands correspondingly greater management commitment. You need dedicated resources and managers' active participation. *If senior people view the project as a part-time venture, it's over before it's begun.* To complete systems implementation, everyone involved must think, breathe and live it.

Make progress manageable   Five-year plans seldom deliver. Few assigned to the project at the start finish it: as new staff take time to get on the project team's wavelength, momentum ebbs and the effort loses direction. Good project management dictates the break-up of large projects into smaller ones. By setting six-month deadlines for any phase or deliverable, you can build progress incrementally.

Be flexible During a large-scale project, the rules change. By the end, many things may be different – technology, business requirements, project sponsors, vendors, the company's customers and product offerings. To avoid disappointing users, accept that the project will have to adapt. Again, projects broken into small segments fare better: if the environment shifts part way through, you're better able to change tack.

Look out for mousetraps As technology advances, it's easy to be sold the latest, better mousetrap – another technical bell and whistle. The trick is to stay open minded but on course. And to fully communicate any changes to users.

Carry on regardless As project staff come and go, get promoted or headhunted, the CFO leans on the experience of the rest of the team, and on sound methodologies, to carry systems change through.

Communicate the plan Far more systems projects fail because of poor communication than because of technology problems. A proper communication strategy – within the overall change strategy – is needed to help make sure that users welcome change, learn better ways to do business, see how technology and procedures enhance the company's competitive position, and contribute to delivering new systems.

MANAGE CHANGE THROUGHOUT

In one respect, successful implementations of new systems are just like any other form of corporate change. They depend on dealing effectively with interrelated issues, across the company – in its processes, organization, people and culture. In other words, you need a full *change management program* – not just talk-and-train sessions in the last half, but a well thought through strategic plan spanning the entire project, from analysis and design to construction and implementation (Figure 8.7).[1] Such a program amply repays the investment of resources required.

Once, CFOs focused on the costs of a systems project – period. Now most appreciate that ignoring the human – including emotional – dimensions of change will deeply undermine any project that depends on people being willing to work in a new environment. In developing a comprehensive change program within the project plan, the CFO needs to forge a broader range of relationships, in particular with the CIO and operations. And the nature of those relationships may be different from any you've had to develop before. From start to finish, systems change had best be a joint

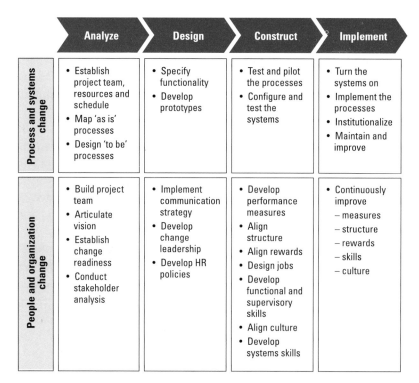

	Analyze	Design	Construct	Implement
Process and systems change	• Establish project team, resources and schedule • Map 'as is' processes • Design 'to be' processes	• Specify functionality • Develop prototypes	• Test and pilot the processes • Configure and test the systems	• Turn the systems on • Implement the processes • Institutionalize • Maintain and improve
People and organization change	• Build project team • Articulate vision • Establish change readiness • Conduct stakeholder analysis	• Implement communication strategy • Develop change leadership • Develop HR policies	• Develop performance measures • Align structure • Align rewards • Design jobs • Develop functional and supervisory skills • Align culture • Develop systems skills	• Continuously improve – measures – structure – rewards – skills – culture

Figure 8.7 **Integrating systems change with process, people and organization change**

venture with the rest of the business. To ensure that you take people with you in achieving change, you must involve stakeholders at every step, and indeed everyone in the company when necessary.

Creating strategy, for both process re-engineering and new systems, also means opening your mind to how vastly different operating contexts can be – and preparing for the different solutions that this might demand. Re-engineering basic functions, like the receivables process, *should* be simple. But if the company uses banks in six European countries and one in Saudi Arabia, for example, a different system will be needed for each one. So re-engineering solutions will also vary for each. And it means a separate collaborative effort with staff on site, country by country.

In re-gearing the corporation for better decision-making, CFOs clearly have their work cut out. To succeed, they need not only to absorb technological know-how, but also to broaden their horizons generally and learn new skills.

CFO's CHECKLIST

USE TECHNOLOGY TO LEVERAGE STRATEGY Systems usually follow strategy, not the other way round. But why strategize in a vacuum? A survey of software packages is likely to reveal advanced capabilities that may raise the company's sights.

ARTICULATE BUSINESS NEEDS IN TERMS OF PROCESS AND INFORMATION NEEDS Before buying technology, the company must know what it wants to do and the information it needs to do it. Break down business needs into process and information needs – and then see what technology best answers them.

LOOK COMPANY-WIDE The only technology strategy that can fully support the business strategy covers the same ground: the entire company. With an enterprise-wide technology vision in place, you can pursue systems goals as resources permit, without wasting time or getting sidetracked.

THINK OF VENDORS AS BUSINESS PARTNERS Go beyond customer–supplier relations with the vendors of your major systems. Vendors must become partners who know the company's technology strategy and goals – and the best ways to achieve them over the long term.

WEIGH ENTERPRISE VERSUS BEST-OF-BREED SOLUTIONS The industry as a whole may move to enterprise solutions. But if you're a niche player or have unique business needs, the greater flexibility and power of best-of-breed – or even custom – solutions may be better able to support the company's value chain.

STEP UP DECISION SUPPORT Operations oriented enterprise and best-of-breed vendors are moving to improve their information access and decision support modules. In the meantime, consider specialist decision support systems for accessing combined financial, non-financial, internal and external information from all existing systems – whether enterprise, best-of-breed or legacy. Consider data warehousing, too, for its information enhancing qualities.

TAKE ACCOUNT OF SUPPORTING INFRASTRUCTURE Technical infrastructure, just as important as core processing and decision support systems, is increasingly complex and costly. Evaluate advanced infrastructure components, including electronic commerce and workflow. And consider the hidden costs of, for example, recruiting or retraining staff, and managing the various vendors that support the new environment.

INTEGRATE ALL DIMENSIONS OF SYSTEMS CHANGE Failed projects are scarcely ever the result of the wrong technology. To get the most from new systems, pay attention to related process, organizational, people, culture and communication issues.

KEEP MOVING FORWARD Despite all their preparatory work, many CFOs hesitate to decide on a new solution. What if something better comes along? But something better *always* comes along. If the business case for change is good, go for it – and don't look back.

CFO at Global Industries Corporation for only three months, Alan Marvin pondered the CEO's passing remark that the finance function had 'some catching up to do'. It seemed every time he asked people to do something that he considered normal practice, they had a good reason why 'it wouldn't work here'. So he knew achieving what he wanted would take time. A few things were obvious: the frequency of technical problems, systems didn't talk to each other, and some finance people acted as if their role was to catch out the business managers. How could he get started?

Marvin decided to have lunch with Adele Islei, his opposite in operations, and Helmut Henk, the marketing VP. He asked them one question: 'What should we in finance be giving you that we're not?'. Two hours later, with a clearer idea of what his customers thought was going wrong, he called his assistant. 'Phil, I need you to arrange a two-day retreat. Clear my diary and the top team's for Thursday and Friday and book a hotel in the mountains for us all. And ask Adele and Helmut to send along two of their best people.'

A year later, Marvin is 'catching up'. The famous mountain meeting set a direction, now fleshed out in a blueprint for the future and a three-year plan to get there. His people are getting the basics right. His managers are leading changes according to plan. And their customers in the business are working with the finance function to benefit the whole corporation.

Earlier chapters concentrate on key areas of *what* should change in the way the finance function serves the business – and *why*. This chapter shifts attention to *how, when, who* and *where*: the nuts and bolts for CFOs determined to engineer radical improvement.

Change may already be under way. Perhaps the biggest business benefits have yet to be targeted. Whatever the case, the CFO as change leader must consider some of the critical issues explored here. What does it mean to create a vision of the finance function's future role? How can you urge people to challenge the way they do things? How do you design a blueprint that spells out what you need to achieve? Where should you focus effort first? Who needs to buy in to the changes? How do you juggle today's priorities and deliver progress tomorrow?

> Set your finance function the challenge of materially improving its value to the business

A phase by phase approach to major change addresses these questions (Figure 9.1). Emphasizing the last and toughest phase – *making it happen* – the chapter concludes by distilling real-world experiences of successful CFOs into a set of *imperatives for transforming the finance function*.

DEVELOPING YOUR VISION

Why do you need a vision of the finance function's future role? Because managing significant change of any kind requires a clear view of the starting point, the finish line, and the route from one to the other. Finance functions that materially improve their value to the business share a common characteristic: their change is *driven by the challenge of realizing a vision* – a vision tailored to the company's own circumstances, strategy and strengths.

However it's articulated, this vision sets out the CFO's aspirations for the finance team. It answers the question: 'How will we know when we're succeeding?'. In doing so, it serves as a crucial underpinning for the whole change process. Thinking through the vision – the sooner, the better – the CFO should make sure it provides:

❶ Develop a vision of the role of the finance function

❷ Confront current reality		**❸ Create a blueprint for the future**	**❹ Plan the change**
• What are people's roles? • What do people *really* do? • What do our customers think of our service? • How does this compare with what we think? • How do other companies do it? • What will success look like?	**Performance gap**	• What services must we deliver? • How must we redesign our processes? • What kind of people do we need? • What technology support do we need? • How should we be organized?	• How should we prioritize potential initiatives? • What quick wins can we make? • How do we manage people through the change? • How can we integrate organizational and cultural change with new processes and technology?

❺ Make it happen

Figure 9.1 **A five-phase approach to developing and delivering a vision for the finance function**

- a compelling case for change
- an assessment of current performance
- a yardstick to prioritize change actions
- benchmarks to drive implementation.

Time and care spent in creating a vision are amply repaid, because a well crafted vision is a powerful tool for communicating with finance people and customers in the business. With it, the CFO begins developing a coherent understanding of the services and value the finance function will deliver in future.

The bigger the gap between your current and desired roles (Figure 9.2), the clearer the picture must be. In many finance functions, change so far

Finance imperative	Scorekeeper response	Business partner response
Influence and support business decisions	Approver, auditor and controller of decisions	Team member and proactive business advisor
Performance management	Historical reporting, budget variance analysis	Balanced measures linked to value driven business strategies
Employ information as an asset	Information is power and should be controlled	Sharing information is power
Organize finance to deliver value	Centralized control focused on accounting	Matrixed organization, embedded in the business, focused on decision-making
Optimize the cost of the finance function	More finance = more control	Lean operations, devolved autonomy, delivering value to the front line
Manage risk	Report bottom line risk	Proactive risk management throughout the business
Co-ordinate value strategies	Control of separate discrete projects	Challenging and integrating change to deliver corporate goals

Figure 9.2 **The vision must recognize the finance function's changing role**

has focused on simply re-engineering processes to cut costs and exploit economies of scale – rather than on finding new ways to improve finance's contribution to the business. CFOs without a strong vision find that the faster they run, the further behind they get, as larger goals recede behind short-term wins and potential synergies are lost.

The worthwhile vision clearly articulates how the finance function will support achievement of business objectives. And it sets out the principles by which finance – its people, processes, systems and organization – will be redesigned, to equip the function to fulfill this future role. In one major multinational, the CFO brought together members of his top team for a series of brainstorming sessions, looking ahead one, three and ten years. Without prior inputs or constraints, their brief was to be as creative as possible, using only their collective instincts. Together they outlined what the finance function could be expected to achieve (Figures 9.3 and 9.4) – an initial hypothesis to be tested and, if need be, updated during later investigation.

By identifying factors critical to the vision's success, the CFO is better able to design, prioritize and monitor change initiatives

236

Yet too many vision statements are bland promises with little to back them up. To be effective, your vision must be specific enough to drive finance strategies and goals and, through them, the values and behaviors of finance staff. By identifying factors critical to the success of the vision, CFOs are better able to identify, design, prioritize and monitor the necessary change initiatives. Often, the finance function is expected to deliver an improved standard of service to the business while reducing its cost base by around 30%. Typically, at least half of current finance activities will fail to meet a critical value added test, and must be either redirected or cut altogether. So the emphasis may be as much on *getting the existing basics right*, so they deliver more value to the business, as on introducing new, leading-edge practices.

Developing an ambitious vision of the future, one finance function realized early on that its credibility to offer strategic financial advice rested first on its ability to produce routine management reports. Simply getting the monthly accounts and forecasts out a lot faster became a critical success factor.

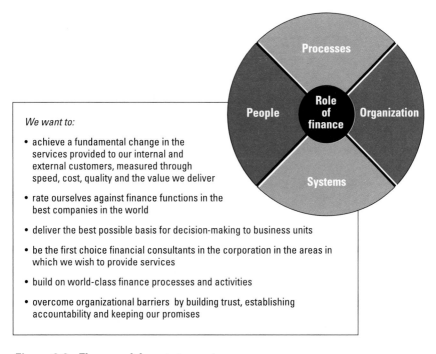

Figure 9.3 **Finance vision statement**

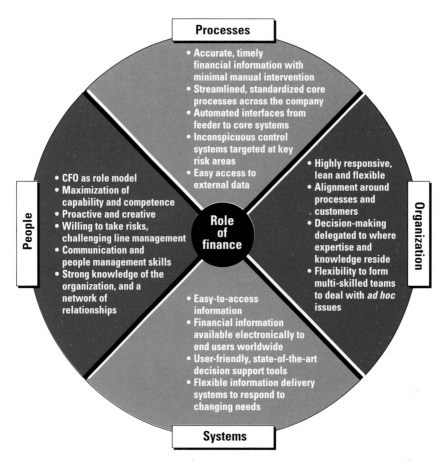

Figure 9.4 **Design principles for the future finance function**

CONFRONTING REALITY

Confronting the reality of where you are now – and comparing this with your vision – lets everyone see the performance gaps that change initiatives must close. Facing people with persuasive evidence of the need for change is the best way to get them asking the right, challenging questions: 'Why do we do things this way? Do our activities add value? How can we improve?'.

To get a better perspective, most CFOs need to do some research, inside and outside the company.

What Do People throughout the Business Think?

Finance is accustomed to shining a critical spotlight on others in the business, rather than on itself. Ask your internal customers – the CEO, business unit heads, sales and marketing, planning, R&D and manufacturing – what they really want and at what cost. And act on the results. Being seen to embark on major change within the finance function telegraphs a forceful message to business managers that begins to alter their perceptions of its potential role. Test the willingness of managers to accept a more proactive role from the finance function. And assess the readiness of finance people themselves to make needed changes.

Experience shows that, inside and outside the function, judgements of finance's effectiveness may differ widely. Don't let finance people rely too heavily on self-assessment. Encourage them to turn to business management for a more realistic view of the quality of service they provide – in other words, to *let customers drive the change.*

Consider how one CFO used a questionnaire to elicit feedback from within the organization. The findings helped validate the finance vision and mold change projects to deliver a service welcomed by the business.

CASE STUDY: Asking the Right Questions

A multinational company devised a detailed questionnaire to uncover perceptions of current finance performance. In interviews, 24 business unit managers and a similar number of senior finance staff were asked to score the finance function on a scale of 1 to 5, on a mixture of hard and soft, technical and service-oriented measures. Topics included: How efficient is finance in managing transaction processing? Does finance provide adequate performance management to support business decisions? Is tax and treasury performance aligned with business needs? Does finance give an effective overall level of service?

Figure 9.5 plots summarized results. After various cost reduction and outsourcing initiatives, people inside and outside the function seemed satisfied that finance operations were both cost effective and service oriented. Broad agreement also existed on the subject of performance management – but here the view was that finance people must improve substantially if they were to lend adequate decision support.

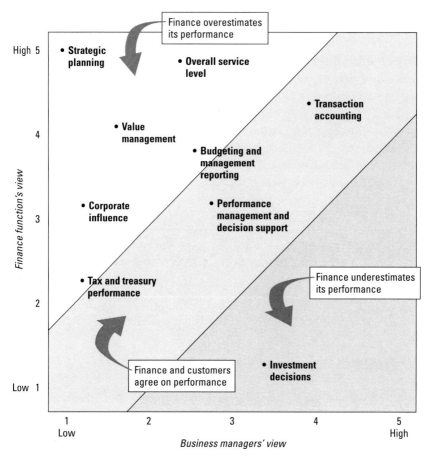

Figure 9.5 **Comparing perceptions of performance, inside and outside the finance function**

Elsewhere, it appeared that finance had been overestimating its performance – for example, in strategic planning ('Consolidating and adding a few high level numbers to our five-year marketing plan does not constitute an effective contribution to strategic planning'), *in tax and treasury* ('The business is increasingly global but tax and treasury are still remote, ivory tower departments. We need them out where the action is!'), *and in budgeting* ('Planning and budgeting are excessively focused on the numbers and forms. The process has become an end in itself, not a means to improving the business').

For this finance function, developing and delivering a vision means making internal changes and, crucially, changing the attitudes of operational line managers – convincing them that finance can add more than overhead to the business. The CFO recognized, at an early stage, that finance professionals could fulfill their potential only by working to establish a valued partnership with the business.

How Do You Compare with Other Companies?

External benchmarking – always painstaking, often painful – offers a bracing dose of reality for entrenched finance functions. By collecting and analyzing benchmark statistics for the size, cost, quality and speed of particular processes, the finance team gets a detailed picture of how its own performance compares with the best.

Since many finance processes are similar in nature across different businesses, it's worth looking outside your industry, as well as inside. Figure 9.6 is part of a typical performance report from the Global

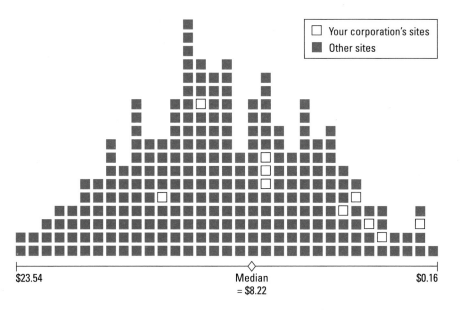

Figure 9.6 **A benchmark report for total cost of expenditure cycle per $1000 revenue**

Benchmarks Alliance, covering a cross-industry membership of some 60 multinationals and more than 650 participating business units.[1] Measures for a member corporation's ten sites are shown graphically in comparison to the Alliance as a whole: note the corporation's two *laggards* (left) and five *leaders* (right). Reports giving peer group comparisons – for example, by geography, revenue size or transaction volume – can turn up other perspectives on the effectiveness of a process or activity.

Benchmarking can also highlight the specific practices that differentiate best performing finance functions – providing ideas for your action plan. For each financial process or activity, review lists of best practices to identify those most relevant to your own operations. Talk to people in businesses with similar finance visions to learn from their experiences. A well designed benchmarking visit can be a useful tool for changing people's opinions and getting them excited about potential improvements. Consider visiting your biggest external customers: meet the people who process your bills. Meet with your biggest vendors too.

Carefully benchmarking the finance function is itself an example of best practice. Few companies derive all the learning they could from their investigation, which yields too much to digest at once. So, be sure to give research the time and resource it requires. Pursue pertinent details: pinpoint ways to avoid mistakes and leapfrog preliminary ideas.

But approach the wealth of information uncovered as a *guide*, not gospel. Over-ambitious re-engineering that lags behind expectations can damage finance's credibility as much as inaction.

DESIGNING A BLUEPRINT FOR THE FUTURE

You should now have a better idea of the changes involved in realizing your vision. In fact, you'll almost certainly have *too many* ideas: you need to review and prioritize opportunities for improvement. Choose options that hold most promise for developing the finance function in line with principles set out in the vision. Use these to design a detailed blueprint – and, at the same time, construct your business case for the new finance function. Doing these tasks in parallel gives the design effort a *results focus*. You could also begin forming your proposals into a change plan, using the process described later in the chapter.

A blueprint for the future of the finance function should define the *processes and services* it will offer, as well as the *people* needed, how they'll be *organized*, and the *systems* that will enable their activities.

What Services Will Finance Offer?

Often, CFOs start by thinking about the services they want to offer and then work backward to the specific processes needed to provide them. You can use the finance value line, described in Chapter 1, as a template for defining how the finance function will deliver value in future (Figure 9.7) – and to help you prioritize and plan changes.

For each service, determine performance measures and targets so that you can assess progress. Where precise measurement is impossible, set directional or relative targets (for example, more satisfied customers, higher quality).

Now comes a marketing campaign to sell finance's ideas. Resourceful CFOs use defined target services and performance levels to trigger discussion within the business. Highlight new and enhanced service areas to make clear the shift you intend to achieve. Experience suggests that the more imaginative the finance team is in demonstrating the improvements it's aiming for, the more support it's likely to win. One CFO set up a permanent vision exhibit showing the services the finance function would offer, with graphics illustrating redesigned processes and case studies of other companies already using elements of the vision.

Here are some points to bear in mind when re-engineering finance processes to deliver new services.

- Invest time in thoroughly preparing process designs. And in testing. And re-testing. Even the most clearly envisioned process will need to be matched to practical realities.

- Make sure the design team has all the training and specialist input it needs. Otherwise it may end up merely *rearranging the furniture* – rather than creating workable process improvements.

- Seek views on the new designs from people in finance and throughout the business, as well as external customers. Will the processes *really* deliver improved service? Will they represent value for money?

- Form a contract with your customers. Help them recognize the value that new processes offer. And explain what information feeds they must provide to make the processes operate effectively.

	Financial strategy	Investment management	Funding, tax and treasury	Cost planning and budgeting	Financial operations	Performance management
Creating value	• Strategic value planning • Mergers, acquisitions, disposals • Managing investor relationships	• Managing programs and projects • Managing assets	• Managing tax regulatory relationships • Developing and delivering tax planning • Processing taxes	• Value planning		• Performance reporting
Supporting value decisions	• Developing business value strategies • Developing business portfolio	• Developing capital/investment plan • Managing and evaluating financial performance	• Managing tax planning • Managing cash • Managing and evaluating financial performance	• Operationalizing value based management • Planning, budgeting and forecasting • Supporting cost management decisions	• Management reporting	• Managing performance framework • Setting targets
Protecting value		• Performing capital allocation	• Managing treasury risk • Managing internal controls		• Managing financial policies and procedures • Revenue/expenditure cycle • General accounting • Transaction processing	

Figure 9.7 **Delivering value across the finance value line**

What Skills Will People Need?

According to our *CFO 2000* survey, by far the biggest barrier to improving finance's role is the current level of competencies among finance staff. It takes radically different skills to deliver the finance visions most large multinationals are developing. As Chapter 10 shows, the skills that CFOs value, as they look to the future, are less and less to do with accounting and control. Instead, they emphasize modern skills of change management, creative problem-solving, business and commercial understanding, communication, and coaching and influencing.

This shift prompts CFOs to rethink their policies for recruitment, training and development, and career management. Quotes from our interviews illustrate how they view the need to develop the right capabilities within their finance functions.

One has begun by exploring the skills sets required. 'We started last year mapping our different competencies and skills. We took a very systematic approach, interviewing 225 of our 600 people in Europe. We're identifying what kind of competencies we have, what we must improve by country and by activity, and then we're making plans both locally and centrally... But all this takes time and you have to push.'

Another CFO is bringing in a new generation of professionals. 'We are changing our finance staff by changing our formal hiring profile. Only the younger, university educated finance people have received a market educated view of finance. They are beginning to talk to the operating managers.'

Many other finance executives say they pay greater attention to continuous education and training. A CFO comments: 'We're trying to upgrade the training we provide for finance professionals to at least 80 hours per year. The training can cover anything from computer courses, accounting standards, mergers and acquisitions, to presentation skills. We see it as a real morale booster. We get better, well rounded employees who are ready for moves and opportunities'.

What Systems Will You Use?

The need to automate processes and controls, to obtain better information from business systems, to provide balanced measures, to slice and dice and drill down – all these point to the finance function's taking a more strategic, integrated view of technology (Chapter 8). The CFO must ensure that the target architecture for financial systems will facilitate achieving the vision. Crucially, it needs to be flexible enough to cope with a fast changing environment: *your systems should leave you unconstrained.*

Too often, companies bemoan their lack of tangible pay-back from implementing new systems. Yet a system is only as good as the people, processes and organizational structures that surround it: these must be updated in consort. If considering a shared services or outsourcing solution, structure it with care – don't lock yourself into an arrangement that might rob the business of key skills and flexibility to change in the future.

How can the CFO help architect the right systems?

- *Develop your relationship with IT* With today's increasing demand for enterprise-wide, fully integrated business systems, finance has a pivotal role to play in understanding needs and defining systems specifications to deliver value and manage performance across the business. The days of IT driven systems may be over, but any systems blueprint will be more robust if designed, tested and modified *in partnership* with the IT department.

- *Educate the business in the art of the possible* It's only once people have had practical experience of, say, data warehousing, that they can relate it to their aspirations. So work with IT professionals to show business customers the benefits of a range of the latest proven technologies.

The CFO of one of the world's largest retailers encourages his finance directors to get closely involved in all IT projects affecting finance. His message: 'You wouldn't let HR hire someone for your department whom you hadn't interviewed. Similarly, never let the IT people build or change a system without your specific input'.

How Should You Organize the Finance Function?

A marked change in finance processes and services invariably means changing the way the function is organized. CFOs with a vision of finance as a business partner have to examine major structural issues and their implications for designing the blueprint.

Our *CFO 2000* survey explores some of the options (Figure 9.8). Today, many finance functions are conventionally structured: nearly half are

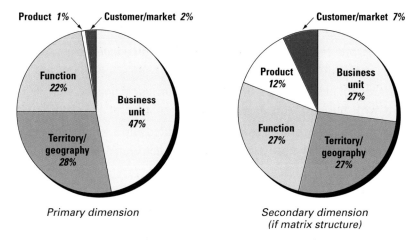

Figure 9.8 ***CFO 2000*** **survey: How is the finance function organized globally?**

organized primarily by business unit and a further 28% by geography or territory. But already, CFOs are responding to business-wide restructuring initiatives that produce ever more sophisticated, matrix managed organizations. In future, traditional business unit finance structures are likely to become less prevalent, as finance is absorbed into operational line management and processes. Instead, increasing numbers of finance teams will be organized along product, customer and market lines – more closely linked to the value chain and better able to flex in response to business needs. At the same time, finance structures built around functions like payroll and treasury will be strengthened by the trend toward shared services and outsourcing solutions.

> Multinational corporations with a vision of finance as a business partner have to change the way the function is structured

With so many choices, how should you proceed toward a structural blueprint? What you decide may trigger big change management challenges Experience shows it's best to aim for as rational an approach as possible – based, step by step, on visible, readily explainable decisions.

The following case study shows how one company used a process of sound structural design to decide the future shape of its finance function. It began with developing and ranking a range of options according to defined design principles. And it ended with setting a *migration path* from the old to the chosen structure.

CASE STUDY: Laying Foundations for Decision Support

The CFO of this multinational wanted nothing less than a world-class finance function. So defining relevant best practices was a priority – not least when it came to structural design. Target best practices included: finance staff to be co-located with business customers, *and* at least 40% of resources to be allocated to decision support. *These were incorporated into a set of principles to guide the design of the new organizational structure: for example,* build business advisor relationships with business units, wherever possible, through local decision support teams.

The next step was to develop structural options – the company considered:

- *a streamlined version of the current departmental structure*

- *a process focused organization*

- *a centralized organization*

- *a customer focused organization*

- *a mixed structure, taking the best of each of the other options.*

Eventually, managers chose the mixed structure as the approach that fulfilled most design principles. After thoroughly reviewing this structure's strengths and weaknesses, they devised a detailed design. Work on the other options was used as added source material for planning the migration path: (1) establish a new top team and streamlined structure, (2) rationalize the central team's structure and shift transaction processing from a functional to a process focus, and (3) devolve decision support into the business.

Today, as stage (2) nears successful completion, the CFO is building local decision support capability in preparation for the final stage.

Obviously, it's essential to align all the different elements of the blueprint – processes, structure, people and systems. Together they must form a clear and complete picture of the future. It's pointless devising a skills set based on empowered finance professionals, for example, if the organizational or systems designs impose undue controls. Integrity of the four combined blueprint elements proves the biggest risk factor in delivering finance visions. So test your whole blueprint – kick the tires, hard – to make sure alignment is tight.

PLANNING THE CHANGE

With a robust blueprint and business case in place, you can begin planning how to move from where you are now to where you want to be. Successful change planning is something of a black art. Some people do it instinctively. But most need a process to help them think through multi-dimensional challenges.

Few CFOs have the management capacity or resources to do all they want to immediately: potential change initiatives must be prioritized by weighing benefits against constraints. Some changes take just hours to accomplish. Many take years. And since interdependencies may exist between planned actions, you need to analyze the critical path. A single initiative is unlikely to deliver complex change, even just in the finance function, and the business as a whole will be pursuing many other initiatives at the same time. So think about how to integrate your own and others' efforts.

A good change plan builds momentum by achieving quick wins. Be sure to include people-centered activities that keep energy levels high. And beware of break points in the project – for example, projects often stumble or stall in making the transition from conceptual activity, like analysis and design, to actual delivery.

One likely problem is that you've identified too many improvement initiatives to deliver in a reasonable timeframe. So in prioritizing initiatives, keep the following questions firmly in mind.

- *How much impact will each initiative have?* Try to gage the extent to which each change will advance the finance function toward satisfying critical success factors for the vision. The benefits may be direct or indirect.

- *How easy will it be to implement and how much will it cost?* Here, the test is based on both the complexity of the task and the level of the finance function's control or influence.

One company's experience shows how important it is to co-ordinate and integrate change initiatives. The finance group used a comprehensive process to prioritize potential changes (Figure 9.9). Inputs from staff and customers, as well as from benchmark comparisons and best practices, helped identify key improvement areas. The aim was to exploit opportunities for *high impact, strategic transformation* – and to maintain and streamline *tactical initiatives*, while leveraging rapid performance improvements from them.

What does this kind of prioritization mean in practice? One CFO decided that, until he could get the management accounts out on time, it would be inappropriate to introduce the concept of value based management. Another reckoned the finance function could achieve the greatest impact by setting up a shared service center for the parent company *before* investing in global integrated reporting and accounting systems. Another delayed a request for a global manufacturing cost model while basic cost accounting was transferred into operations.

Prioritization complete, list your initiatives on a big wall chart or get a project software operator to plot them. Show who'll be involved, the timeframes, and interdependencies. Invariably, the total elapsed time will be longer than you want. But failing to plan for this now means that everyone will be disappointed later, when you fall behind an unattainable schedule.

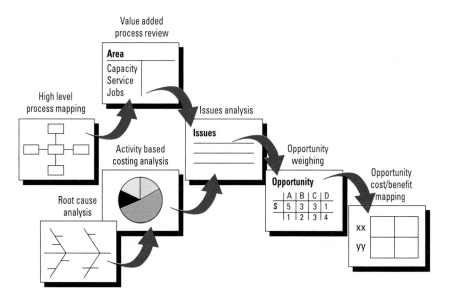

Figure 9.9 **Making objective and thorough decisions about change priorities**

MAKING IT HAPPEN

CFOs who have decided their destination and mapped the route are just warming up. Now the hard work starts! This section collates the experiences of people already implementing their finance visions. Based on what they've found works and what doesn't, it presents *seven imperatives* that any CFO delivering radical change must focus on.

1 Leadership: Get the Right Team around You and Set a Clear Direction

As CFO, you're the only person who can take on the role of change leader. If you harbor any reluctance to drive radical change through the finance function, the project will fail to deliver its full promise.

Listen to the staff of some CFOs who've really made things happen and it's no surprise to hear them characterized as 'unreasonable'. They set 'impossible' targets and refuse to get lost in the detail. One newly appointed CFO lit a number of fires to shock her department out of its complacency. For example, she demanded that financial accountants halve the time taken to close the books in the first quarter, then halve it *again* in the second. Initially, her staff resisted. They hoped the crisis she'd engineered would go away. But by sticking to her guns, she achieved the targets she set.

> Build the most credible team of champions possible – your best, forward-thinking finance people should visibly lead the change effort

Even *super CFOs* can't do this alone. To ensure that the finance function and the rest of the business accept your vision, you need to build the most credible team of champions possible. Your best finance people should visibly lead the change effort, helped by the most forward-thinking staff. Who is assigned to a project is one of the clearest signals of its importance to the organization. But good people are busy people. To get the right members on your team – and get them *full time* – lift them out of daily management by empowering the line to handle routine activities of the function.

Ask yourself: should the team include only finance staff? Adding credible people from other parts of the business can be helpful. Confidence rises and people are less likely to dismiss the team's achievements as just a proprietary finance project.

2 Momentum: Focus on the Vision Always, but the Basics First

It might seem strange to suggest that, in a major strategic program, you begin by concentrating on basic operations of the finance function. But three reasons make this the essential first step.

- Improving the efficiency of current operations is an excellent way of identifying and freeing up high quality, experienced resource – both for your change program and, eventually, for the new activities you'll undertake once your vision is reality.

- Early delivery of benefits signals that you mean business – it lends credibility to the change program, inside and outside the finance function.

- Unless you can secure efficient operation of current activities, crisis management and strategic change may become competing priorities – often the strategic change loses out.

Start the process of getting the basics right as soon as possible. But take proper precautions: put a strict time limit on your improvement strategy and give it measurable targets. People must be clear it's being done *in preparation for even better things*, not as an end in itself.

Your next big challenge is building and maintaining momentum – bringing your change plan to life (Figure 9.10). In a large organization, change can take years and demands discipline, energy and imagination. Make sure people recognize that improvement will come not from a single *silver* bullet, but from *500* bullets. The key lies in successfully managing those critical periods where work is proceeding but real change has yet to be delivered – for instance between initiation and the first quick wins, and again between quick wins and the introduction of new systems.

3 Integration: Use Relationships to Knock down Silos

Finance can't change in a vacuum. The CFO must integrate finance's ambitions with those of the business overall and, likewise, the practicalities of managing the necessary changes, inside and outside the function. Most change drivers in the finance function are rooted in changes needed by the business – for example, the need for greater efficiency to compete in the marketplace or for better understanding of profitability of products,

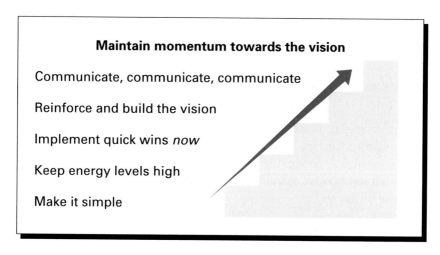

Maintain momentum towards the vision

Communicate, communicate, communicate

Reinforce and build the vision

Implement quick wins *now*

Keep energy levels high

Make it simple

Figure 9.10 **One CFO's instructions to all finance staff at the beginning of their** *Finance Change 2000* **program**

customers and distribution channels. Even the biggest corporation has a finite capacity to deal with change: all areas of the business must prioritize.

Finance is a function with unique reach and power, cutting across all business processes: any significant change in the way finance operates will have knock-on effects on internal customers. Most changes CFOs want to make have impacts outside their own line control. Delivering major improvement becomes even more difficult when it requires the whole organization to change – as when shared services, or new business systems or performance measures are introduced across the enterprise. But played right, pursuit of a new finance vision can give the CFO an unparalleled opportunity to break down functional *silos* and champion integrated change.

Take care not to have your good intentions misread as 'finance trying to take over the business'. You need to build robust relationships, not just to increase your sphere of influence but to make sure you can cope with the strains between people that major change inevitably causes. Strength-ening relationships means improving communication with all key stake-holders. Even *within* the finance function, change can trigger varying technical and emotional responses from people in different specialisms, such as management and operational accountants, and at different seniority levels. But as a rule of thumb, you need influence only 20% of those held in highest esteem to gain 80% of the support your change needs.

4 Excellence: Find Ways to Delight Internal Customers

Your customers may be unaware of the services that the finance function has the potential to provide. So produce prototypes of target services to excite customer interest and create demand. Be sure to involve users in prototype design – avoid the fate of major management information projects that have delivered a lot of extra data but in no way changed how users make decisions!

Too often, finance people themselves cannot readily define what services they deliver – or *could* deliver – to the business. Typically, finance deliverables have evolved piecemeal over the years. No-one has ever asked whether the management accounts add value, or discussed whether a different format might better support business unit decisions. Nor has anyone stopped to take a holistic view of the overall value that finance adds. Your change program gives you the opportunity to rethink it all. Once you've re-examined finance products and the market for them, you'll be ready to enter into negotiations with customers about how to achieve your vision.

> The writing is on the wall: any finance function that continues to believe its responsibility begins and ends with accounting will fail

Improving your service levels means finding new ways to support commercial decision-making. Budget variance analysis, though an important control, never helped inform a pricing decision, resolve a make-buy issue, or improve understanding of product profitability. Working with business customers to tailor what it does, the finance function can give better quality output, in more easily usable formats – providing a transparent cost base and enabling managers to understand the value implications of their decisions.

The writing is on the wall: any finance function that continues to believe its responsibility begins and ends with accounting will fail as a business partner. Yet finance's future role is best built on the foundations of its existing competencies. Successful CFOs are known for *integrating business management information and decision support, enterprise-wide* – ensuring high quality, consistent, well controlled data and insightful analyses. In this way, their finance functions extend naturally from their recognized strengths to provide non-threatening, valuable improvements for customers.

5 Partnering: Build a Bridge with Operations

Re-engineering major transaction processes makes a partnership with operations essential. In most cases, radical improvement means changing processes *end to end*. For example, a large entertainment company started a project to re-engineer payables and, when the procurement group was brought in, decided to seize the opportunity to leverage purchasing across the entire organization. Resulting procurement savings were *25 times* the savings from accounts payable streamlining and the combined project teams implemented dramatic changes.

Such changes often result in significant shifts in personnel and roles at interfaces between the functions concerned. Teamwork is essential: it helps in handling change effectively across functions, gaining participation from major stakeholders, and avoiding the damaging stresses involved in driving change through.

In many organizations, realigning financial transaction processes means moving to a matrix management approach, cutting across traditional functional boundaries. Beware that finance and operations may have different priorities. Operational people excited by the idea of improving efficiency and services may be less interested in control. The CFO's role is to ensure that a balance is struck within matrix management structures.

Even where control is highly important, an effective matrix can be achieved. In the next case study, a CFO who partnered with operational areas of the business was able to break down barriers and reap greater benefits than were otherwise possible.

CASE STUDY: Using Matrix Management to Strengthen Control

Examining how the business collected money from customers and intermediaries, the CFO of a major insurance company found two areas of concern. Processes, structures and systems were functionally based. And process costs were high for what was only adequate performance.

To boost efficiency, the finance function had already partially centralized the collection process. The CFO could either complete this centralization or work with the business to do something more dramatic. Analyzing processes and activities showed that a big collection cost lay in resolving queries between finance and customer services – something that further centralization, he felt, could only make worse. A detailed review of the options available confirmed his fears.

In an adroit move, the CFO decided to include collection activities within customer service teams. This let the teams fulfill their ambition of offering a once-and-done service to intermediaries on new business and queries. And by resolving queries faster, they cut costs and, in turn, receivables balances.

The change carried big control risks – after all, millions were collected daily. So the CFO used IT solutions to design a new, stronger control system into the matrix management structure. For example, users' actions are recorded automatically and permission to make adjustments is withheld, pending proper authorization. Now, customer service process managers have clear accountability.

Apart from welcome cost benefits, the partnership with operations has led to service, speed and quality gains. In the long run, clearer accountability for collection within a matrix management approach looks set to help change the positioning of the finance function and the overall culture of the business.

6 Culture: Create a Value Mindset

Most strategies and change plans work on a one to three-year cycle. But changing a large organization's *culture* can take much longer. So the challenge for the CFO is keeping strategy and culture aligned.

If you need to change culture, the best way is *indirectly*. Don't try making a wholesale change across the finance organization – instead, focus on things that shape new values and behaviors. For example, introducing balanced performance measures across the business is apt to substantially affect the finance culture. Such an initiative changes *what* finance staff work on, and also *who* they work with and *how* they work with these new customers.

But it's a mistake to expect the target culture to simply evolve. You will have to work hard to develop and articulate its critical features – including, for example, how it will take account of international sensitivities within the globalizing business. Then, measure finance people's readiness and ability to change – so that you can direct your efforts toward high priority aspects of the culture. To succeed, you'll need to use many change levers over a period of time: management style, communication, reward systems, skills and career development, performance management, structures, teamwork, working practices and job rotation.

The toughest test comes in a crisis, when the temptation is to go back to what worked before. Only by holding a consistent line over the long term will people believe there's been a genuine shift in *the things that get valued around here.*

7 Benefits: Budget for Radical Improvement

Finance's traditional position in the business is based on an understanding of the need to process business transactions and maintain discipline and control. Too often, the agenda set for finance has been about cutting costs and maximizing efficiency – squeezing the function as merely a business overhead – rather than developing new, higher value adding services. In some companies, this has created enormous barriers: finance professionals face a hard task getting the rest of the business to accept that they can contribute more positively.

CFOs who successfully renew finance's agenda do so by *tuning in to the change agenda of the business.* They craft a business case for finance change that goes beyond financial justification. Using new skills not featured strongly in their past role, they examine the *softer* commercial benefits of changing the finance function – and they *sell* to the business the concept of finance professionals as architects of the corporation's future.

Though your own case for a world-class finance function will be based on specific market conditions, it must come up with answers to three generic questions.

How will finance change strengthen your corporation's competitive position?

- Improved cost, speed and quality of processes (for example, purchasing and billing).

- Support for faster, more reliable, fact based decisions (for example, on pricing).

- Resources allocated to their most profitable use (for example, through customer segmentation).

How will finance change help the business deal with external pressures?

- Enhanced provision, analysis and interpretation of information.
- More forward-looking financial data and balanced *lead indicator* information.
- Improved understanding of the big picture.

How will finance change improve the organizational culture?

- More strategic, longer-term thinking.
- Stronger relationships and better communication with the rest of the business.
- More objective, integrated performance measures.

The CFO of a multinational corporation defined the value proposition for six main streams of the finance change program: treasury, transaction processing, enterprise-wide systems, activity based management, performance management and finance-business partnering. For each stream, finance people developed benefit cases jointly with internal customers – and used these to value the improved service finance would deliver through more efficient processes and better performance management. Crucially, finance's work with the business helped dissolve internal barriers and trigger a rethink of the wider business management process. Able to demonstrate why and what change was needed, the CFO could justify *investment* in finance – and track implementation.

The case for the changes outlined in this book is compelling: if the CFO is not proactive, the business will eventually demand them. Those who are already making the transition know that progress is seldom straight-forward or cheap – and that the many calls on the finance function by the business can force compromise and delay. The super CFOs of the next millennium will need to have an unshakeable belief in their vision and hold a steady course – even under pressure – over several years. But in succeeding, they'll set a new standard for finance professionals as partners in maximizing value.

CFO's CHECKLIST

ENLIVEN WITH A CRISIS, INSPIRE WITH A VISION   Really successful CFOs do more than provide value added advice at board and senior management levels. They energize their finance functions to deliver commercial coaching and consultancy across the whole business. Create a vision that signals your intended shift. If necessary, engineer a crisis to force people to begin responding.

MOVE PHASE BY PHASE TO WORLD-CLASS PERFORMANCE   The pattern of successful change in finance functions is neither one big bang nor lots of minor changes – it's a phase by phase migration. Start with the basics, build capability and credibility continuously, and always aim for the best. The trick is to keep it going and not get stuck on one phase.

GET OUT WHERE THE ACTION IS   You'll find it impossible to advance toward your vision without shifting the finance function's relationship with, and services to, the business. Be prepared to wade right in: don't guess what business customers want – ask them. And keep asking.

CREATE A BLUEPRINT OF THE FUTURE   Finance professionals, often cautious and analytical, are likely to be suspicious of something they've yet to fully understand. If you want to bring about radical change, paint a clear picture of a feasible future. Let your people know where they're going, work with them to draw up a route map that you can all follow – then lead by example.

ARTICULATE THE TARGET CULTURE   Focus your attention on the things that will shape the values and behaviors of finance staff, in line with their changing role. Develop new finance heroes, who are no longer just number crunchers, by training people to become problem-solvers at the front line. Use surveys and measures to establish whether you're on track.

CELEBRATE SUCCESS   Generate excitement by tracking even the smallest victories, publicizing results and rewarding everyone involved. Build enthusiasm and team spirit with every new achievement.

CARRY PEOPLE WITH YOU   As CFO, you can – and must – lead the change. But you won't transform the finance function on your own. So get the right team, build a strong network of supporters and involve key players.

CHAPTER 10
BECOMING THE ARCHITECT OF
YOUR CORPORATION'S FUTURE

Reaching the top of the corporation, Robert Budd became CFO four years ago. He's accomplished a lot in a short time. The corporate finance department is now highly respected, by bankers and management alike, as a major force in international development. Transaction processing takes place in regional service centers, operating under outsourced management contracts. And the internal financial management processes of business units are today so well integrated that local finance functions have lost their identities almost completely. But perhaps his biggest success as CFO has been developing shareholder value models, used to set performance measure targets across the business. Budd's profile with investors and in the boardroom has never been higher. Yet, looking ahead, he realizes he can't rest on his laurels.

The corporation's market value is based on brokers' expectations projected more than ten years out. Budd knows one thing for certain: rapid structural change in the industry will make things very different by 2007. His long-term aspirations for the business reveal major flaws in the corporation's strategy. A fresh business vision is needed. Apparently, the CEO is counting on him to come up with some answers. Is he up to it? Budd has always seen himself as a tough negotiator with sharp analytical skills. Now he needs to be a futurist too.

He wonders what the corporation's customers, competitors and investors will be like in a decade's time. Will the corporation exist in its present form at all? And what of his own role – what will the CFO be doing then? Indeed, will the corporation still need a CFO? What new skills will he have to develop and how will he be measured? Budd decides that by thinking through these personal issues, maybe he'll find some clues to what lies ahead for the business as a whole.

Earlier chapters have concentrated on the CFO's role, *as leader of the finance function*, in applying best practices in the business. But so far, little has been said about the CFO *as an individual* or about the personal ingredients of success. Recounting the views of CFOs of leading companies worldwide, this chapter details how they make an impact on their businesses. Using *CFO 2000* research results, it shows how and where they spend their time, today and in future. An extended case study predicts what life might be like for financial officers in the 21st century. Besides identifying personal characteristics and skills required in coming years, the chapter suggests a development process for getting there.

Finally, a checklist draws together the learning points for you to make a *charter* for your role in the business – a two-way deal that encourages you to perform as *the architect who designs, and oversees building of, your corporation's future.*

A NEW ROLE FOR CFOs

Business partnering, though as a concept not new, is only now beginning to take root. In every industry, CFOs shift from managing the finance function – with an emphasis on accounting and control – to providing leadership for business unit management and, more importantly, working as partners with CEOs. The speed and scale of this trend surprises even veteran business advisors. Today, CFOs figure as major players in driving corporate change and building value.

As already seen, CFOs in global businesses act increasingly as the link between the corporation and shareholders. *This relationship shapes the value agenda of the business.* After all, it's shareholders, institutional or otherwise, who vote daily on whether value is created. As institutional shareholders probe ever more aggressively the corporation's value potential, the CFO often steps into the front line:

- *when things are going well*, the pressure remains to do even better – it takes a proactive stance, building on the success of existing business strategy, to meet rising investor expectations

- *when results are disappointing*, if forecasts are missed and stock market warnings necessary, the CFO must clarify whether the causes are temporary or restructuring of the business is called for – the corporation is often forced into making a response.

In either circumstance, the market looks *to the CEO* for leadership and inspiration, but *to the CFO* for reassurance and a realistic view of what's achievable.

Without question, the CFO's credibility influences investor behavior. His or her ability to switch from high level strategy to the detail of operational reality is crucial. The strong CEO often wants to be partnered by a strong CFO, who does much more for the business than simply raise finance, manage risk and run the finance department. CEOs need financial officers who know the business, who relate well to investors, and who instinctively spot and promote value creating strategies. CFOs in this class become the *alter egos* of their chief executives. They put themselves in a position to add value, not only by acting as counterfoil and constructively challenging their CEOs, but by working independently alongside them as true partners in implementing agreed strategy.

> Today's chief financial officers figure as major players in driving corporate change and building value

Time and again in this book, it's clear that the CFO operates at the *nerve center* of the business – where information flows converge, major business opportunities are filtered, crucial decisions made, and actions sanctioned. To help gage how this role is changing, our *CFO 2000* survey explored the relationships of corporate CFOs inside and outside the business – with the CEO and board of directors, business managers, investors and the finance function. The questionnaire asked CFOs to assess the amount of time spent on these relationships in the last three years, contrasted with what they expect to spend in the next three years.

Today, on average, survey respondents spend a third of their time on the finance function – management activity involving mainly accounting and control. They devote the bulk of their time to other relationships. Time spent with business management averages 25%. Significant, too, is the amount of time spent with the CEO: 21% on average, though for some CFOs, the figure is as high as 40%. Not surprising in themselves, these figures reflect the recurring theme of CFOs' self-image: they see them-selves more as business partners than controllers and accountants. In contrast with the time spent on internal relationships, CFOs typically spend only 11% of their time on investor relations. But this pattern seems set to change in future (Figure 10.1).

Tomorrow, the biggest shift for CFOs is likely to be away from the finance function. Most respondents say they'll devote less time to account-ing and control, and more to business managers and the CEO. And many will respond to another trend: greater emphasis on investor relations.

What type of change initiatives do CFOs work on during their in-creasing time with business management? Survey respondents offer strikingly consistent replies to questions about the initiatives they're involved in and the nature of their role (Figure 10.2). CFOs and their finance teams take a lead role in certain change initiatives and participate in virtually all. Clearly highlighted across the survey population is the leadership role that many CFOs play in four categories of initiative. Topping the list is strategic and shareholder value management, followed

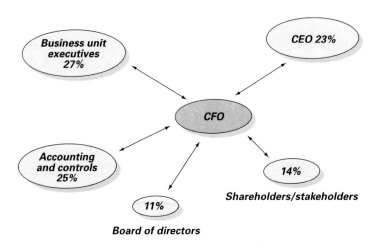

Figure 10.1 ***CFO 2000*** **survey: What per cent of your time will you spend on these relationships over the next three years?**

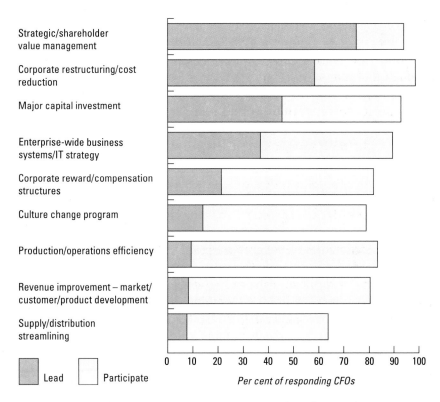

Strategic/shareholder
value management

Corporate restructuring/cost
reduction

Major capital investment

Enterprise-wide business
systems/IT strategy

Corporate reward/compensation
structures

Culture change program

Production/operations efficiency

Revenue improvement – market/
customer/product development

Supply/distribution
streamlining

Lead ☐ Participate

0 10 20 30 40 50 60 70 80 90 100

Per cent of responding CFOs

Figure 10.2 **CFO 2000** survey: What is the role of the finance function in these business initiatives?

by restructuring and cost reduction, major capital investment, and enterprise-wide systems and IT strategy.

Extracts from interviews with respondents illustrate CFOs' attitudes to their role as change leaders.

Moving away from accounting and control... 'Finance has always been a strong function. In the past, the people who saved the company all came from finance. If you didn't have the CFO's approval, you couldn't do anything. When I was a business unit manager, if the treasurer or controller showed up, I felt like I had a problem. And most of the time I did! That doesn't happen any more. We just can't afford to have all these checks and balances.'

Toward strategy and shareholder value... 'In 1995 we established a pay-for-performance plan that went right down to the lowest level employee, based on shareholder return. So everyone in the company became interested in what was happening to the share price. My job was to convince everybody that their effort does make a difference, that everybody has a contribution to make in achieving shareholder value growth. We published regular reports on shareholder return and had line management across the business working to increase cash flows. We encouraged our people working on change programs to think ten years out in the future. We showed our operating people that the present value of the cash flows of the programs they were working on would have an impact leading to a higher stock price. This longer-term view encourages them to seek out bigger ideas, better technology and more innovative solutions.'

... And integrating major acquisitions 'What takes up more of my time now are the issues of integration and efficiency of our international operations. We are a very large company, with operating revenues of over $70 billion, so at my level I deal only with expansion or restructuring plans valued at over $25 million in capital. One particular difficulty we face is improving performance of the businesses we acquire in Central and Eastern Europe and in Asia. I deploy our 160-strong task force to live with the problems locally, to identify how to improve management processes and skills, and to develop business systems.'

These comments are from CFOs of US companies. But the research reflects the varying nature of the CFO's role from company to company and around the world. In Southeast Asia, for example, the chief executive of one company is both a controlling shareholder and the entrepreneur, determined to grow rapidly through acquisitions in diversified activities. In this case, the CFO fulfills more of a technical role in evaluating and controlling risk, rather than as an initiator of external trans-actions. In a second case, in Singapore, the position is very different: the CFO determines company strategy in conjunction with the chairman and executives of the four main businesses. As well as being CFO, he has operating responsibility for the new, smaller but growing, businesses in the group. In another company in the same region, the CFO says: 'Our controlling shareholder's mandate is very simple. By 2000, we aim to produce half a million cars to have critical mass to compete inter-nationally. We must improve internal efficiency, productivity and

> CEOs need financial officers who know the business, and who instinctively spot and promote value creating strategies

supplier cost performance. But our focus is currently on revenue growth. The full financial agenda has yet to be sorted out'.

Despite such variations, one overriding message comes through. For all their basic discipline and training grounded in historical reporting, statute compliance and verification, CFOs are looking *forward*, not backward. Traditional, historically based accounting is likely to converge with a new requirement for value reporting, based on anticipated performance in the future. Technology available today has yet to be applied to the business environment, let alone that being developed for tomorrow. The virtual company is on the horizon. What will it be like for CFOs in future? What skills will be required?

> All their lives, finance people are taught to think backward – yet the best CFOs look forward, imagining what lies ahead

VECTORS OF CHANGE

So little time is spent imagining what lies ahead. Research shows that just 2% of all available executive time is devoted to developing a corporate perspective on the future. Such a low investment is unlikely to keep the company ahead of its competitors and able to create innovative strategies. Going forward, companies must develop managers with an in-built competence to be business futurists.

In his book *Beyond the Next Wave*, Glen Peters describes what he calls the 'vectors of change' – large-scale forces that push the future in different directions (Figure 10.3).[1] Vectors of change provide tools for developing alternative pictures of the future for decision-making purposes.

Inevitably, these vectors will shape your organization and its people. Few companies that began the 1980s as industry leaders ended the decade in the same position. Buffeted by tides of technological, demographic and regulatory change, and the emergence of non-traditional competitors, too many companies seem to be at the mercy of the fates, rather than in control of their destinies. The industrial terrain changed shape faster than top management could re-fashion its basic beliefs and assumptions about which markets and customers to serve, which technologies to master and how to get the best from employees.

All their lives, people are taught to think backward. History, the sciences, management thinking and current affairs are all dominated by

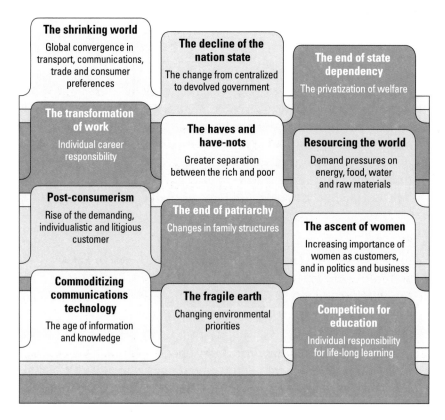

Figure 10.3 **The 12 vectors of change**

the past. Companies run their businesses using management information based on elapsed activities and promote people on the assumption they can repeat past successes. With the value agenda in mind, the CFO should take time with the corporate management team to look at how lives of present and future customers might change, and what products and services they might need. For example, by 2020, China is forecast to be the world's largest economy, dominating the US and Japan. Africa will be the highest growth area, almost doubling its existing population of 750 million people.

How will these changes affect the roles of the CFO and the finance function? The CFO has a key role to play as a strategist and, so, futurist. Considering some of the vectors of change, it's worth beginning to explore their implications.

- ***The shrinking world...*** Internationalization of business and financial services; introduction of common currencies (the euro is nearly upon us); rise of the global investor and global financial markets.

- ***The end of state dependency...*** Increasing numbers of privatized companies across the world (creating new market opportunities but also powerful competitors); growing dependence of an aging population on privatized pensions.

- ***Competition for education...*** Rising perceived value of education; new emphasis on life-long learning (continuous updating of skills); shifting responsibilities for learning, from employers to individuals.

- ***The transformation of work...*** Finance staff taking more responsibility for their own careers; more self-employment and portfolio working (contracts with different employers); substantial rise in tele-commuting; drift to a low wage world, with developing countries as low cost suppliers of computer software and transaction processing services.

- ***Commoditizing communications technology...*** Development of the Internet and Intranets; increasing availability of information services; new risks from information crime; convergence of computing, communications and media; potential demise of the PC in favor of network computing.

The vectors of change may help you develop scenarios setting out the future context in which your business will operate. Create a view of the future for yourself and the finance function. Envisioning what things might be like five to ten years from now will help you make sure you're prepared.

Some food for thought: based on the writings of two senior members of our US team, an imaginary case study creates a vision of the world inhabited by financial officers in 2005.[2] Seen through the eyes of a talented young executive, just promoted to CFO of a leading multinational, this is a world in which a thorough understanding of the business, combined with strong teamworking skills and familiarity with what technology has to offer, has never been more important.

Create a view of the future for yourself and the finance function – make sure you prepare for it

269

FUTURE CASE: Finance in 2005

Halfway through the first decade of the 21st century. Rosemary Ortega has just been named executive vice president (EVP) of the company – a nice set of initials to go with her CPA and CMA. She sits back for an unusually relaxed few minutes and thinks...

The Silicon Path

In the mid-1990s, most of us believed that, if and when it arrived, the future would be much like today. But then – beyond transforming the finance function from clerical bookkeeping to sophisticated analysis – silicon chips changed permanently the way organizations are managed. By the end of the century, accelerating change put everything – the entire general ledger, all the company's customer lists and the complete price book, in full color and with voice annotations – on portable computers.

Every 18 months, personal computers doubled in speed, making the 1998 PC more powerful than the most advanced machines of the previous decade. Now, in 2005, $500 buys a portable computer and personal communications center that runs at one billion cycles per second, with 2.5 trillion bytes of hard disk storage (plus trillions more on CDs) and internal memory of 50 million characters. Power is cheap.

Software designers have long since solved the problems of character recognition, language and software translation, and bandwidth compression. Technology is so much simpler to use. We have voice links that really work and light pens instead of mice. Knowledge management systems with fuzzy logic, real-time artificial intelligence and multi-media interfaces aid data analysis. The ubiquitous, wall-sized telecommunication screen permits inexpensive, instantaneous teleconferencing to all corners of the world.

Reusable program objects have revolutionized software engineering. New systems can be tailored over a weekend and downloaded, via secure optic links, from programmers in New Delhi, Mexico City and Beijing (only a video message away). Integrating systems is not a concern: everything is integrated by modules of software code.

New Finance

By 2000, the finance function was downsized to roughly 30% of its peak. In the mid-1990s, accounting headcount had ranked second to the sales force as a per cent of SG&A, making it an obvious target for process change – and prompting many CFOs to champion a transformed accounting function. This take-charge strategy, stepping up to the challenge early, let CFOs influence the outcome.

The Internet and Intranet enabled dramatically new, more productive ways of working. The most tangible manifestation: bulldozing of the central finance office, which became superfluous when staff were reorganized into devolved business management teams. Finance people now work from home, with home Web pages, video links, and direct access to the business systems and full range of data mining tools. There are no boundaries to sharing, networking and coaching.

Modular, integrated systems have smoothed business reporting. They extract needed data worldwide and prepare journal entries automatically, using agent programs to check transactions. Huge analysis volumes are easily handled by renting transaction access down the wire to on-demand systems providers.

Despite forecasts to the contrary, monthly reporting of financial information has not diminished but grown more important than ever. Sales dollars, order backlog and other key items are available on demand. But once each month, most companies put their financial information together and provide a permanent, comparative historical record – statements that emphasize cash. The money center stock markets and worldwide banking community demand these reports. GlobalBank, particularly, insists on receiving information promptly, with others not far behind. Luckily, our stakeholder information strategy, *implemented in 1999, lets much of this reporting happen invisibly.*

'New systems can be tailored over a weekend and downloaded from programmers in New Delhi, Mexico City and Beijing'

Old style, historical accounting seems a distant memory – wiped out by pervasive use of shareholder value techniques, fully integrated with financial and business management. Today, automated budgeting and profit planning software lets business managers draw down their quarterly budget over the weekend, electronically message it to their direct reports, and then update it using statistical tools provided by the computer. To support value planning, automated sales forecasting uses artificial intelligence routines that interpret each new order and adjust the sales projection and production plan. Our continuous improvement, balanced value processes are beginning to gain acceptance. We now take business decisions at integrated value chain level, understanding the wider implications for the business strategy and partnerships – a great improvement on the seat of the pants guesswork of yesterday's functions.

Taxes remain a major, time-consuming chore. Ironically, neural systems used by state, federal and international tax auditors sharply intensify tax return scrutiny. In self-defense, many corporations are lobbying for a simple, worldwide value added tax. Meantime, our own neural technology – one of the fruits of our software development partnership with NASA – keeps us ahead of the game in delivering world-class tax value plans.

Outsourcing of Treasury

Treasury functions have become even more complex since the turn of the century, when each new computer algorithm added a layer of worldwide financing options. 'Derivatives' may have disappeared but international financing continues to make hedging, swapping and going long or short the daily grist of treasury staff. Banks have taken over most companies' cash management functions, so bank investment specialists have the

'Old style, historical accounting seems a distant memory – wiped out by pervasive use of shareholder value reporting'

information needed to suggest financing options – often designed to shave another hundredth of a basis point off the cost of capital. New schemes offered daily seem just zero-sum games designed to enrich the bank's brokerage department, but companies have to look at them. Product prices leave no room for sloppy expense control!

By 2005, most companies have, like ours, found needed treasury finesse by outsourcing routine aspects of the treasury function – much as we'd all dealt with our tax departments in the late 1990s.

'That reminds me,' thinks Ortega. She turns to the screen on the wall and says carefully: 'Computer – make an appointment for me to meet Doug next week to discuss the improvements we could achieve using the new Price Waterhouse Treasury Portfolio software'.

High Impact Reporting

In progressive companies, the finance team has become the guardian of the information system. Scorekeeping still matters because outside sources' requests for information have increased dramatically. The annual report and quarterly SEC filings remain the official transcript of financial history. But investors, litigators, regulatory agencies and the worldwide media constantly question the organization to verify if information they've somehow obtained is correct. Our recent battle to value our intellectual capital – based on contents of our knowledge management systems – was of epic proportions!

Instantaneous access to information is less than key in running the business. Managerial decision-making means piercing through the erratic behavior of recent results to see future trends and indicators. So the company's performance measurement system, made up of relatively few statistical

'The performance measurement system is like 50 or 60 probes that constantly monitor key company processes'

and financial indicators that assess whether the company's strategies are being achieved, provides the nucleus of managerial insight. Figuratively, these indicators blink red, yellow and green, showing how the company is doing and where trouble spots may exist in the organization. It's like 50 or 60 probes that constantly monitor key company processes.

The finance team long ago abandoned its view of the reporting system as predominantly accounting data. Now, product development lead time, first-time quality, customer satisfaction, out-of-stock conditions, market segment-ation achievement, share price growth and revenue indexes prompt managerial action. Our moves to harmonize our own balanced business scorecard and operational value strategies with those of suppliers and customers have greatly enhanced the value we can deliver.

Assessing New Product Potential

Product and service development cycle times are much shorter. All organizations strive to bring out appealing new products monthly, even if it means obsoleting existing ones. We've almost no choice. Speed to market has been a competitive weapon since the mid-1990s. Today, the finance staff spend much of their time assessing new product potential.

Pricing approaches an art form. Product developers provide factors that can be used to determine costs and the marketing staff gage sales volumes at various net prices, but it falls to the finance staff to wade through these sometimes inconsistent estimates and assess actual future prices. Using advanced simulation engines to model scenarios integrating marketplace, design, production and distribution channels, we've significantly increased the success rate of new product launches.

Quality, Not Quantity, of Finance People

The administrative headcount in the company is smaller, particularly in finance, where remaining staff are highly paid, highly valued contributors to the managerial process – the integrators of information. Knowing where the information is, whether it resides in an internal or external database, they've become singularly effective at understanding its managerial implications.

'Finance staff are highly paid, highly valued contributors to the managerial process – the integrators of information'

Cross-correlation of product development lead times, inventory levels, warranty claims and customer satisfaction surveys provides insight into a product's future market acceptance. Likewise, external information on competitor partnerships, new pricing schemes and upcoming product releases arms management with strategic news.

Much of our high level decision-making takes place on The Bridge *– the purpose built, virtual nerve center of the business. Through this suite of business analysis and communication tools, decision-makers across the organization have easy access to the right people and information. The only problem is the continued failure to agree on Global Time. But one day...*

With many staff groups of the 1990s gone, finance people fill roles as market researchers, capital asset analysts, quality control authorities, pricing advisors, logistical expense experts, information retrieval consultants, merger and acquisition professionals, alliance partnership negotiators and litigation support authorities. Their tiring but exciting lives are satisfying.

Finance also plays several other important roles. Most companies outsource many business functions they once performed internally. The telecommunication service vendor maintains encrypted databases of company records and downloads them, on legitimate request, to the PCs of individuals worldwide. Organizations find it much more economical for the telecommunication company to maintain these databases than it is to update them internally. But the finance function is the keeper of this relationship. Finance staff maintain security codes, agree encryption standards and negotiate terms of the telecommunication partnership. The many mergers of telecommunication, satellite and computer companies in the last decade make choosing the right vendor a vital job.

That is how it is in 2005 and how times have changed!

A CFO in the Making

Looking back, Ortega reflects on what she's done that's pushed her career forward, making her the youngest executive vice president in the company's history and in line for still more responsibilities.

School helped, giving her a good grounding in business strategy, processes analysis and accounting. More to the point, she knew PC software and shared her generation's conviction that silicon chips would revolutionize business. And her ingrained sense of teamwork bolstered her interpersonal skills immensely.

Her first projects drew on her computer skills. She mined answers from a PC quicker and presented them better than anyone else in her employment class. Learning how to tap into the company's general ledger, she spent creative evenings devising a new budgeting system that let everyone complete rolling quarterly forecasts at home on a PC. Soon after, she was named assistant controller.

Her teamwork showed her dedication to the job – and she made good use of the new virtual networks established through the Intranet. About once every six months, she gave users of her budgeting system a software gift: once, a statistical package to correlate expense and revenue items, another time, a user-friendly projection 'mod' for reporting. Soon, all knew that, if faced with an important decision, they should talk to Ortega. She was more knowledgeable than anyone about retrieving data, whether in the company's computers or on the public networks. And she could interpret the information and provide solid suggestions based on the data. Helping to build cross-business support for implementation of fully integrated, enterprise-wide systems, she surprised no-one by being named controller.

Working to be a part of every internal project team, Ortega learned about the company's business functions: product development, logistics, operations, distribution, marketing and sales. On every assignment, she found the data that made the project manager's recommendations look flawless and collected a basket of IOUs in the process. One day, she proposed a new performance measurement system – quickly adopted. It was no fluke: she had fathomed the cross-workings of disparate groups and established measures for each.

The performance measurement system brought her access to most of the company's significant information. Then it was easy to change finance, abolishing obsolete functions in favor of analytical positions grouped around measurement. Always, she worked to cut administrative cost throughout the company: if her staff took on a new role, she carefully documented how it would save money elsewhere. These experiences gave her the knowledge and network to deliver early prototypes of The Bridge.

There was little remorse over outsourcing the company's financial databases. Outsourcing tax was easy. Payables came next and it was her pleasure to be among the first to use the bank's bill-paying service. Invoicing came later but also was easy to eliminate once the electronic shipping network came into existence.

Ortega's star rose sharply when the board supported her views on planning: 'The strategic business plan should be based on future growth targets for shareholder value. The plan for becoming number one in our business sector must include using technology to partner with customers and suppliers – cutting links from the value chain and big chunks of fixed cost burden, making the supply chain more responsive'. She developed The Bridge *concept, now habitually used by top management to devise and report value strategies and to measure progress in improving shareholder value. One tool she pioneered – Visual Finance software, using holographics to describe the company's mission – was a real hit at the AGM and changed the face of corporate reporting. She became CFO.*

For a few years, the company beat everyone in speed to market, product distribution and targeted selling. Less nimble competitors edged toward bankruptcy and could be bought cheaply. Ortega obliged: market share tripled almost overnight.

'Yes, an interesting few years,' she muses. 'But time to get back to business. TransTech Inc has finally agreed to guarantee the United Nations' debt. Are there any implications for us?' She turns to her screen. 'Computer – call Suzuki-San at home in Osaka.' He'll probably be up by now.

WHAT MAKES A SUPER CFO?

It's instructive to look at a hypothetical CFO and the characteristics – insightful, pioneering, persuasive – that make her successful in the 21st century. More can be learned from the best of real-life CFOs in the 1990s – exceptional performers who point the way for others. For example, *Fortune* magazine describes attributes of five so-called *super CFOs*.[3] Individuals like these, the article stresses, 'shape strategy, earn millions – and can be worth billions to a company and its shareholders'. Quotes from the five illustrate qualities that will be increasingly important to CFOs in future.[4]

Creativity... 'I like off-the-wall guys who don't fit the corporate stereotype. At Marriott, the young finance people were on the edge'... 'I'll listen to any idea, no matter how nuts.' *Gary Wilson, co-chairman of Northwest Airlines, formerly CFO of Marriott and Disney.* CFOs needn't be narrow-minded number crunchers. Some are inventive managers – creative and charismatic deal-makers who reap hidden value.

Versatility... 'The modern CFO needs at least three arrows in his quiver that go beyond pure finance: experience in process redesign, a deep understanding of customer satisfaction and product quality, and strategic planning talent.' *Jerome York, vice chairman of Tracinda Corp, formerly CFO of Chrysler and IBM.* Today's best CFOs are superb general managers who, on top of strong financial skills, boast a grasp of operations and a keen sense of strategy. Instead of simply measuring value, they create it.

Intuition... 'Intuition is key. You have to ask, where does this investment put us strategically in 10 years?'... 'When in doubt, act.' *Dennis Dammerman, CFO of GE.* Super CFOs are craftspeople who build businesses for the future, brick by brick. Their strengths lie in their vision and instinct to back key, long-term projects even when short-range numbers look weak.

Drive... 'The only way you can deal with Wall Street's expectations is to perform to them'... 'I see no limit on where the individual can go. There's no reason why a financial executive can't end up being chief executive.' *Stephen Bollenbach, CEO of Hilton Hotels, formerly CFO of Disney.* The CFO's role as deal-maker extends far beyond operations, to forging the company's identity for tomorrow. The Bollenbachs of this world constantly look for ways to raise shareholder value, not just by spinning off assets but by growing – expanding into new businesses and buying companies at the right price.

Rigor... 'Financial types are often accused of being too short-sighted. In our case, the reality is just the opposite'... 'For me, financial models are the key tools in a CFO's kit.' *Judy Lewent, CFO of Merck.* A new group of CFOs push the envelope by employing academic models to weigh investments. To raise the probability of discovering big hits, you must, as in Merck's case, invest in a greater number of promising innovations – measuring the value of projects in the pipeline and formulating alternative scenarios for outcomes at least ten years ahead.

These sorts of qualities differentiate super CFOs from the rest of the pack. *CFO 2000* research shows that many CFOs are beginning to recognize the importance of such qualities in developing the finance function's future role. Survey results confirm the distinct shift away from perceived importance of financial accounting and control, toward a greater emphasis on skills like creative problem-solving, change management and teamwork (Figure 10.4).

We categorize the competencies CFOs require as *foundation* and *leverage.* Foundation competencies are professional, technical and control related – these are minimum competencies for all CFOs. In contrast, leverage competencies allow CFOs to build both the business (strategic thinking, innovation, managing business risk and change) and personal relationships (teamwork and coaching, inspiring leadership).

Our research shows that most, if not all, CFOs rate themselves

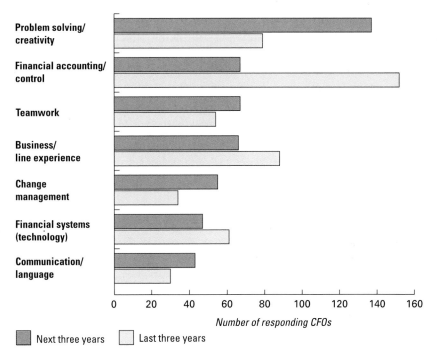

Figure 10.4 *CFO 2000* survey: What two skills are most valuable in developing the role of the finance function?

competent in foundation attributes. But many see further scope for personal development in leverage competencies. This reflects, in part, the conventional career development of CFOs: starting with a foundation in professional accounting (with training in either auditing or industry) and progressing to senior-level financial management, ultimately at board level. It also reflects how fast career tracks are today – it's not unknown for CFOs to be appointed in their early thirties. Of all business functions, finance tends to lead fastest to the boardroom. This leaves precious little time for planned personal development. The CFO's leverage competencies tend to be acquired haphazardly or neglected altogether.

There are exceptions. Some get to a CFO role direct from the world of corporate finance or, perhaps, strategic consultancy. These individuals may have what it takes to contribute quickly to devising and executing major deals – they've been chosen for their leverage attributes – but they can pose dangers for the corporation if these attributes are not balanced with sufficiently strong foundation competencies. A CFO leading a spectacular takeover, for example, at the same time must be sure of complying with company legislation.

Figure 10.5 shows a competencies inventory, bringing together the personal qualities, skills and knowledge CFOs require. Use the table to rate your own combination of *foundation* and *leverage* competencies.

SCALE OF CURRENT COMPETENCE

Key : **1** None   **2** Limited   **3** Moderate   **4** Significant   **5** Specialist

	1	2	3	4	5
1 Professional accounting/compliance					
1.1 Financial and statutory reporting					
1.2 Budgeting, financial planning					
1.3 Balance sheet/cash management					
1.4 Regulatory compliance, internal control					
2 Technical specialist					
2.1 Raising finance					
2.2 Treasury management					
2.3 Tax					
2.4 Legal, secretarial					
3 Managing financial operations					
3.1 Financial systems and processes					
3.2 Group accounting					
3.3 Management reporting					
4 Business management					
4.1 Cost management					
4.2 Project management					
4.3 Performance measurement					
5 External transactions					
5.1 Negotiation, pricing					
5.2 Acquisitions, disposals					
5.3 Investment management					
6 Interpersonal					
6.1 Staff management					
6.2 Communication					
6.3 Delegation					

Figure 10.5a   **Foundation competencies**

BALANCING YOUR PERSONAL DEVELOPMENT

How do *you* rate? No CFO can be expected to score highly on all competencies. There are only so many years in one career. What's important is to achieve *balance* and *progression* – two imperatives for becoming a super CFO.

SCALE OF CURRENT COMPETENCE				

Key : **1** None **2** Limited **3** Moderate **4** Significant **5** Specialist

		1	2	3	4	5
7	**Strategic**					
	7.1 Strategic analytics, business design					
	7.2 Global perspective and reach					
	7.3 Envisioning, scenario planning					
	7.4 Innovation, creativity					
	7.5 Deal origination and flow					
8	**Value based management**					
	8.1 Shareholder value analysis					
	8.2 Investor relations					
	8.3 Value budgeting					
	8.4 Value reporting/scorecard					
9	**Business partnering**					
	9.1 Streamlining, outsourcing					
	9.2 Revenue generation					
	9.3 Risk management					
	9.4 Activity based management					
	9.5 Enterprise-wide IT					
10	**Change management**					
	10.1 *Big-R Re-engineering*					
	10.2 Cross-functional integration					
	10.3 Stakeholder management					
	10.4 Acquisition integration					
	10.5 Building strategic alliances					
11	**Inspirational leadership**					
	11.1 Coaching, motivating					
	11.2 Team development					
	11.3 Questioning, challenging					

Figure 10.5b **Leverage competencies**

- **Balance your leverage and foundation skills** For example, on one hand, devising value creating strategies and, on the other, negotiating and executing successfully the consequential financial transactions. This combination of vision and delivery – the essence of an architect – is what the CFO's role is all about.

- **Continually enhance your skills profile** Standing still is not an option. The external and internal environments change too quickly for current competencies to remain relevant indefinitely. You can go on recruiting additional skills. But your ambition and drive as a leader depend as much on your ability to change *yourself* as on your success in assembling a high caliber team.

The envisioning you've already done – imagining what the business might be like in future and the potential impact on your role – will help you identify personal development needs. Let the priorities of the business for the years ahead (shareholder value, streamlining, globalization) drive your acquisition of leverage competencies (devising and communicating value creating strategies, negotiating outsourced contracts, managing across international cultures).

In deciding which skills to focus on, it may help, too, to think about *role models* who appeal to you. *CFO 2000* research offers examples – three featured here. Robert Hoffman of Monsanto has led major structural change within a relatively short timeframe but with a vision of the longer term. Clark Johnson, interviewed before his death in March 1997, has excelled in international acquisitions and business partnering at Johnson & Johnson. Marianne Parrs of International Paper has concentrated on developing the finance function's competency to add value to the business.

ROBERT HOFFMAN: Releasing Value in the Business

CFO Robert Hoffman is regarded as the financial architect of his company's revolution. Through a series of disposals and major acquisitions, Monsanto shifted from a chemicals to a life sciences company, moving away from low growth, low margin commodity and cyclical businesses into high growth, high margin branded businesses. Accounting for the company's success, Hoffman says a significant factor is its emphasis on strategies that create shareholder *value – supported by economic value added (EVA^{TM}) techniques at all levels, from corporate to business unit.[5]*

He has worked hard to establish EVA. 'In our training, we've introduced the concept of "ambassadors": a healthy mix of operational and finance staff who train the trainers.' Compensation provides appropriate incentives. Pay varies according to shareholder value performance, with increasing variability for higher levels of management. And employees throughout the company are rewarded with stock options. Hoffman and his team use EVA – and the more sophisticated metric, cash flow return on investment (CFROI) – in resource allocation through strategic planning, capital allocation, and the budgeting and reporting processes. As a result, he says, 'managers have been forced to become very smart internal investors'. Overall, the secret, Hoffman believes, is to 'simplify EVA essentials, such as cost of capital and free cash flow, and make them more intuitive for general managers'.

CLARK JOHNSON: Building Partnerships

For Clark Johnson, CFO of Johnson & Johnson, 'influencing the right business decisions is the most important role for finance'. He and his team focus on 'becoming better business partners to improve the company's performance against its many competitors' – the essence, he believes, of enhancing shareholder value. With the company enjoying consistent double-digit growth in earnings per share during the nine years since Johnson became CFO, his approach has surely worked.

Having participated in 26 acquisitions and 12 divestments over the past five years, Johnson (author of a book on integrating acquisitions) understands only too well the critical role the finance function plays once the papers are signed. He says: 'After years of analyzing acquisitions, I learned that failures result more from poor marketing assessments and breakdowns in technology than financial analysis. My finance professionals now spend more time with marketing and operating people to make sure we're part of the process and decisions, as opposed to sitting back and criticizing'.

MARIANNE PARRS: Developing Finance Competency

At International Paper, an industry leader in the Dow Jones Index, Marianne Parrs has risen through the ranks during a 23-year career in the finance function, becoming CFO in 1995. The priorities she sets for finance are to achieve improvements in three key areas.

Productivity... *Parrs' message is: 'Determine whether what you're doing is adding value and, if not, figure out how to get rid of it'. She admits: 'There's nothing like killing a useless report which has been produced for years to give me a personal sense of satisfaction'.*

People... *A 'competency based development' initiative is under way, to ensure that each finance employee develops technical, personal and leadership skills to their fullest potential.*

Partnership... *Parrs believes that 'to be really effective, finance and information systems people need to be partners with business managers'. Finance staff receive hands-on training to teach them to do analytical work aimed directly at improving return on investment in the context of their own businesses or facilities.*

What does it mean to take a planned approach to personal and career development? Most senior executives have personal objectives they update each year, covering anything from ongoing financial targets to *ad hoc*, project based initiatives. Few focus these objectives on what they need to do *as individuals* to realize their full potential. Occasionally, they might indulge in some off-the-job training, perhaps even a Harvard senior management program. More typically, they attend one-day *wonder seminars* run by gurus, hoping for inspiration and a new window on the management world. But such experiences are fleeting.

The most successful senior finance executives take seriously the business of planning and pursuing their own development over time. Many of them:

- gain substantive, structured experience outside the finance function (one finance director who became CEO of a leading retailer insisted on spending three months working in store operations)

- visit other world-class companies (a CFO who wanted to see the best shared service centers in action undertook a tour covering three continents)

- maintain personal links with business academics (the CFO of a major international manufacturer has received regular coaching, over many years, from a professor in advanced cost management).

A personal development plan should cover things that you, as an individual, find difficult to face up to: *your behavior* (are you setting the right example in cross-functional working and sharing credit for successes?), *your inhibitions* (are you genuine in your desire to see change in your own backyard and to respect local cultures when making decisions?) and *your ambitions* (are you confident and clear about what you want to do?). Your personal objectives will be worthwhile only if they take you beyond what you're comfortable with. Your plan should be medium to long-term and linked, wherever relevant, to company strategy and culture change. And, above all, it must be measurable, so you know where you're going and when you've arrived.

The balanced business scorecard for measuring performance at corporate, business process and activity levels (Chapter 3) can be a useful approach in devising measures to improve performance at personal level. The aim – to balance your development between financial and non-financial criteria and between external and internal priorities – is demonstrated in Figure 10.6, which shows an example of a personal scorecard for the CFO.

Typically, people's *planning* for personal development is more structured than their *monitoring* of what actually takes place. Yet useful mechanisms exist for measuring achievement and seeking feedback, even on intangibles like behavior change. Techniques for 360-degree appraisal may sound simple in theory but often prove difficult to apply in practice, especially at senior management level. In Price Waterhouse, the partners developed a target culture profile for the global consulting business. To measure individual partners' progress in adopting target behaviors, feedback is obtained from:

- *subordinates* – anonymously, they feed back to an independent third party how well they feel they've been coached, managed and supported during assignments; this information is analyzed statistically and passed confidentially to the partner concerned

- *peers* – partners (across national borders) rate each other on how

External stakeholder measures	Process measures
• Shareholder relations • Customer, competitor and market analysis • Alliance partnering, mergers and acquisitions candidates	• Effective control processes • Development of enterprise-wide processes and systems • Efficient financial transaction processing • Effective management information and decision support
Financial measures	**People measures**
• Share price performance • Targeted value creation • Optimization of business and financial risk • Cost effective finance function	• Finance skills and discipline to meet business needs • Finance teamwork • Integrated business and financial organization • Communication of financial skills across the business

Figure 10.6 **A CFO's personal scorecard**

much help and advice they receive, on a scale from intermittent to substantial and recurring

- *coaches* – all partners, as mentors to other partners, have rigorous training to become more effective as coaches; top-down guidance goes beyond the typical routine of objective-setting and annual performance reporting to focus more on how and where individuals can exploit their potential as leaders.

For the CFO, useful feedback could also come from external sources, such as analysts and investors. The process needn't be formal. Some of the most insightful feedback is picked up in ordinary conversation, simply by asking and listening – another reason for the CFO to maintain open communication lines with key stakeholders.

REALIZING YOUR VALUE

The recurring theme of our research is the importance of measuring and improving shareholder value. Such measures feature highly in the CFO's personal objectives and performance feedback. Almost all CFOs expect their remuneration to include incentives based on measurable financial targets, such as profit and sales revenue growth – as well as, increasingly, less tangible targets such as leadership. *CFO 2000* survey results show that part of the remuneration for four out of ten CFOs is linked directly to share price.

> As their responsibility for corporate success grows, chief financial officers earn higher status and rewards

In the last decade, as their responsibility for corporate success has grown, CFOs have earned higher status and rewards. Some variation exists between regions and sectors, but generally a CFO's remuneration is around 70% of a CEO's – rising to around 80% when the CFO is also deputy chief executive.

In the 1980s, incentives and bonus schemes represented about 12% of the average CFO's remuneration package. Today, bonuses for performance and profitability average nearer 40% and, for some, can be as high as 200%. Increasingly complex, these schemes often involve both short and long-term plans, with a proportion of the bonus paid in equity with vesting restrictions to *lock in* the CFO for a set period. Recruiting a new CFO, a company may have to pay a sign-on bonus to buy out options, and other unvested incentive remuneration, that the executive will lose on changing jobs.

Why not link your personal wealth targets more directly to those you set for your company? As one institutional investor points out, a company's share price can rise or fall with a change in the CFO. By making more transparent your contribution to increasing shareholder wealth – and communicating the results to investors – you should be in a position to tie the drivers of your reward package to the growth in company value.

Like the other chapters, this ends with a checklist of key messages. You may want to use these to draw up a *charter* for your role in the business – describing what you'll contribute, and what you'll need in return from the CEO and other major stakeholders in your future. The charter could contain *criteria for measuring your success* in, say, improving shareholder value, developing the finance function, and partnering the business – as in the following example.

One year from now...

- Share price outperforms the industry average and grows by at least 25%.

- All finance processes are simplified, with more than half standardized worldwide.

- Finance leads the way in implementing enterprise-wide streamlining and business systems.

- Activity based budgeting is fully implemented.

Three years from now...

- Share price increases two-fold.

- All finance processes are standardized and regional shared service centers operate in each of the three continental theaters.

- Successful integration of one or more acquisitions, together equivalent to at least 50% of current shareholder value.

- CFO becomes deputy chief executive.

Six years from now...

- Share price increases four-fold and the company is rated number one in its sector on all value driver benchmarks.

- All finance and support processes worldwide are outsourced to strategic partners.

- The company is structured as value centers, and all employees use a value based scorecard for performance measurement.

- Finance leads some, and participates fully in all other, significant new revenue-generating initiatives.

CFO's CHECKLIST

THINK LIKE A FUTURIST   Use the *vectors of change* to paint a picture of your company and its industry in the next century, anticipating radically different customer and competitor scenarios. Set targets for shareholder value five to ten years from now. Make sure they will put you at the top of your industry league table.

ACT LIKE AN ARCHITECT   Calculate the fundamental value of your current business design and what it will deliver in future. Add your view of incremental values attributable to new projects and products the corporate management team currently envisions. Determine the gap between these calculated values today and your future aspirations. Identify options for filling the gap – for example, through alliances, acquisitions or a step change in organic growth. Design the business model for the future and present it to your investors and colleagues. Working with the CEO, set the longer-term course for the business.

BE THE CHANGE INTEGRATOR   As the company undergoes its transformation, ensure that re-shaped business processes support the business vision. Align new processes with the competencies, systems and performance measures needed to achieve long-term financial targets. Assess the shareholder value contribution of individual change initiatives – discarding some, reinforcing others. Persuade your stakeholders to back the change, using an integrated *value proposition* – the business case, expressed in value terms.

DEVELOP A BALANCED PERSONAL SCORECARD   Together with corporate management colleagues, construct personal scorecards that measure your individual contributions to achieving the vision. As CFO, your scorecard should balance your performance in meeting both *external* requirements of investors and *internal* needs of the business, as well as *financial* and *non-financial* criteria.

GET FEEDBACK ON YOUR PERFORMANCE   Declare to your stakeholders your personal performance measures and aspirations. Get their commitment to change by asking them for feedback. Conduct regular peer group reviews to check how well you're helping others to succeed, and improving your own skills and behavior.

PLAN YOUR SKILLS INVENTORY FOR THE 21ST CENTURY   Make a realistic assessment of your current *foundation* and *leverage* competencies. Envision what you will be doing five years from now. Thinking about the changing emphasis in your role, create a personal development plan.

GROW YOUR VALUE WITH CORPORATE VALUE   Link your personal earnings targets to those you set for the company. Make your contribution to boosting shareholder wealth more transparent: use the value agenda to demonstrate how you make a difference. As CFO, everything you do should have a value impact. If you are judged and rewarded accordingly, you can earn a bigger slice of a bigger business.

NOTES AND REFERENCES

Chapter 1

1) As part of the research for this book, Price Waterhouse commissioned the Conference Board to conduct a worldwide survey of the views of CFOs on their changing role: the resulting report summarizes *CFO 2000* questionnaire responses, received in late 1996 and early 1997, from a total of 300 CFOs. Highlights appear in relevant chapters, along with extracts from face-to-face interviews with participating CFOs.

2) Glen Peters, *Beyond the Next Wave: Imagining the Next Generation of Customers*, Pitman Publishing, 1996; citing George Yip, professor of strategy at Anderson School of Management in Los Angeles (page 25).

3) Stephen Gates, *The Changing Global Role of the Finance Function: A Research Report*, The Conference Board, 1994.

Chapter 2

1) Michael Price, 'An Investor Calls', *Management Today*, December 1995.

2) In 1996, Price Waterhouse commissioned Taylor Group Inc to survey the views of senior analysts at 30 leading US investment management firms.

3) EVA™ was developed by Stern Stewart & Co. For discussion of the relative merits and demerits of various valuation techniques, see Randy Myers, 'Metric Wars', *CFO*, October 1996.

4) Alfred Rappaport, *Creating Shareholder Value*, Free Press, 1986.

5) ValueBuilder™ is Price Waterhouse's value modeling software.

6) Adrian J Slywotzky, *Value Migration*, Harvard Business School Press, 1995.

Chapter 3

1) Bill Birchard, 'Making It Count: How Innovative Companies Really Use the New Metrics', *CFO*, October 1995.

2)   EVA™ was developed by Stern Stewart & Co.

Chapter 4

1)   Michael E Porter, 'What *is* Strategy?', *Harvard Business Review*, November–December 1996.

2)   Price Waterhouse's Global Benchmarks Alliance is a confidential database supplying members with detailed metrics and descriptions of best practices for finance processes including accounts payable, accounts receivable, financial reporting, shared services and use of IT. It covers more than 60 leading multinationals in a range of industries.

3)   ACTIVA is Price Waterhouse's client/server leveraged ABM software.

Chapter 5

1)   The Economist Intelligence Unit, *Managing Business Risks: An Integrated Approach*, 1995. (Part of the *Creating the Future* series.)

2)   Rory F Knight and Deborah J Pretty, *The Impact of Catastrophes on Shareholder Value*, Templeton College, 1996. A research report sponsored by Sedgwick Group. (Part of *The Oxford Executive Research Briefings* series.) It should be noted that the incidents which are the subject of this research are those defined by the insurance market as *catastrophes*, usually meaning the loss extends just beyond the first layer of insurance cover. This differs from the definition of catastrophic loss used for the purposes of this chapter – that is, the inability of a business to achieve its strategic objectives.

3)   The Price Waterhouse Change Integration® Team, *The Paradox Principles: How High-performance Companies Manage Chaos, Complexity and Contradiction to Achieve Superior Results*, Irwin, 1996.

4)   Price Waterhouse's international study of *Corporate Treasury Control and Performance Standards* was conducted in 1995 and 1996.

Chapter 6

1)   Procurement Analysis Workbench™ is a decision support software

system developed by Price Waterhouse and Analytics Inc, a specialist purchasing consultancy. A multidimensional data warehouse, the Workbench is designed to hold accurate, high quality information on a company's full range of procurement activities.

Chapter 7

1) The shared services diagnostic tool forms part of a senior executive workbook developed by Price Waterhouse. Designed for use during workshop discussions, the workbook helps executives establish the readiness of their businesses for different types of finance process re-engineering and begin planning appropriate actions.

Chapter 8

1) Figure 8.7 is based on BetterTech™, Price Waterhouse's methodology for managing the people and organizational issues of large-scale, process and systems driven change.

Chapter 9

1) Price Waterhouse's Global Benchmarks Alliance is a confidential database supplying members with detailed metrics and descriptions of best practices for finance processes including accounts payable, accounts receivable, financial reporting, shared services and use of IT. It covers more than 60 leading multinationals in a range of industries.

Chapter 10

1) Glen Peters, *Beyond the Next Wave: Imagining the Next Generation of Customers*, Pitman Publishing, 1996.

2) Daniel P Keegan and Stephen W Portik, 'The 21st Century Financial Officer', *Management Accounting*, December 1995. Reprinted from *Management Accounting*. Copyright by Institute of Management Accountants, Montvale, NJ, December 1995.

3) Shawn Tully, 'Super CFOs: They Can't Jump... But Some Earn More Than Deion Sanders', *Fortune*, 13 November 1995.

4)   Other quotes from Ann Monroe, 'A Dozen Who Made a Difference', *CFO*, February 1995; Ida Picker, 'Troubleshooting for Jack Welch', *Institutional Investor*, July 1995; and an interview with A R Sales, treasurer of Arvin Industries, 'No Guts, No Glory', *Financial Executive*, March/April 1996.

5)   EVA™ was developed by Stern Stewart & Co.

INDEX